WRITING BROADCAST NEWS

WRITING BROADCAST NEWS—
Shorter, Sharper, Stronger

A PROFESSIONAL HANDBOOK

Mervin Block

Bonus Books, Chicago

Library of Congress Catalog Card Number:
86-70705

International Standard Book Number:
0-933893-20-5

Bonus Books, Inc.
160 East Illinois Street
Chicago, Illinois 60611

96   95   94   93   92   10   9   8   7   6

Printed in the United States of America

To my parents

CONTENTS

1

DOZEN DEADLY SINS

As a working writer, you already know that writing is work. But you might not realize that you do much of your work before you write—and after. *Before* is when you grasp the ins and outs of writing, *after* is when you spot any flaws and see how you can improve, how you can make your scripts more speakable, understandable, recallable—and commendable.

The best way to do that is to apply the rules. Some of them you know. Some, you may not even know that you don't know. And some, you may not care for. But just as rules govern broadcasting, rules also govern newswriting. So in the interest of better broadcast newswriting, we're going to start by looking at rules. Not that this is a rule book. Rather, this is a professional writer's handbook, a guide to making scripts shorter, sharper, stronger.

You may think rules are for use when brains run out. Or that rules can be made only by rulers. So I'm going to rule out any *diktat, ukase,* or *fiat*—none of those European imports. And certainly no *bull.*

Instead, unless my editor overrules me, I'm calling these rules *tips.* My mental computer, though, has programmed them as rules for *me.* They weren't handed down to me at Mount Sinai; I've never even been in that hospital. For more than 20 years, I've absorbed them while writing in network newsrooms and refined them while teaching in college classrooms.

I shy away from asking anyone else to live by my rules. But I'm not mealymouthed, so I'm not going to say that you *might consider trying* them. I am saying that whatever you call them, you can put them to work for you. And they do work. As many ads for kitchen gadgets say, they're simple, reliable and fully tested. If you apply the rules—no matter how experienced you are—you're bound to write better.

When I started writing news for broadcast, I knew only one or two rules: type on one side of the page, do not split words from one page to

1

the next. But over the years, I picked up some sensible rules on news-writing from old pros, I dredged up some from my memory of a college class in broadcast newswriting, and I devised some from insights gained through writing day after day after day. I also assimilated rules laid down by various writing experts, including Strunk and White—and *they* do call them rules.

Besides all the things I learned to do, I learned many things not to do. And I learned a lot from my mistakes. Mistakes are often our best teachers, so the sooner you make your first 5,000 mistakes, the sooner you'll be able to correct them. With all that experience, now I can at least recognize a mistake when I make one.

The first right thing to do is often not doing the wrong thing. The Ten Commandments tell us what to do by telling us mostly what *not* to do. And the scholar Maimonides said the Bible sets forth 248 positive and 365 negative commandments. Not that I want to turn a script into Scripture, but if the Good Book can see the positive purpose of negatives, we should have faith.

In a burst of originality, I've labeled the most important no-nos the Dozen Deadly Sins. Right after them, I list the Venial Sins. Then, pivoting from Don'ts to Do's, I list what I call the Top Tips of the Trade.

You've already learned some of these how-to techniques, but although we're taught once, we must be reminded many times. So these reminders and tips will help make you a better writer.

The tips and reminders—or rules—are omnidirectional: They cover radio and television, and they apply to all kinds of newswriting, from 20-second stories to two-hour specials, from anchors' "readers" to reporters' "wraps."

I'm starting with the Don'ts because by understanding them a writer can readily see what may be even more important than the Do-Thises to produce good broadcast copy. Just as a musician can perform his magic by knowing which notes *not* to play, the writer who knows what to avoid is on the path to writing well.

Here are the Dozen Deadly Sins—not necessarily in order of sinfulness. Remember, scripts will suffer from—if not die for—your sins.

■ *Starting a story with "as expected."* Don't. Almost every time I hear an anchor say that, I find it's something I had not expected. Hadn't even *sus*pected. I think most listeners tune in to hear the *un*expected. Most of us, even seers, have no intimation of what to expect. I remember hearing a story that began:

> As expected, President Reagan has appointed Martha Seger to
> the Federal Reserve Board.

As expected? By whom? Not your average listener! I, for one, had never even heard of her. If everyone *had* heard of her and if her appointment were widely expected, then when the appointment finally came, it would have already lost much of its news value. What are listeners to think when they hear "As expected" and the story turns out to be about something they had never heard of, like a Martha Seger? Would they feel left out, put out, put down? Often, when newswriters start a story with "As expected," they do so because *they* had been expecting a development. Or their producer had told them to keep an eye out for a story that the wires had said they'd be moving shortly. So the writers have been scanning the wires expectantly. After hours of expectation, the story finally arrives. And without any thought, without thinking of the listeners they're going to be talking to—listeners who aren't newshawks, listeners whose reading is limited to program listings—they hurriedly write the words that have been on their mind. And, as expected, they start with that news-appetite depressant "As expected" or "As predicted." Which, predictably, takes the edge off any story. Even more of a turn-off for me is a negative version that I've heard with my own ears—no one else's: "Not unexpectedly." Another variation: "The *long-awaited* appointment of _____ _____ to the _____ _____ _____ was made today by Governor Grosvenor." It certainly wasn't "long-awaited" by listeners, probably only by the appointee.

■ *Starting a story with "In a surprise move."* Don't. A typical example:

> In a surprise move, the Interstate Commerce Commission rejected
> the proposal to merge the Santa Fe and Southern Pacific
> railroads.

I had long forgotten about the proposal, which the ICC had been considering for two-and-a-half years. How could I be surprised when I wasn't even aware that it was pending? For whom was the rejection a surprise? Rail and trucking industry insiders, perhaps, but for the rest of us, news is full of surprises.

■ *Starting a story by saying someone "is making news," "is in the news," or "is dominating the news."* Don't. Just go ahead and tell the news. That's what a newscast is for. That's why they call it a newscast.

Everyone who's mentioned in a newscast is "making" news, so when writers say someone "is making news," they're wasting time, theirs and their listeners', time that could be spent reporting news. Another waste of time is the lead that says someone "made history today" or "entered history books today." Only historians will decide, and that may be a long time off. Equally foolish is the lead that says, "They're rewriting the record books today in. . . ." Just tell the news, and if someone broke a record that's worth reporting, say so. Simply.

■ *Starting a story by saying, "A new development tonight in the. . . ."* Don't. Every item in a newscast is supposed to be new, based on a recent development. Some writers try to go beyond that opening by saying, "A *major* new development tonight. . . ." What's to be gained by saying, in effect, "The story you're going to be hearing next is new"? Or what's the point of saying, "Our top story tonight is. . . ." If it's the first story, it must be the top story. Let's just go straight to the news.

■ *Characterizing news as "good," "bad," "interesting," or "disturbing."* Don't. Just tell the news. Let the listener decide whether it's good, bad or interesting. What is good for some is bad for others. What seems, at first glance, to be good, can turn out bad. What's good for a city-dweller may be bad for a farmer. What's good for Luke Skywalker may be bad for Lucy Streetwalker. Bad news for Main Street is often good news for Wall Street. The plunge in oil prices seemed like good news, but in many places in this country, it turned out to be bad news. So the best course is: Just tell the news. Even more undesirable for newswriters—but not necessarily for comedians—is the good news-bad news combo: "Governor Gibson had good news and bad news today. He said he's going to push for a tax cut—but not this year." What makes it objectionable is that it has become tattered. But I do think it's unobjectionable to use the "good news" approach when the news is indisputably good for a specific group or person: "The I.R.S. had good news today for taxpayers." Or "Governor Wilson received good news and bad news today. His good news: He was put on probation. His bad news: He has to make restitution." Otherwise, the time-consuming, judgmental "good news" label is bad news. And please don't call a story "unusual." We don't report the usual, do we? Not usually.

■ *Starting a story with a participial phrase or a dependent clause.* Don't. That's not the way we talk. It's not the way other people talk. It's not the way you can help listeners latch onto a story and lock in on it.

Would you ever phone a friend to report some gossip and say, "Trying to concentrate on her job hunt so she can change careers, Ellen quit her job today"? You'd probably say: "Ellen quit her job today. She wants to get into something else, so now she'll be able to concentrate on finding a job."

Yet, some newscasters often use the type of participial phrase seen in that first sentence. Stories that start with participles are usually weak and murky. That's because they require too much of listeners. The participial phrase with its secondary information that listeners hear at the start means nothing until they hear the next cluster of words. Then the listeners have to rearrange both clusters so they make sense. And how many listeners have the time, the ambition and the aptitude—all while the wordathon rolls on?

Once you establish the subject in the first sentence, it is O.K. to start your second sentence with a participial phrase. If you do start it with a participial phrase or dependent clause, the subject should be the same as in the first sentence. Otherwise, you're creating the same sort of burden for listeners.

To make the subject of the story clear and unmistakable, the best pattern for writing your first sentence, at least, is subject-verb-object: Start with the subject, go to the verb and follow with the object. In sum: S-V-O. The closer the verb follows the subject, the easier for the listener to follow. If you put a subordinate clause after the subject, you're separating the subject from the verb. So try to avoid subordinate clauses that separate subject and verb. The greater the distance between subject and verb, the greater the difficulty for listeners. They hear only one word at a time, so that by the time they reach the verb, they have to make an effort to go back mentally and try to figure out who's doing what. While they're trying to do that, they might lose the train of thought. And if they lose it, they probably won't be able to get back on board.

Consider a listener trying to sort out this imaginary lead:

A million-dollar jackpot winner—burdened by heavy debts, a critically ill wife and a son accused of beating up a policeman—shot and killed himself today.

Might sound to some listeners like a policeman committed suicide. This is an exaggerated example, but it illustrates one of the problems caused by subordinate clauses. Do you think listeners—most of whom are only half-listening—can sort that out? And still keep up with the flow of the story? If the information in a subordinate clause is essential, put it in a sentence of its own. Perhaps you could rewrite that lead this way: "A million-dollar jackpot winner cashed in his chips today." No, I'm kidding. That lead is in poor taste; we mustn't poke fun at someone's misfortune. Try this: "A man who won a million dollars in the lottery shot and killed himself today. He was heavily in debt, his wife critically ill, his son in jail." When you go with S-V-O, listeners know the subject; they don't have to exert themselves to grasp the thread. And they can hang on to it. Listeners are not supposed to do the work; you are. Listeners have only one chance; they can't refer to a previous word or sentence; they can't set a story aside and go over it at their leisure; they can't ask you what you mean. But they can turn to another newscast. So as you write, think of your listeners and write for *them*.

■ *Starting a story with a quotation.* Don't. Listeners can't see quotation marks. And they can't see your script.

When an anchor starts with a quotation, listeners rightly assume that the words are the anchor's own. It's especially confusing for listeners when the anchor opens with a startling or potentially controversial assertion. So if attribution is needed, the best way to proceed is to put the source, or attribution, first. The best way to remember this is: Attribution precedes assertion. When we converse, we put attribution first. We don't even stop to think about it. Our conversation follows that pattern naturally. People talk like this: "He said, 'Blah-blah.' And she said, 'Hah-hah.'" If your news director ever rebukes you, you might tell a friend in the newsroom. Without pausing for an instant, you'd put the attribution first: "The Boss told me today I have to learn how to park my bike straight." You certainly wouldn't say to your friend, "'You have to learn how to park your bike straight.' That's what the Boss told me today." Yet, you'll hear anchors start a story with a quotation that sounds as though they're expressing their views or saying something else that is unsettling or jarring, maybe something like this:

> City Hall needs to be taught a lesson. That's the opinion of a
> retired councilman, Boris Bravo. He told a City Council meeting
> today. . . .

A listener might take that first sentence as the start of an editorial. Better: "A critic of City Hall says it ought to be taught a lesson. The critic, Boris Bravo, is a retired councilman. He told a City Council meeting. . . ."

Here's another type of strong lead that we hear without any preceding attribution:

Anyone who chews five sticks of gum a day can ensure healthy gums and teeth. That's the finding of a ten-year study released today. The study was done by researchers in Asunción, Paraguay, and it shows that. . . .

All it shows, in fact, is that some newspeople have to work harder at understanding how people speak and how they listen. (See pp. 137-141.)

■ *Starting a story with "There is," "There are," or "It is."* Don't. They're dead phrases. And they're wordy and wasteful. The strength of a sentence lies largely in a muscular verb. A sentence gets its get-up-and-go from an action verb like "shoot" or "hit" or "explode." Or hundreds of others that express action. Although "is" and "are" are in the active voice, they are not *action* verbs; they convey no action. They—and other forms of *to be*—are known as linking verbs. They link the subject of a sentence with a complement, another noun or adjective, a word that identifies or describes the subject. Linking verbs, including *seem, become, feel* and *look,* don't have the power to drive a sentence forward, merely to keep it idling. When you start a sentence with "There is," you're just marking time until you introduce the verb that counts, even if it's only another linking verb. Take this first sentence from a network story:

There's growing speculation in the credit markets that the Federal Reserve is going to ease up again in the face of slow economic growth.

First, lop off *There's.* Then rewrite: "Speculation is growing in the credit markets that. . . ." By deleting *There's,* you're making the sentence tighter. And by making it tighter, you're making it stronger. There are instances, though, as in this sentence, which says something exists, when *There are* may be appropriate.

■ *Writing a first sentence in which the main verb is any form of "to be," like "is," "was," "were," and "will be."* Don't. It's not wrong, just weak. Sometimes it's acceptable, even desirable, but in most cases, it's best to search for an action verb. Here's a sentence I hear on the air occasionally:

The President is back in the White House.

Factually and grammatically, that sentence is unobjectionable. But the "is" lacks movement; it merely expresses a condition or a situation, not an action. The next sentence is better because it has an action verb that indicates someone has *done* something. "The President has returned to the White House." Or "The President has arrived back at the White House." Sometimes, though, the use of "is" in the first sentence is suitable when the sentence is short and the story is big: "The teachers' strike is over." Another appropriate use of "is" in a first sentence: "Mayor Smiley is dead." That sentence gets its strength from "dead." Which reminds me of another tip: certain one-syllable words—like "dead"—gain extra impact when used as the last word of a sentence. First, let's look at this sentence: "The death toll in the X-Y-Z crash has now risen to 149." That's a big number, but it's not presented in the most memorable way. The sentence is all right, but the word "death" doesn't have the impact of "dead," particularly when "dead" is used as the last word. By the time the listener hears "149," he might not remember that it refers to the dead, not to "casualties," which refers to dead *and* injured. Now let's revise the sentence: "The toll in the X-Y-Z crash has now risen to 149 dead." See the difference? Rather, *hear* the difference?

One of the biggest weaknesses in broadcast news stories is the opening sentence. Too many limp. Or just lie there. Every lead can't be a grabber, but what listeners hear first can be crucial as to whether they keep listening. So newswriters should strive to use action verbs. This broadcast story illustrates how not to do it:

> There was another clash in Britain tonight between police and gangs of youths. The latest incident was in the northern London district of Tottenham, where hundreds of youths overturned cars, threw gasoline bombs and set fires. Several policemen were reported injured. The incident followed the unexplained death of a West Indian woman during a police search of her home.

Now let's see where that lead went wrong. The writer had plenty of action that he could have reported with vigorous verbs. Instead, he began with the flabby "There was." And he weakened the sentence with "another." Used so soon, "another" makes almost any story less newsy. After all, the main point of the story isn't that the two groups clashed *again*. The story is that they clashed. If it weren't a sizeable clash, it probably wouldn't be worth reporting at all. And the writer sapped a good verb, "clash," by using it as a noun. Further, "youths" is not a conversational word. Another point: the name of the London district is not worth mentioning, nor that it's in the north.

Now let's look at one way to pep up the first sentence of that story: "Hundreds of young people in London went on a rampage tonight: They overturned cars, threw gasoline bombs and set fires." Which approach sounds stronger?

■ *Starting a story with the name of an unknown or unfamiliar person.* Don't. An unknown cannot be the reason you're telling the story; you're telling it because of an unusual occurrence that just happens to concern that person. If the name means nothing to listeners, they're quite likely not to pay close attention and thus miss the crux of the story. The best way to introduce an unknown is with a title or a description: "A New York City milkman, Gary Goldstein [he took that name because it's a blend of Guernsey and Holstein], was awarded five million dollars in damages today for. . . ." But many stories don't need a name: without it, a story flows better and runs shorter. What does an unknown name in another city mean to you? Or your listeners? If you're writing about a fugitive or about a runaway, then a name may be essential. Before you use a name, ask yourself whether the story would be incomplete without it. Would any listener be likely to phone your newsroom and ask, "What's the name of that Albanian you just said was arrested in Turkey for cavorting in a Chicken Man costume?" (If you ever hear a listener say "cavort," try to get *his* name.) It's O.K., though, to start a story with names of people with official titles, prominent people whose names are in the news constantly: President Bush, Prime Minister Thatcher, Pope John Paul, Secretary of State Baker. Also, your governor, mayor, police chief and a few others. And for them, we drop first names. We can also start a story with someone who has star quality, whose name is widely known, but we use a first name and precede the name with a label: "The actress Bernadette Peters," "The painter Pablo Picasso," "The author Kitty Kelley." But we do not use a middle name or middle initial—unless. Unless we're writing about someone whose middle name is (or was) tattooed on his chest, say, John Paul Jones. Also, skip initials unless the person you're writing about has long been identified by an initial, say, Joe E. Brown, J. Edgar Hoover, Robert Q. Lewis, Edward R. Murrow, Edward G. Robinson. Another exception: use of an initial may be desirable if you're trying to avoid a mixup with a widely known person who has the same name. Broadcast newswriters customarily omit "Junior" and "the Third" after someone's name—unless not using them might cause confusion with prominent namesakes. But there's no need to use someone's first name *and* a nickname, say, House Speaker Thomas "Tip" O'Neill. Go with one or the other, preferably Thomas, but not both. We just don't have time for nicknames, especially those silly uses of first names with standard diminutives, like Edward "Ed" Cooper, Thomas "Tom" O'Connor and Joseph "Joe" Collier. (Have you ever known a Joseph who was called Tom? Or an Irving called Sam?)

Even when you do use a name in a story, try to use as few names as possible so listeners can keep their eye on the ball. Names make news, but there's a time and place for everything, including those two clichés.

A companion rule: Don't start a story with the name of an unknown or unfamiliar entity or concept.

■ *Starting a story with a personal pronoun.* Don't. Here's an example of a story that starts with a personal pronoun:

> He said he'd never give up his campaign to stop the X-Y-Z project, and today Morgan Murgatroyd took his case to. . . .

Whenever I hear a story start that way, I wonder whether I missed the beginning, which would have identified "he." Or I think I might have been only half-listening. If you put yourself in the shoes of a listener, you'll see that an ordinary listener might be just as confused by such a lead. A newspaper feature can start with "he" because a reader generally can first see who "he" is in a headline or a photo. But we don't talk like that. That's another argument for relying on the best pattern of all: Subject-verb-object, good old S-V-O. And avoid premature pronouns.

■ *Writing a first sentence that uses "yesterday."* Don't. People tune in expecting to hear the latest news, the later the better. They want to hear news that has broken since they last heard or read the news. Imagine tuning in an evening newscast and hearing an anchor starting to talk about something that happened "yesterday." "Yesterday"? I thought yesterday was gone for good. Who cares about yesterday? I want to hear what happened today, especially what's happening now. "Yesterday" is still common in newspaper leads, but for broadcasting, it's too old, too dated, too rearview-mirrorish. If you have to lead with a story that broke yesterday, try to update it so you can use a "today." Or use a present tense verb without a "yesterday" or "today." Or use the present perfect tense. It expresses an action carried out before the present and completed at the present or an action begun in the past and continuing in the present. If you find out, for example, just before tonight's broadcast that the mayor's wife was kidnapped last night, you can write around "last night" or "yesterday" by making use of the present perfect tense: "Mayor Hudson's wife *has been* kidnapped." A script mustn't deceive listeners by substituting "today" for "yesterday," and you mustn't try to pass off yesterday's news as today's. Exercise ingenuity in figuring out how to write a first sentence without harking all the way back to yesterday. Nowadays, yesterday is long gone. A worse sin than using "yesterday" in a lead is using yesterday's news. Where appropriate, try to give your story a forward thrust, not a backward glance.

■ *Writing a first sentence that uses the verb "continues."* Don't. It doesn't tell a listener anything new. It doesn't propel a sentence or a story forward. It merely tells the listener that something that has been going on is still going on. That alerts the listener to the realization that this is going to be a story that's just more of the same: not news, just olds. News is what's new. When you have to write a long-running story—a siege, a hijacking, a hunger strike, a drought—search for a new peg. If there is none, find a different angle of attack, move in from a different direction, and steer clear of "continues." Focus on whatever's going on today that wasn't going on yesterday. And try to find a verb with verve. In a second or subsequent sentence, "continues" is not objectionable. But it's nonsensical for someone to end a story with "The controversy continues."

Another word I avoid: "details." Whenever I hear "details," I think of the fine print in a lease or a contract, the specs for a stereo component, or something else where I'm loath to go into detail. I suspect that most listeners view *details* with the same dislike or lack of interest. Yet we often hear anchor lead-ins that end with this kind of introduction to reporters: "Sally Golightly has the details." It's better to say, "Sally Golightly has the story." Or "Sally Golightly has more." Or "Sally Golightly reports on how this might affect you." Or "Sally Golightly reports [a fact from Smith's script]." Or find other words; just don't bother me with *details.*

■ *Starting a story with "another," "more" or "once again."* Don't—with few exceptions. It's a turnoff. If you start a story with "another," it sounds as though whatever the story turns out to be, it's similar to or a continuation of a story told previously, a story that's not new or not much different, perhaps just more of the same. A broadcast example:

> Another jetliner tragedy in Britain today. A chartered airliner
> caught fire on take-off in Birmingham, and 54 passengers
> were killed.

The story is newsworthy on its own merits, not because it was the third airline accident in a month. To stress that it's the third in a short time, I'd put that fact in a sentence of its own: "A British jetliner caught fire on take-off in Birmingham, England, today, and 54 passengers were killed. It's the third airline disaster in less than a month." New York City averages four homicides a day, yet who'd ever think of starting a story,

"Another man was murdered in Manhattan today"? Or "Another tourist was mugged in Central Park today"? Want another?

Starting a story with *more* also signals the listener that what's coming is more of the same. It'd be better for you to skip *more* and proceed directly to whatever the new "more" is. One reason so many broadcast stories start with "more" is that it's an easy way to go: "More headaches for the President today," "More wrangling on Capitol Hill today," "More arrests in the Acme Power case." (As for sentences without verbs, that's another story. For another time.)

■ *Starting a story with a sentence that has a "no" or "not."* Try not to. Recast a negative lead into a positive. Instead of saying, "The President is not going to take his planned trip to Tahiti," it's better to say, "The President has canceled his trip to Tahiti." In some cases, a listener might confuse "not" with "now." We shouldn't go overboard worrying about possible listener confusion, but it's the reason we don't write "*a* million"; instead, we write, "*one* million"—lest a listener mistake *a* for *eight*.

■ *Cramming too much information into a story.* Don't. Too many facts, too many names, too many numbers, too many words are too much for listeners. They just can't process a steady flow of facts. Brinkley has said the ear is "the worst, least effective way to absorb information." (*David* Brinkley, not Christie.) No matter how complex the story, our job is to compress the facts and give the listener not just the essence but a highly concentrated essence: the quintessence. Architect Ludwig Mies van der Rohe, a minimalist, used to say, "Less is more." His critics retorted (not in unison), "Less is less." And I say, when it comes to lead sentences, "More is less." Moreover, more is a bore.

■ *Using newspaper constructions.* Don't. This is an example of a common newspaper construction:

> The chairman of the Senate Foreign Relations Committee said today Moscow should stop threatening Washington. Senator John Walton said. . . .

Most newspaper readers would probably see that Walton is the person described in the first sentence, the committee chairman. But in broadcasting, the nature of the medium leads many listeners to assume that the Walton in the second sentence is someone else and that Walton is adding his voice to the chairman's. In broadcasting, it's better to write, "The chairman of the Senate Foreign Relations Committee, John Walton, said

today. . . ." Or "The chairman of the Senate Foreign Relations
Committee said today. . . . Chairman John Walton told. . . ." That
makes Walton's identity unmistakable. For writers with a newspaper
background, a reminder. Don't write in an inverted-pyramid style. Leave
that to newspaper people. If you haven't worked on a newspaper or don't
know what an inverted pyramid is, you have one less habit to undo. In
journalism school, I was taught in a class in broadcast newswriting not to
use newspaper terms. After it sank in, it struck me as reasonable. Why
should we, in a far different medium, use lingo devised for another
medium, one that broadcasting tries to be different from? Yet I hear
newscasters refer to people or stories "in the headlines." What headlines?
Are they plugging newspapers? And some newscasters talk about their
"front page," their "sports page," their "people page," their "back page,"
even their "cover story." "Cover" for TV? Yep, and they aren't referring
to dust covers. Another publishing word borrowed by broadcasters is
"magazine." It's also a place of storage and a storehouse of information,
so perhaps its use in broadcasting can be justified. But "pages"? The only
pages I know in broadcasting run errands.

While I'm at it, I might as well point out a newspaper ritual that
some broadcasters follow, probably without due thought: reporting the
composition of a jury by sex. How many times have you heard a story
that starts, "A jury of seven men and five women convicted a Hicksville
man of murder today"? Or, even worse: "The seven-man, five-woman
jury deliberated for three hours"? The length of deliberations may be
worth mentioning only if unusually long or unusually brief. Otherwise,
who cares? Every jury takes a certain time to reach a verdict. But every
jury—except a grand jury, which has 23 members, and a six-person
jury—consists (excluding alternate members) of the same number of
citizens, 12. No matter how many are men, how many women, the total is
always 12. Listeners who hear that five women—or seven—sat on a jury
are not learning anything of consequence. So why take valuable air time
to tell the composition of the jury? I haven't heard anyone report the
makeup of an appellate court—"a panel of two men and one woman."
Nor have I heard anyone report a decision by the U.S. Supreme Court—
"the eight-man, one-woman court." If a rapist is convicted by a jury of 12
women, the makeup of the jury is newsworthy. Except for unusual
circumstances, the makeup of a jury, a committee, or a legislative body
is irrelevant.

Other usually meaningless figures: the number of counts in an
indictment. Circumstances alter cases, as we say in court, but it's usually

better to skip the number of counts and just say a man was indicted for allegedly defrauding investors of 10 million dollars. If he was indicted on 3,000 counts—one for each complaint or each offense—I would use that. Why? Because that's the highest number of counts under one roof since a Hapsburg ball.

Another newspaper ritual that wastes listeners' time—and yours: saying that the person just indicted "faces 765 years in prison." Assuming the indictment is not dismissed, assuming he goes to trial, assuming he's convicted, assuming a judge imposes the maximum, assuming the conviction is not overturned, assuming the sentence is not commuted, he'll never serve 765 years. Never in a million years.

In addition to avoiding newspaper rituals, broadcast newswriters should avoid newspaper words. Papers use them because they're short enough to be shoe-horned into headlines, but people don't use them in conversation: *vie, nab, oust, laud, foe, woe, don, probe, yegg, slate* (for *schedule*), *decry, fray* (don't write that someone "was shot in the *fracas*"), *top* (as a verb), *cop* (as a verb; I don't use it even as a noun), *hike* (as a synonym for *raise*), *pact, aid* (as a verb meaning *help*), *eye* (as in this headline: "Sneaker-Maker Nike Eyes China's Two Billion Feet"), *seek* (except in a combination like "heat-seeking missiles"), *ink* (as a synonym for the verb *sign*), *felled* (as in "Ship's Crew Felled by Food Poisoning"), *garbed, clad* (except as a suffix, as in "iron-clad"), *blast, rap* and *hit* (when they're intended to mean *criticize*) and *up* as a verb: "The workers want to *up* their pay." Which reminds me of a title for a *Reader's Digest* article: "How We Upped Our Income; How You Can Up Yours." Those short words can be squeezed into one-column heads in papers, but they're not words that we use when we talk; not even newspaper copy editors *say* them.

Another newspaper word to be avoided is *slay*. It's a good Anglo-Saxon word, but it's not so strong as *kill* or *murder*. And *slay* is not conversational. I don't know anyone who says *slay*. Nor do I know anyone who uses the past tense, *slew,* or the past participle, *slain.* So don't use *slay* unless you're talking about dragons. Or Santa.

Also: When writing about a young person, don't call him, her or it a youth, as in: "Police are also questioning the youth about several other murders." It's not uncouth to say *youth: Youth* has long been used to describe a young person, especially a young man between boyhood and adulthood, but *youth* is a print word, not a talk word. Have you ever used it in conversation? Do you ever hear anyone else use it? If so, please report him to the Bureau of Youth Abuse.

Other words that should not be used in broadcast copy are several commonly used in print: *former, latter, respectively.* Our reason for not using them: Listeners probably won't remember names or items mentioned even seconds earlier, and they certainly can't peek at your script to check.

■ *Losing or not reaching a listener.* Don't. Don't lose a listener and don't fail to reach one. The best way to keep a listener is by talking to him, not at him, and by working at it, not by making him do the work. He won't, so you have to. Writing *is* hard work; anyone who says it's easy is someone who hasn't tried it or doesn't know how to do it well. The work of writing, it is said, can be easy only for those who have not learned to write. Telling a long, complex story in 20 seconds is a challenge for any writer. Telling it well is even harder. As Confucius should have said, "Easy writing, hard listening. Hard writing, easy listening."

■ *Making a factual error.* Don't. This is the deadliest sin of all. It causes you to lose authority and credibility. And eventually you lose audience.

You may think you've caught me in a factual error. I called those the Dozen Deadly Sins and, like a good writer, you counted the sins and found 19. No, I didn't miscount. Rather, to atone for all my sins over the years, I'm doing penance by renouncing an additional seven deadly sins. Thou shalt not commit any of them.*

When you write your next script, keep them in mind. You'll see how avoiding the Deadly Sins can help make your copy more lively.

But if you want to win a Peabody and not wind up a nobody, here's perhaps the most important rule of all: To *improve* a story, go ahead and break a rule.

---

*The writer Justin Fishbein says there's only one of the Ten Commandments he hasn't violated. Which one? He says he has never made a graven image.

2

VENIAL SINS

A rung or two down the scale from the Deadly Sins are the Venial Sins. Deadly they may not be, but sins they are:

■ *Starting stories with pre-fabricated phrases.* Don't. Among the most frazzled: "This is the story of," "It's official," "Once upon a time," "Now it can be told," "It shouldn't come as any surprise," "It had to happen eventually," "Mayor Mozzarella made it official today," "The mayor fired the opening shot today in the . . .," "When was the last time you . . .?" "Believe it or not!" "[Lebanon] is no stranger to violence," "[Orville Oliver] is no stranger to politics," "For City Hall today, it was the best of times, it was the worst of times," "It was business as usual today at. . .," "What we know now is. . .," "It's that time of year again," "Here we go again."

■ *Ending stories with pre-fabricated phrases.* Don't. Some to shun: "Police are investigating" (Since when is that news?), "What happens next remains to be seen," "Only time will tell," "Now the ball is in the mayor's court," "Don't count him out yet," "As Yogi Berra put it, 'It ain't over till it's over,'" "It'll probably get worse before it gets better," "The full story is yet to be told," "In the final analysis," "No one knows what the outcome will be," "No one knows for sure," "The final chapter is yet to be written," "There's no end in sight"—and variations without end.

■ *Using pre-fabs anywhere.* Don't. Most of these word packages are the kinds that secretaries can type on a word processor with one keystroke, like "In response to your letter" and "Very truly yours." Lawyers call these groupings "boilerplate," strips of words that are extruded into contracts automatically with little thought or effort.

16

Among pre-fabs in broadcast news: "At a hastily called news conference," "At a crowded news conference," "In a prepared statement," "In a bloodless, pre-dawn coup," "In an abrupt about-face," "None the worse for wear."

■ *Wasting words.* Don't. Not only do they waste time but they dilute the impact of what you say. Here are some words that almost always are excess baggage:

In order—as in "They went to the White House *in order* to protest the President's action." In almost all cases, when you delete *in order,* the sentence means the same.

In the process of—as in "The mayor is now *in the process of* deciding whether to run for another term." Without *in the process of,* the meaning is the same.

Literally, actually, really—as in "The umpire *literally* walked off the field." Or "The sheriff *actually* saw the collision." In both cases, the adverbs add nothing. *Really.*

Suddenly, gradually, finally—as in "*Suddenly,* he fell off the bridge." No one falls gradually. Remember that scene in *The Sun Also Rises* when Bill asks, "How did you go bankrupt?" And Mike replies: "Two ways. Gradually and then suddenly." *Finally,* those adverbs usually add nothing to a sentence but bulk.

Flatly—as in "She *flatly* denied it" and "He *flatly* refused." A denial is a denial.

Personally, officially—as in "The governor *personally* favors taking steps to stop the project." *Unofficially,* those adverbs only delay delivery of the news. Another adverb that's often unnecessary: *formally. Seriously.*

Local and *nearby*—as in "The injured were taken to a *local* hospital." Or to "an *area* hospital." (I'm unaware that *area* is an adjective, except in "area code" and "area rug.") Where else would they be taken, to an out-of-town hospital? If anyone is taken to a distant hospital, it may be worth reporting. If anyone is taken to a nearby hospital, it's not worth mentioning. But if they're taken to a hospital just across the street, that may be part of the story. Otherwise, listeners assume the injured were taken to the nearest hospitals. And I prefer to have ambulances *take* people, not *rush* them. Ambulances do rush; but I find *rush* in copy is too breathless. And please don't write that the injured were taken to three *different* hospitals. That's a common lapse to which a good writer cannot be indifferent.

A total of—as in "A total of 50 people were hurt." A total waste.

Then—as in "He was arrested and charged, then freed on bond." When the chronology is obvious, *then* is usually unneeded. Sometimes, all that's needed is *and:* "He was arrested, charged and freed on bond."

The fact that—as in "The fact that there are two suspects means that police have a lot more work to do." Better: "Police have two suspects, so they have a lot more work to do." Another example: "The marchers were protesting the fact that the government refused to release the two prisoners." Better: "The marchers were protesting the government's refusal to release the two prisoners." Whenever you find *the fact that* in a sentence you've written, try to rewrite it. When you eliminate *the fact that,* you almost always can improve your sentence. That's a fact.

Meanwhile—as in "Meanwhile, the White House said it's examining the situation." I hesitate to say there's never an occasion to use *meanwhile,* but I've never run across it, except here. Even more wasteful than *meanwhile*—which means "at the same time" or "in the intervening time"—is the meaningless *in the meanwhile.* If you need a transition from one item to a *related* item, you can use other devices. One: you can start the second item with a dateline: "In Washington, the Administration said it's examining the problem." Two: you can link the second item by starting it with a word like "later." Three: you can think of another way. Whatever you decide on, don't use as a transition the all-purpose "on another front"—unless you're writing about a war with several fronts. Or unless you're talking about a weather front. Also avoid using as a transition "closer to home." We generally hear that after a foreign story or one from out-of-town. If anything, the new item is *at* home. After many a calamity, we hear this transition: "On a lighter note." It implies that what we just heard was light and what we're going to hear is even lighter. After a recent bombing, one anchor said, "On a *much* lighter note. . . ."

Speaking of strained segues, and that's another type of transition to avoid, this was broadcast on a New York City TV station: After an anchor described John Glenn (erroneously) as "the first man to orbit the earth," his co-anchor said, "And speaking of the earth, the earth has weather, and here's our weatherman." And speaking of weathermen, they, too, can chill me. We're "sitting under a convective flow," a weatherman said on a New York City station. A "convective flow"? What's that? And a Los Angeles meteorologist reported "a split flow in the 500-millibar chart," whatever that is. Made me think of splitting for Malibu. Or Malabar.

Let's just hope we don't hear an anchor use this old Monty Python line as a transition: "And now for something completely different."

■ *Using non-broadcast words.* Don't. A non-broadcast word is one that's not likely to be readily understood by almost all listeners. A listener who's baffled by a word on a newscast probably doesn't reach for a dictionary, assuming one is within reach. How many listeners understand *infrastructure?* Or *draconian?* Or *Byzantine?* Another non-broadcast word that I've heard on a newscast is "vagaries." How many listeners know what they are? Or confuse them with "vagrants"? I don't have a list of non-broadcast words, but here are some warning signs: If you suspect that a word you're considering is a non-broadcast word, you're probably right. If you've never run into the word before, never used it and never heard anyone else use it, or if you have to look it up in the dictionary, it almost certainly is a good word not to use, so drop it. Some newswriters think that by slipping in a big word now and then they'll make an impression. Well, they do make an impression: unfavorable. Here's a word that we hear on the air often during political campaigns, but one that deserves retirement: *gubernatorial.* I doubt that anyone outside newsrooms ever uses it, not even gubernators.

And don't dare use *energumen, epigone, eristic, hebdomadal, maieutic, periphrastic, psephology, stochastic, tergiversation, velleity* or any other sesquipedalian words unless you're bucking to understudy Bill Buckley.

The best policy: Save the big words for Scrabble.

■ *Using hollow words.* Don't. They're usually combined with words that do matter, but they themselves usually do nothing but take up time. The hollow words, when used in certain combinations, are: *activity, incident, condition* and *situation.* For example, newscasters talk about "the shooting *incident.*" All they need say is "the shooting." No need for *incident.* (Incidentally, a shooting is hardly an incident; an incident is usually a minor event, say, a jostling on the bus.) They also talk about "the famine *situation.*" Some weathercasters talk about "thunderstorm *activity.*" They need mention only "thunderstorms." And they say "the storm *condition*" will last several hours. That sentence, too, would be stronger if it were un*conditional.* I've also heard weathercasters talk about the temperature's reaching "the 45-degree *mark.*" And the temperature's falling to zero *degrees*. Zero *is* on the scale, but zero is not a degree and certainly not *degrees*. Zero is zero.

We also hear newscasters talk about a trial that has been "one-month *long*." Better: "The trial has lasted one month." And some newscasters say something like this: "The test will run for a three-month *period*." Better: "The test will run three months." Period.

■ *Using vague words.* Don't. One of the most popular is *involved*. When I hear that someone was *involved* in a crime, I don't know whether that person committed it or was a victim. Or a witness. Whenever possible, be specific.

■ *Using vogue words.* Don't. A few that shouldn't find their way into your copy: *meaningful, opt, parenting, parameters, peer, sibling, supportive, viable, wellness.*

■ *Using weasel words.* Don't. I'd change the slogan "Never say die" to "Never say pass away." You may think you're being more solemn and respectful by saying someone *passed away* or *expired*. Not at all. The nice-nellyism may be well intended, but it's merely wordy and indirect. (Even hairstylists prefer euphemisms: "Never say 'dye.'")

Some squeamish writers also say "attack" instead of "rape," but an attack covers many kinds of assaults. So stop squeaming.

■ *Using windy words.* Don't. Some newswriters use windy words to inflate their stories or because they're not aware of simple synonyms. Some newswriters use *commence* when they could easily say "start." But they may think "start" is too common a word, that they ought to give their copy class. No point in putting on airs, though, when all you're doing is slowing listeners' comprehension, adding length to a story and lessening its effect. They also say damage is *extensive*. But, depending on what they mean, why not say the damage was "heavy" or "widespread"? Other highfalutin words that we hear too often: *utilize* instead of "use," *implement* (verb) instead of "put into effect," *implement* (noun) instead of "tool." And please don't use *initiate* unless you're writing about a fraternity.

You have no need to say *approximately* when all you need is *about*. Mark Twain said: "I never write 'metropolis' for seven cents when I can get the same . . . for 'city.'"

■ *Using weary words.* Don't. A weary word in my book, and this *is* my book, is one that through overuse has been used up. The first one that comes to my mind, and it comes often to many minds, is *controversy*. That's why we hear newscasters refer to a new controversy brewing, or a controversial candidate, a controversial bill, a controversial plan, a controversial movie, a controversial action, a controversial faction. In fact, almost everything is controversial, perhaps even this denunciation. To avoid controversy, I suppose I should say *almost* everything is controversial. In some quarters, even Santa Claus in controversial. Some people object to him because they regard Christmas as a sacred day but one that is mocked by the creation of Santa and his commercial ties. That also goes for the Easter Bunny. Even Jesus was controversial. And still *is*. That's one reason that, worldwide, Christians are a minority. Who or what is *not* controversial? That's why Congress debates bills, people argue over candidates, and objectors circulate petitions. Some broadcast newswriters who want a strong word for a lead promptly latch on to *controversy* or *controversial*. That's the easy way out. Or in. What they apparently don't realize is that the more they use those two words, the less they mean. (See pp. 176-177.)

■ *Using wrong words.* Don't. Make sure you know what a word means before you use it. The best way to make sure is to check a dictionary. One of the most frequently misused words is *dilemma*. It's almost invariably intended to mean *problem, plight* or *predicament*. In fact, a *dilemma* is two alternatives, equally undesirable.

And watch out for words with contrary meanings, like *sanctions*. When newscasters speak of nations' "imposing sanctions," they mean "penalties." But dictionaries' first definition of the noun *sanction* is confirmation or approval. And the verb *sanction* means *approve*.

■ *Using foreign words and phrases.* Stop. (See p. 168.) Many listeners have all they can do to understand basic English. Governmental surveys estimate the number of illiterates in this country at more than 17 million. And not everyone classified as literate is a prospect for a Ph.D. So writers should stick to English, the only language we expect listeners to know. Most of them don't read the *New Yorker,* don't work the Sunday crossword puzzle in the *New York Times.* And don't use or hear foreign words in conversation. Those are the people we're writing for, people who speak plain English.

I don't want to seem persnickety, but we should also avoid *per.* That's not a peremptory command. As with other tips, or principles, or rules, or whatever you call them, I'm not saying, "Never, ever, under any circumstances whatsoever." All I'm saying is, whenever possible, avoid it.

Instead of writing "55 miles per hour," for example, write "55 miles an hour." Most experts oppose the use of *per* where *a* or other familiar English words will do. A high school textbook—published in 1908—said of *per.* "A Latin preposition not sanctioned in English." Instead of *per week, per* pound, write *a week, a pound.* Avoid *per se, per annum, per capita, per diem* and *per deum*—unless you write with divine inspiration.

Also avoid *amicus curiae, caveat emptor, en route, gratis, ipso facto, quid pro quo, sine die, sine qua non, status quo, via, vis-à-vis,* etc., especially *et cetera.* Avoid almost all other Latin words and terms. I say *"almost* all other" Latin-based terms; a few are permissible because they are so deeply rooted in common speech: one is "percent." If I may digress, use *percent* (from the Latin *per centum,* meaning "by the hundred") only after a number. Don't say, "A large percent were out of work"; it is correct, though, to say, "A large percentage were out of work." A few Latin words *may* be acceptable *in extremis*—when no English equivalent is available or when Latin can be readily understood. The Latin term *in absentia* may be acceptable when reporting the case of a defendant who was sentenced even though not present: *Absentia* does sound like "absence." I think it may be better, though, to say "He was sentenced although [he was] absent." Another Latin term that may be acceptable is *persona non grata,* the diplomatic term for someone declared unwelcome—not to be confused with *persona au gratin,* a diplomatic big cheese. Otherwise, foreign words are just not *apropos.*

Not long ago, the columnist Mike Royko took a swipe at Americans who use foreign words: "Just as irritating as restaurants are books and magazines that slip French words in and expect us to understand them. That's why I gave up reading the *New Yorker,* which is one of the worst offenders. I don't know why that magazine does it. Half of all New Yorkers I've known can't speak understandable English, much less the language of the bwah and fwah."

Newswriters should avoid not only foreign words but also words with roots in Latin and Greek. Instead, they should use—whenever possible—words of Anglo-Saxon origin. So shun *facilitate* (help, ease), *endeavor* and *attempt* (try), *triumph* (win), *insurgent* (rebel), *exonerate* (clear), *extinguish* (put out), *conflagration* (fire), *altercation* (fight), *lacerations, abrasions* and *contusions* (cuts, scrapes and bruises).

Exception: Although it's a blend of Greek *and* Latin (from the Greek for "at a distance" and the Latin for "see"), your listeners shouldn't have any trouble understanding *television.*

Another language to keep away from is the language of law, exemplified by *therefore* and *nevertheless.* Here are the basic English equivalents: *therefore* = so, *nevertheless* = even so, *notwithstanding* = despite. I also skip *however.* Instead, depending on the story, I use *though, yet, still* or, most often, *but.*

■ *Resorting to clichés.* Don't. One cliché is not worth a thousand pictures. The only picture a cliché usually brings to my mind is that of a weary writer. I hear so much copy clotted with clichés that my mind curdles. I heard a Los Angeles TV newswoman report that an executive was confident that the movie industry, stung by an investigation, would get a "clean bill of health." I'd like to see one of those bills of health, clean or soiled. And I'd like to see one of those "bargaining tables" I hear about so much. Or a "bargaining chip." Or even a bargain. A New York City TV reporter, covering a double murder, said, "The police have their work cut out for them." Made me wonder: Had the victims been dismembered? Another reporter said three fugitives had everyone "on pins and needles." (That script should have been spiked.) Often, when a blackout, blizzard, flood or shutdown hits a community, a newscaster says, "Residents are taking it in stride." I never hear, though, that anyone is *not* taking it in stride. The only place I know where everyone takes things in stride is a marathon. And a network newsman has kept calling gold "the yellow metal" and silver "the gray metal." Fortunately, I've never heard him call copper "the red metal" or U.S. currency "the green paper."

Another cliché: "met behind closed doors." Example: "The President and his national security adviser met behind closed doors." Where else would they meet, for Pete's sake, on a bench in Lafayette Park? Some writers have people *huddling* behind closed doors. If you think the secrecy of a meeting is unusual or significant and worth taking time to mention, you can write, "The committee met in closed session." Or "met in secret." Or "met privately." And I wouldn't let people *huddle* unless there are eleven of them and one is a quarterback.

Also objectionable in news scripts are catchphrases lifted from commercials: "As for your umbrella, don't leave home without it." Also: "They got their prison terms the old-fashioned way. They earned them." My advice: Don't reach out and touch any of them. Other clichés to avoid—almost all the time: song titles and lyrics. How many times have you heard this lead-in to a voice-over, "It rained on the city's parade. . . ."? How many times have you written it? Promise not to do it again?

The most cliché-clotted copy I've ever heard on the air:

Robert Kennedy *dropped the other shoe* today and *threw his hat into the ring* for President, and now it's a *whole new ball game.*

As Shakespeare put it, and he *was* tuned in: "They have been at a great feast of languages, and stolen the scraps."

When it comes to scrapping clichés, experts, as usual, disagree. Most experts say clichés cause air pollution. A few experts say some clichés have *a saving grace.*

The granddaddy of good grammar, Henry W. Fowler, condemned clichés, but he said writers would be needlessly handicapped if they were never allowed to use, among others, *white elephant, had his tongue in his cheek, feathering his nest.* Fowler observed, in *Modern English Usage:* "What is new is not necessarily better than what is old; the original felicity that has made a phrase a cliché may not be beyond recapture." As George Burns put it, "If you stay around long enough, you become new."

"Use a cliché only with discrimination and sophistication," Theodore M. Bernstein wrote in *The Careful Writer,* "and . . . shun it when it is a substitute for precise thinking."

But for George Orwell, all clichés were *dead as the dodo:* "Never use a metaphor, simile, or other figure of speech which you are used to seeing in print."

The columnist Colman McCarthy told how, as a college English major, his required reading list was crushing. So he adopted a method suggested by the writer John Ciardi: "Read a writer's essay, poem, story or column until the first cliché. At that collision, stop. Then drop."

I don't want to be an absolutist and say, "Never use a cliché." I wouldn't knowingly use one in a script, but I wouldn't want to exclude the possibility that one day I might think of a cliché that conveys a thought better than any other combination of words that I can think of. The only time I deliberately use a cliché is when I can turn it inside out or upside down. For example, the cartoonist John Caldwell has uncorked "The early dog gets the worms," "There is no free brunch" and "What goes up must calm down."

■ *Stretching for synonyms for words that are easily understood.* Don't. Some writers dread using the same word twice in a 20-second story, not to mention twice in one sentence. Perhaps they fear someone might think that anyone who uses *said* twice in a story has an anemic vocabulary. So they figure the best way to dispel any such notion is to find another way to say *said*. But for writing broadcast news, the best verb to express oral communication, usually, is *says* (or *said*). Someone (I forget who) has compared *says* to a skillful stagehand: He does his work well, moves the show along and stays out of sight. Some synonyms for *said* lead to a script that's either stilted or tilted. Copy that sidesteps *said* is stilted, in most cases, when it uses *state* and *declare*; they're best reserved for formal statements or declarations. Copy may be tilted when the writer uses as a synonym for *said* a verb that might reflect on the person who was doing the saying, or calls into question his veracity. Here are a few such verbs: *admit* ("He admitted having a car"); *insist, maintain, claim* ("He claims he wrote the book himself") Because of what I was taught by Prof. Curtis MacDougall at the Medill School of Journalism, I do not use *claim* as a synonym for *asserts*; I use *claim* only when I talk about someone's claiming his baggage or claiming his stake. But the first American Heritage dictionary, published in 1969, said that in the sense of asserting as factual or maintaining a position in the face of possible argument, *claim* is "established." The dictionary's example: "The Air Force claims that the battleship is obsolete." The entry says 69 percent of the American Heritage Usage Panel found that use of *claims* acceptable.

Several other verbs are often used as the equivalent of *say*, but they are not the same. One is *explain*, as in: "He explained that the Bears won." That's hardly an explanation. *Explain* should be reserved for explaining plans or puzzles, or at least for situations that require some explaining. It's not to be used as Ring Lardner did, facetiously, in *You Know Me, Al:* "'Shut up,' he explained."

Another verb not to be substituted for *say* is *point out*. Save *point out* for pointing to facts, not mere assertions that may or may not be true. It's wrong to write: "He pointed out that his contract is still in force." He says it is, but maybe it isn't. This would be an appropriate use for *point out:* "He pointed out that the largest state is Alaska."

Also used as a synonym for *say*, incorrectly, is *laugh:* "She *laughed* that losing isn't everything." People do laugh, but they don't laugh anything. Better: "She said with a laugh that she would try again" or "She laughed and said she'd try again." And don't let anyone *chirp* even if you're quoting a jailbird who has turned canary.

Another problem crops up when a writer uses *said* before the subject: "Said one official: 'We're very disheartened about the outcome. . . .'" The writer might have been trying for a change of pace or for what he thought was streamlining, but in placing *said* before the subject, he's transgressing against the fixed word order of the normal sentence and violating conversational style. People don't talk like that. They don't say, "Said the magazine renewal letter: '*Time* is running out.'" It's unnatural. Says who? Says me. But don't just take it on my say-so; listen carefully to what people say and how they say it. Wolcott Gibbs of the *New Yorker* once wrote a profile of *Time's* co-founder, Henry Luce, and parodied *Timestyle,* which often ran counter to standard English: "Backward ran sentences until reeled the mind . . . Sitting pretty are the boys . . . Where it will all end, knows God!"

Enough *said?*

Some writers who shy away from simple words or avoid using a simple word more than once in a story look for what's called an elegant variation. If they were to write about bananas, they would, on second reference, talk about "elongated yellow fruit." It's easier for a listener if we use "banana" twice in 20 seconds, even three times.

■ *Hotrodding.* Don't. As you probably infer, this is high-powered writing. Hotrodders pepper their copy with words like *special, major, important, extra, unique, unprecedented, crisis.* In some stories, those words may be apt. But everything can't be special. "Where everybody is somebody," William S. Gilbert wrote, "nobody is anybody."

Hotrodders turn a spat between two public officials into a *clash.* And officials *lash out.* When they meet, it becomes a *summit* or a *confrontation* or a *showdown.* When an official announces a campaign or a drive against almost anything, it becomes a *war.* So we have a *war* against crime, a *war* against drugs, a *war* against illiteracy, a *war* against pornography, a *war* against scofflaws. After being bombarded by all these *wars,* a listener loses his understanding of war. So far, luckily, I haven't heard of a *war* against potholes.

Hotrodders make awards *prestigious,* experts *respected.* A trend becomes a *revolution,* a disclosure becomes a *shocker,* increased costs *astronomical* (because they've *skyrocketed.*) Two other popular words in the lexicon of hotrodders: *mystery* and *mysterious.* I learned long ago, as a newspaper cub (when I was what you might call an inkling), that rewritemen would use those words when they were short on facts and long on fancy. If they had a few more facts, they'd have no mystery.

And no discussion of hotrodding should overlook *spectacular.* Broadcasters often apply it to fires or to fire footage (And they're not all fire buffs—or firebugs). Sportscasters often apply *spectacular* to a base-ball player's catch, a football player's run, a tennis player's serve, a golfer's drive, not to mention the Amalfi Drive. In fact, *spectacular* seems to be an all-purpose adjective, one that a writer can use whenever he can't think of anything else to hold his audience.

One way to avoid many of these sins is not to write on a hypewriter. Yes, I know we're not writing a paper for a scholar, nor are we writing patter for a barker. Not that we're members of the priesthood. Nor candidates for sainthood. It's just that we want our copy to be true and trustworthy. And free of all sin.

3

TOP TIPS OF THE TRADE

Now that we've looked at the Don'ts, let's look at the Do's. I call them the Top Tips of the Trade. Whatever you call them—tips, reminders, principles, guidelines or rules—they'll help you do a better job. And they'll help your listeners.

First, the tips, then, after the list, an explanation:

1. Start strong. Well begun is half done.
2. Read—and understand—your source copy.
3. Underline or circle key facts.
4. Don't write yet. Think.
5. Write the way you talk (unless you're from the Bronx).
6. Apply the rules for broadcast newswriting.
7. Have the courage to write simply.
8. Refrain from wordy warm-ups.
9. Put attribution before assertion.
10. Go with S-V-O: subject—verb—object.
11. Limit a sentence to one idea.
12. Use short words and short sentences.
13. Use familiar words in familiar combinations.
14. People-ize your copy.
15. Activate your copy.
16. Avoid a first sentence whose main verb is any form of *to be: is, are, was, were, will be.*
17. Avoid *may, might, could, should, seems.*
18. Put your sentences in a positive form.
19. Use present tense verbs where appropriate.

20. Don't start with a quotation or a question.
21. Use connectives—*and, also, but, so, because*—to link sentences.
22. Put the word or words you want to emphasize at the end of your sentence.
23. Use contractions—with caution.
24. Pep up your copy with words like *new, now, but, says.*
25. Watch out for *I, we, our, here, up, down.*
26. Omit needless words.
27. Hit only the main points; trash the trivia.
28. Don't parrot source copy.
29. Place the time element, if you need one, *after* the verb.
30. When in doubt, leave it out.
31. Don't raise questions you don't answer.
32. Read your copy aloud. If it sounds like writing, rewrite it.
33. Rewrite. The art of writing lies in rewriting what you've already rewritten.

Now let's examine those tips in slo-mo:

1. *Start strong. Well begun is half done.* The most important words you'll write in a story are those that come first, what Prof. Mitchell Stephens calls "the lead's lead." So bear down on your first sentence. "Start strong" doesn't mean, make the story stronger than the facts warrant; it doesn't mean, exaggerate, distort or misrepresent. It means, put all your mental power into the start. Your first words may well determine whether listeners keep listening. So focus on your first words and your first sentence. If you set sail with even a small compass error and it's uncorrected, you'll end up far off course, even on the rocks, or at the bottom. A bad beginning, as Euripides told me, makes a bad ending.

2. *Read—and understand—your source copy.* Read it to the end. Don't write a story after reading only two or three paragraphs. If you don't understand something, don't use it. After all, if *you* don't understand it, how can you write it so your listeners will understand? Too many writers lift words and phrases from source copy and transplant them into their own copy without knowing what they mean. When an editor or producer asks what something in the script means, many a writer replies, "Well, that's what the wire copy says." Don't be a copycat.

3. *Underline or circle key facts.* By marking your source copy—preferably with a red or orange pen—you'll see instantly what's

important and what you have to consider including in your script. This can be a big help so you can boil down what's important and interesting to what's essential. Your markings will also help when you check the facts in your completed script against your source material.

You'll do a better job of deciding which facts to use as you develop your news judgment. So it's beneficial to ponder the question "What is news?" One of the best answers is provided by an authority on journalism, Prof. Melvin Mencher. He says: "Most news stories are about events that (1) have an *impact* on many people, (2) describe *unusual* or exceptional situations or events, or (3) are about widely known or *prominent* people." He goes on to say, in *Basic News Writing,* 2d ed.: "The presence of one or more of the four additional determinants will heighten the news value of an event. The four are: *conflict, proximity, timeliness and currency.*"

The more you learn about what makes news, the better you'll be able to write news.

4. *Don't write yet. Think.* Don't just do something; sit there. Allow time for incubation and meditation. Not much time, but some. Even if you're fighting the clock, you may be able to take as much as 30 *seconds.* And if you're working on a script for tomorrow, you can afford more than that.

I once had a producer who often snapped: "Write. Don't think."(He became a network vice president.) Unless you're up against a deadline, with no time to spare, take time to think. Even if it's for only 30 seconds, think: Think what the story is all about; think what the heart of the news is; think of the best way to tell it. Think.

5. *Write the way you talk (unless you're from the Bronx).* If you don't talk good like a good writer should, perhaps you should become a Trappist (and close your trap).

No one writes exactly the way he talks or talks the way he writes, so writing for broadcast is a compromise. But keep in mind that you're writing for people who can't read your script, people who can only hear it—and hear it only once. One way to make sure they get it the first time around—and they do get only one crack at it—is to use everyday language.

You have no need to stoop to the style of Dick and Jane, but you should write it in a straightforward, linear fashion—without detours or zigzags—so ordinary listeners can grasp it word by word, word for word,

word after word. It's that unswerving directness—and adherence to rules—that enables listeners to follow the thread of your story.

6. *Apply the rules for broadcast newswriting.* Our source copy does not play by our rules. Most wire service stories—except for the broadcast wires—usually cram the *who, what, when, where, why* and *how* into the first paragraph or two. There's a good reason: When a newspaper sets a story into type and it's too long for the allotted space on the page layout, an editor is most likely to trim it from the bottom, lopping off entire paragraphs.

One reason newspaper people put the best first is that if they're writing against a deadline, they don't know whether they'll be able to get more than a few paragraphs into the next edition. So they figure they had better jam their best material into the lead. Writing in a pattern known as the inverted pyramid, they set down facts in descending order of importance. The most expendable material they write last. So newspaper reporters develop the habit of front-loading, putting all the best material at the top.

Another obstacle for us: Some wire copy is written in wirese or journalese, a quaint tongue that we have to translate into basic English. As newspaper style developed over the centuries, it deviated further and further from the way people speak. Read a newspaper or wire service lead aloud, and you'll be reminded how different they are from us, how print style does not meet our needs. That's why we have developed our own broadcast style, one that's geared to a receiver far different from the eye: the ear.

People who read newspapers are able to give them their full attention. And they can read whatever they wish, at their own speed, and re-read it and mull it over. They can't do that with *our* stories, so we have to adjust our language to allow for the peculiarities of their listening apparatus, which processes information relatively slowly. That's why we have to make our copy simple, clear and direct.

Set your mental processor so it adjusts every sentence to conform with the rules. The ultimate test for all writing, though, is not whether it follows the rules but whether it works. Even so, writers who've mastered the rules know that rules help *make* it work.

7. *Have the courage to write simply.* (Thank you, Prof. Wilbur Schramm.)

8. Refrain from wordy warm-ups. ("Refrain from" may seem like a Don't, but don't let that throw you. The Don'ts in this list show us what to Do.) Get to the point. But what if you don't get the point or don't even see the point? If you've read the source copy, marked it, thought it through and are still stumped, put your source copy face down and tell the story to your keyboard. If you do that, without glancing at the source copy, you'll probably confine yourself to the most memorable highlights, which is just what you're supposed to do. Don't fret about producing perfect copy; just put your words down in rough form. You may not be sure what you want to say until you see what you've said. Read your script and black out any words that are unneeded. If you don't need to keep them in, you do need to keep them out. Prof. Joe Durso Jr. tells his students to start their stories as if they had rushed into their dorm and said to a roommate, "Guess what just happened." And go on from there. "One day in class," Durso recalls, "a frustrated student blurted out, 'I just didn't know what to write.'" So Durso told him: "It should be 'I didn't know what to *say*.' Don't *write* your stories, *tell* them. It'll come a lot easier."

Or try this: Pretend you're telling the story to a friend by phone. As long as we're pretending, let's say your friend is out of town and you're out of pocket. You wouldn't rattle on and on, digress or say any more than it takes for your friend to get just the gist. You'd tell the story hurriedly, and you'd hit only the high points. You wouldn't tell your friend in the curt style of a nine-word telegram (isn't the tenth word usually *love*?). You'd tell your friend in a conversational style. And once you delete a few unnecessary words, you'll have your lead. Or at least a good framework.

If you find that that doesn't do the trick, do this: Try to visualize tomorrow morning's newspaper and its front page. How would the banner stretching across the top of the page capsulize the story? Which few words would a headline writer choose to condense a complex event? If you put your mind to it, you can often get a handle on a story that way. And go from there. But not always. If a gas tank blows up and kills 50 people, a banner might read, "50 DIE IN BLAST." For us, even after expanding that scanty line with verbs, articles and a few facts—"Fifty people are dead in the explosion of a gas tank in Hackville"—the result is undesirable. The reasons: Once you say 50 people are dead, the story runs downhill; *are* is weak, as is any form of *to be; explosion* conceals an action verb, *explodes;* the place-name is mentioned last. Even so, the banner gives you the bare bones; you have to take that skeleton and flesh it out into a story in broadcast style: "A gas tank in Hackville blew up today and killed 50 people." Why didn't I write "blew up today, *killing* 50 people"? Because a finite verb, one with a tense (*killed*), is stronger than a participle *(killing)* with its *ing* ending. (See Freeman's rule 5 on p. 133.) Your second sentence usually answers questions raised by the first: Did anyone survive? What caused the explosion? Did the victims work there? Any homes damaged? What's the impact on Hackville? Too many questions for one sentence, so the third sentence answers unanswered questions. And the fourth sentence, if your story runs that long, answers questions not answered by the third sentence. They should flow so smoothly and seamlessly that a listener isn't aware of the careful construction and your labor.

When I'm stuck in trying to figure out what a story's all about, I've found that trying to picture the front page of tomorrow morning's newspaper works best for me. Some newswriters start by shutting their eyes; some stare into space, as though they expect to see cue cards; some hop right to it and bat it out one, two, three. Some try to see the event in their mind's eye. Your mind's eye can see plenty, from a nuclear explosion to a sunset in Sarasota. The network newswriter Carol Pauli says she has seen even more: "Mind's eye has seen the glory of the coming of the Lord."

The best way is the one that works for you. If you haven't found it, keep at it anyway.

9. *Put attribution before assertion.* This is one of the hard and fast rules that a writer mustn't play fast and loose with. If you're sure your information is factual, you may be able to go ahead without using attribution. Or at least you may defer naming the source. But if you're going to write a story that seems iffy, or at least not solid, let your listeners know who's behind these assertions at the outset. We don't credit the wire services for their material because, in a sense, they work for *us*. If a wire service moves a big story that seems improbable, a network will quickly try to pin it down itself. If a networker cannot verify it and the story is too big to ignore, a newscaster will start the story this way: "The Associated Press says the chief justice of the United States is going to undergo a sex change." If the story were less startling, or less unlikely, the broadcaster might delay identifying the source but would make clear that the information is not in the realm of established fact: "The chief justice of the United States *reportedly* plans to retire soon." The next sentence would explain *reportedly* by linking it to the people

doing the reporting: "The Associated Press also reports he's going to move to Hawaii. The A.P. says the chief justice has told associates he wants to. . . ." That's the same way we handle big stories broken by newspapers: "The chief justice of the United States reportedly is entering a monastery. The *New York Times* also reports he plans to. . . ." No responsible news organization wants to say, on its own authority, with no confirmation: "The chief justice of the United States is entering a monastery." Nor does it suffice—having already jarred the listener—to report the chief's impending departure and then say, "That's what the *New York Times* reports today." Another offense against good judgment occurs when the newscaster presents a shocking assertion in a way that implies it represents the newscaster's fact-finding or thinking: "Good evening. The United States should bomb Moscow back to the Stone Age." Then the second sentence pulls the rug out from under the opening: "That's the opinion of Councilman Tom Troy." The opinion of a councilman? Does his area of incompetence extend beyond his ward? My opinion: that's unfair to listeners. They should know up-front who's doing the saying so they know how much weight to give it. And also so they don't think the anchor himself is sounding off. All of which underlies one of the immutable basics of broadcast newswriting: Attribution precedes assertion. (See pp. 137–141.)

10. *Go with S-V-O: subject-verb-object.* That's the standard pattern of sentences for people who speak English. The closer the verb follows the subject, the easier for the listener to follow. Yes, I've said that before (see p. 10), and I reserve the right to say it again. Start sentences with the subject, go straight to the verb and then the object. Avoid subordinate clauses. In re-reading your script, if you find a subordinate clause that contains essential information, put it in a separate sentence or incorporate the information in other sentences. "Avoid commas," advises Prof. Mackie Morris of the University of Missouri. "A comma demands a hitch in reading," he says, "and the resulting jerkiness frustrates the listener. Avoiding commas also will eliminate subordinate clauses. Such clauses kill the impact of copy, especially if they come at the top of a story or sentence."

11. *Limit a sentence to one idea.* This makes it easier for the listener to understand a story that he can't read, let alone re-read. By keeping to one idea to a sentence, a writer best serves his listeners by uncomplicating stories, by simplifying (but not over-simplifying) them, by reducing difficult, complex stories to their gist.

12. *Use short words and short sentences.* Think small. The words that people use most frequently tend to be short. We don't want to use baby-talk, but we do want to make ourselves understood to people who may be only half-listening, people on the go, people who have many things on their minds, people who might be listening amid hubbub, people who have no chance to check your script, who can't rip out your story and go over it at their leisure, people who can't ask you what you mean. They're accustomed to hearing words the same way they absorb them in a conversation, in a linear fashion, and they're best able to understand them that way: short words, short sentences. People are most comfortable with short words. Look at how we've shortened "telephone" (*phone*), "airplane" (*plane*), "parachute" (chute), "automobile" (*auto*), "refrigerator" (*fridge*).

13. *Use familiar words in familiar combinations.* Using familiar words is not enough. We have to use them in ways that listeners are accustomed to hearing. A broadcaster recently said, "The economy shows growth signs." All good, plain words—but. We don't talk that way. And, I hope, don't write that way. We'd say, "The economy shows signs of growth."

14. *People-ize your copy.* Write about *people,* not about *personnel.*

Whoever wrote this wire service story should be reported to the Missing People's Bureau: "Tribal factions angered over a beer hall dispute fought with sticks and iron bars Sunday at Kloof gold mine west of Johannesburg, killing seven black miners and badly injuring 39, police said." For use on the air, this "A" wire story needs major surgery. "Faction" is an abstraction, so we shouldn't write about factions fighting. Our listeners can't see factions, but they can see people. So we should talk about members of tribes, or blacks, or black tribesmen.

Another type of story that often needs people-izing is a statistical release. Instead of borrowing references to "a decline in births," we should, where possible, write about "fewer babies." Instead of writing about "unemployment," we should, where time and context permit, talk about "people out of work." Instead of talking about "deaths," we should, where appropriate, talk about "*people* killed" or "*people* who died."

People want to hear about *people.* Abstractions don't breathe—or bleed. Besides humanizing stories, we should also be on the alert to localize them, to bring a national story down to a local level, to report its local effects.

15. *Activate your copy.* Start with action verbs. And write in the active voice.

If your copy lies there limply, give it some life with verbs that move. The passive voice is weak because the subject of the sentence does not act but is acted on. In some cases, comparatively few, if the subject is more important than the act, the passive may be preferable: "Mayor Byrd was hit by an egg. . . ."

I wouldn't say, "The passive is to be avoided." As an activist, I say, "Avoid the passive." Act now.

16. *Avoid a first sentence whose main verb is any form of to be: is, are, was, were, will be.* Those are all linking verbs, so they merely link a subject with a predicate that identifies or modifies it. Other linking verbs include: *appear, become, feel, has, have, had, look.* In certain contexts, they may link, but they don't *do* anything. A transitive verb transmits an action to a direct object: "A truck *hit* a school bus. . . ." There, the subject acts on the object. An intransitive verb expresses an action or a state without reference to an object or complement (a noun or an adjective): "A truck *blew up* outside City Hall today." *Is,* though, transmits no action. Do not confuse this advice against using *is* when it serves as an auxiliary (or helping) verb in the formation of tenses: "Mayor Holmes *is searching* for a new. . . ." Stronger, though, than a verb form that ends with an "ing" is a finite verb, one with a tense: "Mayor Holmes has started to search for a new. . . ." But *is* alone merely says someone or something exists or else describes it: "Mayor Holmes is a man with a plan." *Is* lacks energy. It doesn't move; it doesn't tell us something happened; it just is. *Is* does have a place in language, but not in a lead.

Even so, in a few leads, *is* may be O.K.: "Senator Hooper is dead." Or "The war is over." Those sentences get their punch from their brevity and the impact of the news. That first example also benefits from its strong last work, "dead." "Dead" gains extra impact from being a one-syllable word ending in one of the consonants that can close a sentence with a thud. Or thwack.

But *is*'s valid uses in leads are few. Shakespeare knew. The great strength of English, the educator Ernest Fenollosa wrote, "lies in its splendid array of transitive verbs. . . .Their power lies in their recognition of nature as a vast storehouse of forces. . . .I had to discover for myself why Shakespeare's English was so immeasurably superior to all others. I found that it was his persistent, natural, and magnificent use of hundreds of transitive verbs. Rarely will you find an 'is' in his sentences. . . ."

And as the poet Robert Graves said, "The remarkable thing about Shakespeare is that he really is very good—in spite of all the people who say he is very good."

This tip is the reverse of one of the Deadly Sins (see p. 7), but it's worth saying twice. Even thrice.

17. *Avoid may, might, could, should, seems.* They, too, are linking verbs, but they're even wimpier: They don't say anything for sure. Whenever possible, make a definite statement, not one that has the ring of *maybe yes, maybe no.* Can you imagine a strong script that starts with a sentence riding on *seems?* That's even weaker than *is.* At least, *is* says something is. *Seems* says only that it *may* be. So another word to avoid in a lead is *may.* Even softer is *might,* which in the present tense (*might* is also the past tense of *may*) indicates a possibility that is even weaker than *may.*

If the facts of the story suggest that something *may* occur, I think through the lead carefully to try to find a way to say something definite. Instead of saying, "The space shuttle Liberty may finally get off the ground today," I'd say, "The space shuttle Liberty is going to try again today to get off the ground." The second lead may be only marginally better, but at least it has more strength than *may,* which carries the implied burden of *may not.*

18. *Put your sentences in a positive form.* Try to avoid *not* and *no.* That old song says it best: "Accentuate the positive, eliminate the negative, latch on to the affirmative, don't mess with Mister In-Between."

19. *Use present tense verbs where appropriate.* The verb that most often can be used in the present tense is *say.* You might even be able to use the present tense throughout your story, or you might shift in the second or third sentence to the past tense. Example: "Governor Hawley says he's going to visit China. His goal, he says, is to push for business for the state's farms and factories. The governor told a dinner audience in Middletown tonight that he plans to leave the first of next month." Note: In the second sentence, the attribution is delayed. That's all right because the first sentence led with attribution. It is O.K. to defer attribution until after the first few words; it's definitely a no-no—make that No-No—to defer attribution until the end of any sentence. (See pp. 137-141.)

A newspaper or wire service reporter would end a sentence with "the governor said" or "according to the governor." We don't talk like that and we don't write like that. The second sentence needs attribution because we don't know of our own knowledge what his true goal is; it may be no more than a free vacation.

20. *Don't start with a quotation or a question.* Some writers do so occasionally for a simple reason: going with a quotation or a question is an easy way to start. But, in the case of quotations, it's wrong. And you can quote me. They're wrong on several counts: a listener assumes the words are the anchor's own, people don't talk that way, a quotation is rarely the most important part of a story. And anyway you can probably boil it down and say it better.

Question leads? I wouldn't go so far as to recommend that you ban them, but I think you should limit yourself to one every other year. Our job is to answer questions—not to ask them. (See pp. 154–156.)

21. *Use connectives—and, also, but, so, because—to link sentences.* Connectives bridge sentences and let listeners see how they're tied together in one fabric. That makes it easier to follow the thread.

No matter what your sixth-grade teacher told you, feel free to start a sentence with any of them. Example: "Mayor Collins was indicted today. A grand jury charged him with grand larceny—stealing more than 10-thousand dollars from petty cash. *Because* of the indictment, the mayor said, he's going on indefinite leave." *Because* connects that sentence to the one before, and *indictment* also helps the listener even though *indicted* was used in the first sentence.

Also use possessives—*his, her, its, their*—to tie sentences and facts together. Instead of talking about "*the* car," you can make it "*her* car." If you think listeners would have any doubt about who *he, she* or *it* refers to, don't hesitate to repeat the noun itself: "The car crashed into a home, and *its* roof caved in." The antecedent of *its* is *home,* but some listeners might take it to mean that it was the *car* whose roof caved in. To remove all doubt, delete *its* and substitute *the home's.* Although we have to be frugal in using words, don't fret about repeating a word to make sure a sentence is clear. You have to write not only so that you're understood but also so that you can't be misunderstood.

"If you must use a pronoun," says Prof. Mackie Morris, "make sure the pronoun agrees with its antecedent and appears close to the antecedent."

22. *Put the word or words you want to emphasize at the end of your sentence.* And don't take the edge off by ending it with weak, incidental or irrelevant words.

Emphasis has not received enough emphasis in books about writing, according to Theodore A. Rees Cheney in *Getting the Words Right.* He writes, "A word or idea gains emphasis (and is therefore remembered) if it is positioned right before the period that ends the sentence. . . ."

That type of sentence, by saving its impact or meaning until the end, builds tension and suspense. "The most emphatic place in clause or sentence," F.L. Lucas writes in *Style,* "is the end. This is the climax; and during the momentary pause that follows, that last word continues, as it were, to reverberate. . . . It has, in fact, the last word."

In contrast to that type of sentence, known as periodic, the cumulative sentence makes a statement and keeps on going, adding subordinate elements, like modifiers, clauses and phrases, as it rolls along, which is what this sentence is doing before your very eyes, accumulating more add-ons. It could have ended after any of the last few commas. For good reason, this type of sentence is also called loose.

"There is a slackness to a loose sentence, a lack of tension," says Thomas Whissen in *A Way With Words.* He calls it comfortable and easy to write, but he observes, "There is no real build-up, no anticipation, no excitement."

Strunk and White tell how to deal with emphasis in *Elements of Style:* "The proper place in the sentence for the word or group of words that the writer desires to make most prominent is usually the end."

"Unless you have good reason for doing otherwise," David Lambuth says in *The Golden Book on Writing,* "put your most important word or phrase at the end of the sentence. The most important word is usually a substantive [a word or group of words having the same function as a noun] or verb. Don't sacrifice the strategic final position to a preposition or even to an adverb, unless it really is the most significant word—which it sometimes is. The well-known advice against ending a sentence with a preposition is valid only against unimportant prepositions. In certain cases, a preposition is the most emphatic word to end a sentence with."

One of the benefits of the periodic sentence is that it builds up to the main point. Unlike the loose sentence, it does not make its point and then dribble downhill. As Lambuth says, "Build *up* to your big idea, not *down* from it."

Most sentences in newspapers and wire copy are loose. And most of us, when chatting, use loose sentences. If we had the time to think over our thoughts thoroughly, we'd use far more periodic sentences: they carry the most impact and are the most rememberable.

Bell Labs has found that people remember best what they hear last, so if you want your words to sink in and to be remembered, use periodic sentences. Not exclusively, but frequently.

Let's look at how you can transform leads that rely on loose sentences to those that put the emphasis at the end of the sentence, where it should be. Here's a lead that was broadcast on a network:

> Matters went from bad to worse between the United States and Libya today.

The news is the slide from bad to worse. But it lies in the middle of the sentence, which means it's buried. That's the worst place to put the most important fact. Better: "Relations between this country and Libya have gone from bad to worse."

Here's another network example that needs restructuring:

> Union Carbide said today that *equipment trouble and workers who didn't know what they were doing* were to blame for this month's chemical leak at the company's Institute, West Virginia, plant that sent more than a hundred people to the hospital.

That's some sentence! Not a good one, but a long one. And a busy one. Too long and too busy. Imagine reading that on air. Imagine listening. Imagine trying to understand it. And trying to recall it.

I've italicized the key fact—what's responsible for the leak. (Or, at least, what the owner says is responsible.) So the key fact should not be submerged in the center of that morass. As it stands, the most memorable part of the sentence is given over to the people hospitalized, a fact already reported many times. Applying the principles of emphasis, here's one way to improve that sentence: "Union Carbide says the leak at its plant in Institute, West Virginia, was caused by equipment trouble and workers who didn't know what they were doing." The original sentence was 41 words; the rewrite is 26 words. Shorter, sharper, stronger.

23. *Use contractions—with caution.* Contractions are conversational and time-savers. But some contractions can cause confusion; the most common is *can't.* Even careful listeners—and they're not plentiful— often miss the final *'t.* So they think they hear *can,* contrary to what the story is trying to stress: *cannot.* So we run the risk of confusing listeners when we use a negative contraction if the loss of the final letter leaves only the positive form. But some contractions are safe to use even if a newscaster swallows the final *'t* or a listener has a hearing problem:

among them, *don't, won't.* Even if a listener misses the final *'t,* he's not going to mistake the sound of *don't* (dough) with *do* (due).

24. *Pep up your copy with words like new, now, but, says.* Not only does *new* signal a listener that he's hearing news, it also can compress a mouthful into one short word. Instead of writing, "The government issued a report today that says . . . ," we can start speedily, "A *new* report says . . . ."

Now has two good uses: it shows that an event is going on at this very moment, and it indicates a reversal in course. For example: "Sheriff Gooch has denied he was on duty when. . . .But *now* he says. . . ."

25. *Watch out for I, we, our, here, up, down. I* is open to misunderstanding when used in a direct quotation in a story: "The mayor said, 'I had it coming to me.'" The listener has reason to believe the mayor is talking about the anchor. *We* usually puzzles me. Is the newscaster using it so she can avoid *I?* Is she referring to her newsroom, her community, or what? *Our* is too possessive unless you're writing about something that is yours, something that belongs to you or your station. Avoid *"our* troops" unless our station maintains a militia. As newspeople, we report from the sidelines, not as participants or partisans.

Here should be deleted from copy. Whenever I hear *here,* I wonder whether the speaker means "here in our newsroom" or "here in our town." The center of a listener's universe is where he is. And, no matter where he's listening, in his mind, he *is* here. We also hear newscasters start stories like this: *"Here* in Hicksville. . . ." Hicksvillians (Hicksvillains?) know they're in Hicksville, so they don't need to be reminded.

As directions, *up* and *down* are objectionable for similar reasons. From the place where you broadcast, a town to the north, Hangtown, is *up.* But don't say, *"Up* in Hangtown. . . ." For folks farther north, Hangtown is *down.* Another adverb to watch for is *out,* as in *"Out* in Far Corners." People there regard themselves as insiders. In their worldview, every place else is *out.*

26. *Omit needless words.* (Thank you, Strunk and White.) Try to rid your copy of *thats, whiches, who ises, ofs* and other space-eaters. As you read your script, you may spot a few space-eaters sneaking in. In most cases, they can be deleted with no loss of meaning—and with a gain in clarity. One reason to rid your copy of needless words is that they lengthen your sentences and force your listeners to work to extract the

substance. Bear in mind: the fewer words you use to tell a story, the clearer and more forceful the story.

The importance of examining the need for every word is pointed up in a joke told by Harold Evans in *Newsman's English:* A London fishmonger had a sign that said: FRESH FISH SOLD HERE. A friend persuaded him to rub out the word FRESH; he wasn't expected to sell fish that wasn't fresh. Then the friend persuaded him to rub out HERE; he's selling it, naturally, in his shop. Then the friend urged him to rub out SOLD; he isn't expected to give it away. Finally, the friend persuaded him to rub out FISH; you can smell it a mile off.

27. *Hit only the main points; trash the trivia.* Because the wires carry something doesn't mean we should use it. Some wire service reporters write long because they haven't learned to write short. Some write long because newspaper clients have oodles of space to fill and some shovel in wire copy by the yard. And, anyway, those high-speed printers have to have something to spew out round the clock. But *we* have to be highly selective. The minutiae that a newspaper might print are, for us, nonessential.

See to it that every word you use is essential and that you use nothing that's superfluous. Whatever you say, say only once. Life is too short for any repetition.

28. *Don't parrot source copy.* When a wire story has a clever play on words, or an unusual combination of words, avoid borrowing that language. One reason: if we do borrow it, a listener who recalls hearing those very words on an earlier newscast on another station may say, "So that's where those jerks get their news!" We should rewrite wire stories in our own words. Sometimes, though, wire copy on certain events is phrased in such a way that we dare not substitute a synonym lest we inadvertently deviate from what's accurate. Even though broadcast wires are supposed to be written for the ear to accommodate subscribers, the quality of the copy is uneven. Not all of it is written by people who are adept. But why parrot what any writer has said? Aren't you a better writer?

29. *Place the time element, if you need one, after the verb.* The listener who turns on your newscast tonight has every reason to believe that all your stories are today's news, not yesterday's, not tomorrow's. What will catch the listener's ear and prompt him to keep listening is an action verb, not a "today."

30. *When in doubt, leave it out.* Go with what you know. Just before airtime, when we handle so much copy, we probably can't find answers to all our questions about the source material, resolve ambiguities, or reconcile discrepancies. Don't assume. Don't speculate. We deal only in facts, not in conjecture. The wires are not infallible. Far from it. Their stories are gathered, written and edited not by superhumans but by imperfect people like us.

If your source copy is a press release, you have to be even more careful. Wire service stories are written by newspeople who work for news agencies and, in effect, work for us. They're hired for journalistic skills. And they're trained to report objectively.

But press releases are written by people who do not work for us. With few exceptions, they're not paid for their objectivity, devotion to the public weal and dedication to truth. Whether they call themselves press agents, press information officers or public relations counselors, they work for private parties. And the press releases, which they sometimes call *news* releases, are written for the benefit of their private interests, not our public interests. Sometimes their interests and ours intersect, and we find a release that's worth using. But it may or may not be accurate, it may or may not be complete, it may or may not be fair.

The press agent is not a disinterested party. His motto is, "Whose bread I eat, his song I sing."

If you decide to use a press release or a part of one, make sure you rewrite it. First, verify that the person named as the sender did send it, that it's not a hoax. Even if it's not a hoax, remember that the release comes from someone who is, in effect, a salesman, trying to "sell" you a story, one written to advance his interests, not necessarily yours. If you doubt any key points in the release, pick up your phone and verify them on your own. If you can't verify them but decide to go ahead anyway, be sure to attribute them to someone named in the release. Many press agents are honorable people, and they write releases that are honest. But some press agents slip in a few curves. It's your job to detect them—and reject them. "The most essential gift for a good writer," as Hemingway said so elegantly, "is a built-in, shockproof shit detector."

Another source of problems—and opportunities—is telephone tips. People phone newsrooms with all sorts of motives: some callers are looking for rewards, some are looking for kicks, some are looking for vengeance. Any caller can identify himself as just about anyone else. Listen carefully, ask questions and treat a call as potentially newsworthy. When you hang up, though, don't go straight to your keyboard. Verify anything you wish to use. And don't rely on dialing back the number the caller just gave you and checking the information with him.

Some pranksters delight in phoning in obituaries. Never use an obit without first checking the undertaker. And watch out for mischief-makers. I remember a cub reporter who was refused service by a Chicago nightclub because he wasn't wearing a tie. So he walked across the street to a saloon, where a TV set was carrying a telethon. In a twinkling, he had an inspiration. He phoned the telethon and said he was the manager of the nightclub and wanted to make a contribution to fight the dreaded disease: $5. Announcement of the paltry gift made the famous club look like a den of tightwads. And the reporter got his revenge; yes, I did.

Don't take that as advice to hang up on callers. Or to ignore them. Another reporter, Martin J. O'Connor, used to say that he didn't care if a tip came from Judas Iscariot, that as long as he could confirm it, he'd run with it. Once you confirm a story, it's yours.

31. *Don't raise questions you don't answer.* Don't insert a fact that cries out for clarification. Not long ago, I read a script about a fire in a trailer park. The script said a man was killed in a trailer, "where he lived with a companion." But no one told us whether the companion survived, nor whether the companion was a colleen or a collie.

32. *Read your copy aloud. If it sounds like writing, rewrite it.* What counts is not how it looks on paper but how it sounds. If it sounds un-conversational, as though written for the eye, rewrite it. When you read it aloud, you also might catch any unfortunate sequence of words. For example, a BBC news reader (as the Beeb calls anchors) said, so the story goes, that in a croquet match Lord Hampton "had been playing a round" with Lady Fairfax. If the reader had read his script aloud, he might have caught that double-meaning. I'm not saying a writer should have a dirty mind, but it helps. And it also helps to have a mind that's nimble enough to catch single words that seem safe on paper but can lead to complications. For example: "query." You may never be tempted to use "dastard," but be careful of "duck" and "finger" (as verbs), "shift" and "Uranus."

The broadcaster who wrote this news item also should have listened to his script:

> An Interior Department report on Teton Dam is still pending. So are Congressional studies of the Bureau of Reclamation and other dam-building agencies.

The writer should have caught "dam-building agencies." The listener can't see the hyphen, so the phrase sounds like a curse. If you read your script aloud to yourself before turning it in, you'll catch seemingly innocent combinations of words that sound damning.

33. *Rewrite. The art of writing lies in rewriting what you've already rewritten.* Check all names, dates, amounts, facts with the source copy. Take time—and make time—to give it a good going-over. Is every word necessary? The rule: If it's not necessary to leave it in, it is necessary to leave it out.

After you get rid of any clutter and trim flab, ask yourself: Are the words right? And in the right order? And does it read right?

Also: Is every bit of information right? Accuracy is essential. As one news agency used to say, "Get it first, but first get it right." (The agency had trouble getting it either way—and went the way of all flash.)

Extra time is scarce in newsrooms, particularly as air time approaches. But if you can start writing earlier, can skip the chitchat and can bear down on writing, maybe you can save enough time to rewrite your copy. And re-rewrite it. The importance of rewriting is illustrated in George Plimpton's interview of Hemingway for the *Paris Review:*

P: How much rewriting do you do?

H: It depends. I rewrote the ending of *Farewell to Arms,* the last page of it, thirty-nine times before I was satisfied.

P: Was there some technical problem there? What was it that had stumped you?

H: Getting the words right.

Getting the words right!

But we don't have as much time as a Hemingway. We write in haste but can't revise at leisure. If we're working on a piece that doesn't have to go on the air tonight, we can let our script sit overnight and cool off. The next day, we're refreshed and we can read it as though it's new. And we can go over it energetically. Maybe this time, after another rewrite or two, we can get the words right.

Murphy's Law has it right, but I've devised Mervy's Corollary: "Whatever *can't* go wrong, will." So reread, recheck, reflect, relax. Also: pray. And keep your résumé up to date.

After you read a wire story or other source copy, you have to apply all those top tips instinctively. You can't take time to review each one step by step, like an airline pilot going down his checklist for takeoff. You have to absorb the tips so they become second nature and you're able to apply them on autopilot. Then your scripts will be all set for air.

4

LEAD-INS, LEAD-OUTS, VOICE-OVERS

Now that we've seen how stories can take off, let's see how we can make some other things fly, or at least get off the ground: lead-ins, voice-overs, tags, tease(r)s and one-minute newscasts.

The tips and rules that guide us to better stories also serve us in writing all these other items. But each of them has its own peculiar needs.

Lead-in

An anchor reads this to introduce a reporter's narrative, live or taped, or a natural sound cut, say, of a shouting match. The lead-in sets the scene and identifies the reporter or the people who are the loud speakers.

The lead-in's job is to alert listeners and prepare them for what's coming, the important, exciting, fascinating, or amusing story that's about to unfold—without using any of those adjectives. But the lead-in is more than a billboard for the coming attraction. It sets up what follows so it makes sense to a listener, and it supplies a crucial fact or two that may be missing from what follows. So lead-ins have to do more than just lead in. Sometimes a lead-in doesn't have to spell out the "where" if the reporter immediately says where he is.

Lead-ins—like everything else—should keep listeners listening, either through the impact of hard facts told well or the engaging grace of a light touch. A lead-in should arrest listeners in a gentle, polite way. Not an easy assignment, especially when the reporter's story that the lead-in introduces is, shall we say, a 97-second weakling. And not when we have to comply with the truth-in-advertising laws, never promising more in the lead-in than the piece delivers.

All we need is the same skills that we use in writing stories and scripts of any type, the kind of writing that's best suited for broadcast news: simple, straight, brisk.

The two main varieties of lead-ins are—surprise!—hard and soft. For a hard-news story covered by a reporter in the field, the anchor opens with the essence of the story before intro-ing the reporter. As with the Deadly Sins recited at the outset of this book, the Don'ts are especially important in writing a lead-in:

■ *Don't use the same key words that the reporter uses.* And don't introduce him or any speaker with the very words that he starts with. Violation of that rule produces "the echo-chamber effect." It sounds—and resounds—like this: "Good evening. Governor Goober warned today he's fed up with state employees who loaf on the job." Instantly, we hear Goober say: "I'm fed up with state employees who loaf on the job." Listener: "Haven't I heard that somewhere before?"

Or the anchor leads in with something like this: "Old MacDonald said today he's going back to his farm. Sally Simpson reports he has been pining for his pigs, ducks, and cows." Then she begins, "MacDonald has been pining for his pigs, ducks and cows." This leaves the listener higgledy-piggledy, and the duplication wastes time and crowds out other material. Instead of starting the second sentence with the reporter's name and stepping on the reporter's lines, the anchor could have said, "He [MacDonald] has been working as a bricklayer, but now he has decided to throw in the trowel. Sally Simpson has the story." By saying she has the story, the anchor is signalling the listener that the best is yet to be.

If possible, a writer should prepare a lead-in only after reading the text of the cut or reading the reporter's script, or at least talking with the reporter so the writer knows what the reporter is going to say, or so the reporter knows what the lead-in is going to say.

■ *Don't steal the reporter's thunder.* Although the lead-in for a hard-news story should hit a few highlights, the anchor shouldn't skim off all the reporter's best material. Otherwise, the reporter's account will seem anticlimactic, and it'll sound as though the reporter got his news from the anchor. Or, as they say so delicately in the barnyard, the reporter will be left sucking hind teat.

■ *Don't write a soft lead-in for a hard-news story.* A soft lead-in may work for a feature story, but a hard-news story calls for a hard-news lead-in. A lead-in is something like a store's display window. A dime store doesn't dress a window with diamonds. And a diamond merchant doesn't display dimes. Hard news, like diamonds, deserves an appropriate showcase.

■ *Don't write a lead-in that conflicts with the reporter's script.* This may seem abecedarian (no kin to ABC's Sid Darion), but every once in a while we hear a reporter say something that contradicts what the anchor's lead-in has said. That's a mislead-in.

■ *Don't overstate or oversell.* The lead-in should not promise—or suggest—more than the reporter is going to deliver. It should adhere to standards of journalism, not hucksterism.

■ *Don't be vague.* Sometimes, because of the way newscasts are put together, we don't know precisely what the reporter in the field is going to be saying, or which segment of a speech is going to be used, so we have to write "blind"—without saying anything specific, putting down only enough words to allow the control room to roll tape: "The chairman of the city transit agency, Lionel Train, spoke out today on the agency's problems." Writing "blind"—like flying "blind"—can be risky. But wherever you can, say something substantive: "The chairman of the city transit agency, Lionel Train, said today he'll clean up the agency's problems within six months."

■ *Don't use a faulty "throw line" at the end of the lead-in to introduce a reporter.* If the next voice we're going to hear is not that of the reporter but of a woman taking an oath of office, you'd confuse a listener by saying, "Jerry Jarvis has the story." One way to handle that "throw-line" is to say, "Jerry Jarvis looked on as Mary Barton took the oath."

Most lead-ins run less than 20 seconds, and a few run barely 5 seconds. No matter what it takes to do the job, no matter what the length, every word matters. And the shorter the lead-in, the greater the need for every word to carry its weight.

Voice-overs

If you're in radio, you don't have to worry about V/O's, the scripts that are read over silent videotape. And if you're in TV, you don't have to worry either, as long as you observe these tips:

■ *View the footage before writing.* If this seems obvious, think of all the V/O's you've heard on air that didn't fit the picture, obviously.

If pre-viewing the footage is out of the question, try to get a shot list (a.k.a. shot sheet, shot card, spot sheet and breakdown sheet). It lists the scenes, describes the contents in a few words, the running time of each shot and the cumulative time. Even if you do pre-view the footage, make a shot list. Without a list, by the time you get back to your keyboard, you might forget whether the third scene shows injured people or overturned trailer homes, and you might need to know for certain.

Your words don't have to match the picture every step of the way. They should add to what viewers see, tell them, perhaps, what it's all about, why it's going on and help them understand what they're seeing. An instant or two before each new scene comes up, if necessary, start to identify the setting and the main characters. In some pieces, "spotting" a new character—by name or job description—is imperative. We call this "writing to picture," "cuing words to picture" or "keying." If you want to write about something the camera did not shoot or the tape doesn't show but that is pertinent, we "write away from picture." At the start of a V/O, it's usually best for the script to match the picture to help establish what it's all about. It's safer to write away from picture after the viewer gets the picture.

■ *Don't state the obvious.* For too many writers, this is not so obvious. That's why we hear lines like: "This is the man," "This is the lake," "This is the man jumping into the lake." Viewers see that. We can augment what they see by putting the picture in perspective. We can inform them that the water temperature was 35 degrees, that the man weighed 250 pounds and that he didn't know how to swim.

■ *Avoid "Here we see," "shown here" and "seen here."* If we're seeing an overturned mobile home, the script needn't whack viewers over the head with a "here." If something needs to be explained or spelled out, do it unobtrusively, without fanfare.

■ *Don't tell viewers to "watch this."* If you wish to direct your viewers' attention to something that's about to occur in a long shot, do it politely. Please. Let's say that in a few seconds a man in the mob is going to pull a gun and fire. Unless viewers know in advance, they might not be focusing on that part of the screen and might miss the best part of the action. We can tip them off without issuing orders: "A man on the far right, the man in a khaki jacket, pulls out his gun and fires at a policeman."

■ *Don't fight picture.* That means, our words shouldn't be at odds with the pix. We shouldn't say, for example, zookeepers recaptured two monkeys at the very moment viewers are watching someone holding two children.

■ *Avoid the newspaper use of "left to right."* If several people are on the screen and you need to "spot" someone, you can refer to "the half-pint in the ten-gallon hat" or "the woman with the whip." (Her escort is the assistant to the House majority leader, the whip. Don't you dare use "half-pint" unless you're writing about a mug.)

■ *Don't overwrite.* Don't try to squeeze too much copy into the script, making the V/O run longer than the footage. If you have a feature or a soft-news story and don't have to "hit" any scenes, try writing loose. That way, the words don't overwhelm or drown out the picture.

■ *Don't overload your listeners with facts.* Viewers are busy viewing. They're not giving their undivided attention to the words, and too many facts—or words—can cause a sensory overload.

■ *Make use of natural sound and silence.* Don't feel obliged to cram words into every single second. If the footage has natural sound, say, a gurgling brook, let the picture and sound carry the scene. Even when the footage is silent, you can sometimes skip the narrative. Pause. Occasionally, a few seconds of silence can be eloquent. And, depending on the scene, the anchor's (or reporter's) silence can underline the drama. What kinds of scenes? Perhaps a fireman breathing life into a baby, a lottery winner exploding with joy, a pole vaulter flinging himself over the crossbar.

■ *Put the "where" at the top of the V/O.* If the anchor's lead-in doesn't name the place, see to it that it's identified at the outset. Sometimes, though, it's acceptable to identify the place only with a "super." Viewers should know right away what they're looking at, where it was shot and when.

■ *Read your V/O against the footage while an editor or deskmate watches.* This is the best way to catch mistakes and weaknesses. If you time each segment of your copy as you write it, the final run-through should be O.K.

Tag

This is the sentence or two that sometimes follow a story or V/O. Some people call it a tag line, lead-out, write-out, cap or button. The tag is supposed to add a bit of information, perhaps an important fact that couldn't be fitted into the lead-in. Or perhaps it's an updated casualty figure. Or late news that should accompany the story that has just been reported. Maybe it's a P.S. that rounds out the story. Or maybe it's a correction of something that the correspondent had recorded but that couldn't be edited. Or it might be an anchor's comment or aside. Whatever you call it or whatever you put into it, keep it short and to the point.

Some anchors begin their tags by saying "Incidentally" or "By the way." But my advice—and I hope someone asks—is, refrain from those transparent efforts at being casual. If an item is indeed incidental, it doesn't deserve valuable air time. If the item is not incidental—and most of the time, it is, or should be, significant—it shouldn't be minimized by being called incidental.

Tease(r)

A tease is designed to inform viewers what lies ahead, to pique their curiosity and lure them into staying tuned. A tease requires more than compression; it requires crushing. Or squashing. With only several seconds to work in, a writer has to have a big vocabulary of small words. He also has to be creative, be imaginative and have a disdain for the rules. Many times, there's not enough room for a complete sentence, so he has to use a line that's like a headline: "Murder at the Waldorf." I like that. A good tease. It lacks a verb, but it packs a punch.

One of the dangers in condensing a story into a headline is that by reducing and rounding off, we can easily warp it. And warping can lead to slanting. No matter how catchy the tease you've just written, no matter how clever, ask yourself: Is it deceptive? Does it hint of more than the newscast is going to offer? Does it mislead listeners? If your answers are No, No, No, then Go, Go, Go.

How often are you annoyed after finding that a newspaper headline isn't supported by the story? Most often we see headlines like that in tabloids at supermarket checkout counters, but the headlines are beyond checking out: "Siamese Twin Girls Born Pregnant" and "Man Gives Birth to Test-Tube Twins." I haven't heard anything that phony in tease(r)s, but I do hear some that seem to be flirting with fakery. You can avoid being a flirt—even though you're handling a tease—by applying the same standards you apply in writing stories. In writing teases, or anything else, you can't always follow writing rules, except the unwritten rules to be fair and factual.

Otherwise, you might find yourself the target of a comedy sketch. So don't write a tease that seems like a parody of itself, like this one: "TV teases taken to task. Tape at ten."

One-minute newscasts

Someone I know has written them at all three networks, a sort of latter-day minuteman: me. Usually, excluding commercials, they run about 40 seconds, but sometimes they exceed a minute. Whatever the length or brevity, they represent a challenge that's anything but minute. Fitting four or five stories into 40 seconds is as tough as stuffing six pounds of suet into a five-pound sack. Once, at least, I stuffed seven stories into 50 seconds, a series of short bursts. If you think a network evening newscast is merely a headline service, then a seven-item minicast should be called an index.

Writers who do these 'casts frequently develop a knack for ultra-compression. Whoops; that *frequently* is a squinting modifier. It seems to be looking in two directions at the same time and might modify *do* or *develop*. I edit myself as I go along, almost unconsciously, so I'll re-do that sentence to read, "Writers who frequently do these casts develop a knack for ultra-compression." And that's what it takes to develop the knack—frequency.

As with any kind of writing or performing, improvement comes through doing it. And reviewing it.

5

STYLE

Style is not like fast food. You can't walk in and say, "I'd like a style. To go."

Sorry, it's no go. Style is intangible. You can't just pick it up or buy it. You can't walk into a barbershop *or* a workshop and sit back and wait for a style to be bestowed on you. And you can't casually borrow a writing style, one that stamps your copy as something special. Although style is not yours for the asking, style is gettable.

When I say "style," I mean *what* you say and *how* you say it, the words you choose, how you use them, the way you weave your sentences. That's *writing* style, not the kind of style that style manuals deal with, the basic work rules for a newsroom, designed mainly for uniformity.

Most writers are individualists, and they want personal styles. They want their scripts to differ from all those other people's. And many of those other people also want a distinctive style to make *their* copy stand out. *And* themselves.

Many new writers who yearn for a style shoot for the stars; they try to pattern their writing after that of newscasters widely known for their style. Some newscasters do have recognizable and admirable writing styles, but some establish their reputation for style through a combination of elements that have nothing to do with writing: presence, personality and presentation. If you want to develop *those* qualities, you'll have to read another chapter. In another book. By another writer.

Style is more than an unusual, or unique, way to say something. Trying to define style, a Frenchman said, is like trying to put a sack of flour in a thimble. There are no rules, no books, no one true style. If it's so hard to put your finger on, how can you get your hands on it? Put thimbly: from reading, listening and learning, from writing, writing and writing. By writing, the proverb goes, you learn to write.

A dictionary defines style as "distinction, excellence, originality and character in any form of artistic or literary expression."

Distinction. Excellence. Originality. That's a lot to aim for. Sure, we write about momentous events, but we spend more of our time writing about crimes, crashes and coroner's cases. It may seem hard to make copy about the commonplace different. For if we all write about the same things, follow the same rules and use the same basic language, how can we develop a style that's noticeable?

Don't worry about acquiring your own style. While you work on your craft and hone your skills, style will come to you. The acquisition of style may be a process of decortication, a stripping or peeling away. As a writer learns to get rid of non-essentials, what's left eventually is style. But a writer mustn't work too hard at attaining a style or the excessive effort will show. No matter how you go about it, the attainment of style must not become your main goal. Your most important goal is to communicate clearly, to tell a story well, so well that a listener understands it instantly and easily. To do this, we have to write simply. We mustn't strain and stretch to strut our stuff—and that's the kind of sentence to get rid of, a succession of hissing sibilants. Alliteration and other devices of rhetoric do work on occasion, but they have to be used with care. And anyone pursuing style should not sacrifice substance for style: Style is no substitute for substance. According to the publisher Aaron Cohodes, the best way for a writer to be different is to be better.

Not only shouldn't we labor to draw attention to our scripts, we shouldn't draw attention to ourselves. Our focus should be on our listeners. They're the people we should be directing our attention to. Them.

Still, you might say, there must be more to style than that platter of platitudes. Right you are when you are right! There is far more, and the more we learn about writing, the more we write, and the more we work at it, the more we'll realize that style—a style worthy of being called a style—is not so easy to come by.

To say that style is elusive is not to say just what it is. Perhaps some of the best stylists can tell us—and tell us how to acquire it. They can say it far more succinctly and interestingly than I can, and they have, so let's turn to our guest lecturers:

> "The virtues of good style are more negative than positive. The man who knows what to avoid is already the owner of style."
>
> HENRY W. FOWLER

"Everyone recognizes it, everyone describes it, but no two people agree as to its exact nature."

HENRY SEIDEL CANBY

"The fundamental rule of style is to keep solely in view the thought one wants to convey. One must therefore have a thought to start with."

JACQUES BARZUN *(quoting an unnamed French stylist)*

"A good style must, first of all, be clear."

ARISTOTLE

"In language, clearness is everything."

CONFUCIUS

"If any man wishes to write in a clear style, let him first be clear in his thoughts."

JOHANN WOLFGANG VON GOETHE

"First, clarity; then again clarity; and, finally, clarity."

ANATOLE FRANCE

"Whatever we conceive well we express clearly, and words flow with ease."

NICHOLAS BOILEAU

"People think I can teach them style. What stuff it is. Have something to say and say it as clearly as you can. That is the only secret to style."

MATTHEW ARNOLD

"Style is a sort of melody that comes into my sentences by itself. If a writer says what he has to say as accurately and effectively as he can, his style will take care of itself."

GEORGE BERNARD SHAW

"The indispensable characteristic of a good writer is a style marked by lucidity."

ERNEST HEMINGWAY

"Lucidity is the soul of style."

HILAIRE BELLOC

"Nothing is so difficult as the apparent ease of a clear and flowing style. . . . Those graces which, from their presumed

facility, encourage all to attempt to imitate them, are usually the most inimitable."
CHARLES CALEB COLTON

"Clear writers, like clear fountains, do not seem so deep as they are; the turbid looks most profound."
WALTER SAVAGE LANDOR

"Proper words in proper places make the true definition of style."
JONATHAN SWIFT

"Get your facts right first; that is the foundation of all style."
GEORGE BERNARD SHAW

"Your writing style is yourself in the process of thought and the act of writing, and you cannot buy that in a bookstore or fix it up in a seminar."
WILLIAM SAFIRE

"There is such an animal as a nonstylist, only they're not writers—they're typists."
TRUMAN CAPOTE

"I've been called a stylist until I really could tear my hair out. And I simply don't believe in style. The style is you."
KATHERINE ANNE PORTER

"Style is everything and nothing. It is not that, as is commonly supposed, you get your content and soup it up with style; style is absolutely embedded in the way you perceive."
MARTIN AMIS

"Style is the physiognomy of the mind."
ARTHUR SCHOPENHAUER

"A man's style is in his mind's voice. Wooden minds, wooden voices."
RALPH WALDO EMERSON

"Style is what gives value and currency to thought."
HENRI FRÉDÉRIC AMIEL

"Style is the essence of thinking."
ROBERT LOUIS STEVENSON

"Style is the dress of thoughts."

LORD CHESTERFIELD

"Style is the dress of thought; a modest dress,
Neat, but not gaudy, will true critics please."

REV. SAMUEL WESLEY

"Style is organic, not the clothes a man wears, but the flesh,
bone, and blood of his body. Therefore it is really impossible to
consider styles apart from the system of perceptions and feelings
and thoughts that animate them."

J. MIDDLETON MURRY

"The style is the man himself."

GEORGE DE BUFFON

"Montesquieu had the style of a genius; Buffon, the genius of
style."

BARON GRIMM

"A man's style is nearly as much a part of himself as his face, or
figure, or the throbbing of his pulse. . . ."

FRANCOIS DE SALIGNAC DE LA MOTHE-FÉNELON

"Style is the hallmark of a temperament stamped upon the
material at hand."

ANDRÉ MAUROIS

"A good style must have an air of novelty, at the same time
concealing its art."

ARISTOTLE

"Carefully examined, a good—an interesting—style will
be found to consist in a constant succession of tiny, unobserv-
able surprises."

FORD MADOX FORD

"No style is good that is not fit to be spoken or read aloud
with effect."

WILLIAM HAZLITT

"A good style should show no sign of effort. What is written
should seem a happy accident."

W. SOMERSET MAUGHAM

"There is no such thing as good style or bad style. The question is, does it accomplish its intention?"

CHRISTOPHER MORLEY

"Be plain and simple, and lay down the thing as it was."

JOHN BUNYAN

"Simple style is like white light. It is complex but its complexity is not obvious."

ANATOLE FRANCE

"When you doubt between words, use the plainest, the commonest, the most idiomatic. . . . Eschew fine words as you would rouge, and love simple ones as you would native roses on your cheek."

AUGUST W. HARE

"As for style of writing, if one has anything to say, it drops from him simply and directly, as a stone falls to the ground."

HENRY DAVID THOREAU

"Only great minds can afford a simple style."

STENDHAL

"Style is hard to pin down. The difficulty recalls Justice Stewart's remark about obscenity; he couldn't define it, but he knew when he saw it. Whatever it is, style provides the individual hallmark that writers stamp upon their work—but that metaphor is inapt, for it suggests that style is something you put onto a piece after you've finished it, as if it were ketchup on chili, or lemon on fish. Style doesn't work that way. It's more of a marinade, permeating the whole composition."

JAMES J. KILPATRICK

"A pure style in writing results from the rejection of every-thing superfluous."

ALBERTINE ADRIENNE NECKER DE SAUSSURE

"In what he leaves unsaid I discover a master of style."

FRIEDRICH VON SCHILLER

"A strict and succinct style is that, where you can take away nothing without loss, and that loss to be manifest."

BEN JONSON

"Without style there cannot possibly be a single work of value in any branch of eloquence or poetry."

VOLTAIRE

"Writing, when properly managed, is but a different name for conversation."

LAURENCE STERNE

"A style, representing the sum total of choices made in daily speech and writing, expresses our individual connection with that vast and confusing body of knowledge known as language."

CHARLES W. FERGUSON

"He who thinks much says but little in proportion to his thoughts. He selects that language which will convey his ideas in the most explicit and direct manner. He tries to compress as much thought as possible into a few words. On the contrary, the man who talks everlastingly and promiscuously, who seems to have an exhaustless magazine of sound, crowds so many words into his thoughts that he always obscures, and very frequently conceals them."

WASHINGTON IRVING

"Words are like leaves; and where they most abound, Much fruit of sense beneath is rarely found."

ALEXANDER POPE

"Obscurity and affectation are the two great faults of style. Obscurity of expression generally springs from confusion of ideas, and the same wish to dazzle, at any cost, which produces affectation in the manner of a writer, is likely to produce sophistry in his reasoning."

THOMAS BABINGTON MACAULAY

"The way of speaking that I love is natural and plain, as well in writing as speaking, and a sinewy and significant way of expressing one's self, short and pithy, and not so elegant and artificial as prompt and vehement. Rather hard than harsh, free from affectation . . . not like a pedant, a preacher or a pleader, but rather a soldier-like style. . . ."

MICHEL DE MONTAIGNE

"Words in prose ought to express the intended meaning; if they attract attention to themselves, it is a fault; in the very best styles you read page after page without noticing the medium."

SAMUEL TAYLOR COLERIDGE

"A good narrative style does not attract attention to itself. Its job is to keep the reader's mind on the story, on what's happening, the event, and not the writer."

LEON SURMELIAN

"A pen may be just as usefully employed in crossing out as in writing."

QUINTILIAN

"In composing, as a general rule, run your pen through every other word you have written; you have no idea what vigor it will give to your style."

SYDNEY SMITH

"One should not aim at being possible to understand, but at being impossible to misunderstand."

QUINTILIAN

"The chief aim of the writer is to be understood."

JOHN DRYDEN

"Intense study of the Bible will keep any man from being vulgar in point of style."

SAMUEL TAYLOR COLERIDGE

"He that will write well . . . must follow this counsel of Aristotle, to speak as the common people do, to think as wise men do."

ROGER ASCHAM

"To tell about a drunken muzhik's beating his wife is incomparably harder than to compose a whole tract about the 'woman question.'"

IVAN TURGENEV

"I am well aware that an addiction to silk underwear does not imply that one's feet are dirty. None the less, style, like sheer silk, too often hides eczema."

ALBERT CAMUS

"Those most likely to talk about it [style] are least likely to have it. Style in writing compares to intonation in speaking. It may be harsh; shrill; nasal; affected; a soft Southern timbre, or a cockney vivacity. It is as personal as clothes or complexion. It can be controlled and educated, but beneath control it must partly remain instinctive, unconscious and organic. As in clothes so in

literature it is most admirable when least obtruded.
Its very plainness implies high cost; the cost of thinking
and study."

CHRISTOPHER MORLEY

"[The beginner should shun] all devices that are popularly
believed to indicate style—all mannerisms, tricks, adornments.
The approach to style is by way of plainness, simplicity,
orderliness, sincerity."

E.B. WHITE

"To eliminate the vice of wordiness is to ensure the virtue of
emphasis, which depends more on conciseness than on any other
factor. Wherever we can make 25 words do the work of 50, we
halve the area in which looseness and disorganization can
flourish, and by reducing the span of attention required we
increase the force of the thought. To make sure our words count
for as much as possible is surely the simplest as well as the
hardest secret of style."

WILSON FOLLETT

"For a man to write well, there are required three necessaries: to
read the best authors, observe the best speakers, and much
exercise of his own style."

BEN JONSON

"Crisp writing usually has a good deal of shortening in it."

ANONYMOUS

"There is no way of writing well and also of writing easily."

ANTHONY TROLLOPE

"You want to fix up your writing, parse your sentences, use the
right words? Fine, pick up the little books, learn to avoid
mistakes, revere taut prose and revile tautology. But do not flatter
yourself that you have significantly changed your style. First,
straighten out yourself so that you can then think straight and
soon afterward write straight."

WILLIAM SAFIRE

"Style comes only after long, hard practice and writing."

WILLIAM STYRON

"Now do it—with style."

MERVIN BLOCK

6

ALL ELSE

Q. What else can be said about broadcast newswriting?

A. Plenty else.

Q. O.K., let's start with one else: What are the tricks to writing news?

A. The only trick is to know how to write, and the secret is to make it all seem like it's not a trick.

Q. Huh?

A. We don't engage in tricks or trickery.

Q. Well, what about short cuts?

A. There are no short cuts, no gimmicks, no simple steps, no easy solutions, no magical cures, no quick fixes, no can't-miss measures, no one-fits-all answers. If there ever could be one single answer on how to become a better newswriter, it would be: Work, learn; work, learn; work, learn. Work *works*.

Q. But learn from whom?

A. From someone who's better.

Q. What if I'm the best in my shop?

A. "Best in my shop" may be a modest boast indeed. "The best" may not be much better than the rest. Unfortunately, many newcomers—and oldtimers—regard themselves as masters. That's why there are so few masters.

Q. What about getting *outside* help?

A. Most newsrooms don't get outside help. And newspeople, like most other people, find it hard to improve when they have no one to learn from but themselves.

Q. What about learning from writers with more experience?

A. Learn from anyone who knows more than you. The best writers know how much more *they* have to learn. At the age of 70, an accomplished French writer said, "Every day I am learning to write."

Q. So what's the answer?

A. Whether you become a writer or a Writer depends on you.

Q. How so?

A. If you want to improve, and apparently you do, you'll have to do it yourself.

Q. Explain yourself.

A. Experts say good writing cannot be taught but can be learned.

Q. What do *you* say?

A. I say it *can* be taught and *can* be learned.

Q. How?

A. By you, as part-time teacher and full-time learner. The author and teacher Jacques Barzun says all good writing is self-taught: "Almost any professional writer will tell you that nobody can teach another person to write. . . . But all writers admit that they were helped by criticism; somebody showed them the effect of what they had written—the unintended bad effect. In doing so, the critic pointed out where the trouble lay and perhaps what its cause was. . . . The truth remains that the would-be writer, using a book or a critic, must teach himself. He must learn to spot his own errors and work out his own ways of removing them."

Q. Who else?

A. Another author and teacher, John Ciardi, says: "A writer can develop only as rapidly as he learns to recognize what is bad in his writing. . . . [The bad writer] never sees what he has actually written. . . . He does not see because, in plain fact, he cares nothing about it. He is out for release, not containment. He is a self-expressor, not a maker. . . ."

Q. Anyone else?

A. Prof. David L. Grey says Ciardi's comments suggest the best response for the beginner who asks, "How can I learn to write?" Grey says the response is: "Do you care enough to work at it? Or, rephrased: How are your motivation and willingness to accept criticism? Are you willing, literally, to sweat over words? And is your primary purpose random self-expression, or is it to communicate something systematic-ally to someone else? Such a philosophy for writing requires corraling the ego, as well as self-discipline and practice. It demands . . . a willingness to 'grope' relentlessly for the best word and set of words. And it demands active seeking out of the best library and human sources of information and insight."

Q. Any other advice?

A. Pay attention to the author William Zinsser. He tells writers, "You must take an obsessive pride in the smallest details of your craft."

Q. What else?

A. Listen to the best newscasters and the best reporters, even if it means (sob!) turning to another station or network. Listen carefully. Tape newscasts that have the best writing. Play them back. Replay them. Analyze them. See what makes the best writing the best. Read some of the books listed in the back of this book. "The man who does not read good books," Twain said, "has no advantage over the man who can't read them."

Q. Why haven't you mentioned humor?

A. That's funny; I thought I had. Humor is hard to write and harder to write about. In news scripts, it's especially fragile. Most news stories don't lend themselves to humor, unless you're a Mark Russell. And he's not a newsman.

Too much of what is intended as humor in newscasts is contrived and heavyhanded. Most often, the best humor in a newscast depends on humorous aspects of an event itself, not in the newswriter's effort to turn it into a laugh. In fact, most real humor in newscasts produces a smile or a glint of appreciation, not a guffaw. Too much of what we hear on the air sounds as though it has been pounded out with a sledgehammer. What's needed is the delicate brush of a watercolorist.

"Everything is funny as long as it happens to someone else," Will Rogers said. We might have fun *with* someone else, but never do we make fun *of* people. Misfortune is not a matter for jest. We don't make fun of those who've just lost a game, a home or a contest.

One last thought about humor: If you write something that is humorous, don't apologize for it. That's one of the four "nevers": Never volunteer, never complain, never apologize, never explain. Don't tell your listeners, by word or gesture, that you're uncomfortable with something that's supposed to be humorous. If you're uncomfortable, rewrite it. Or kill it.

Q. What about puns?

A. As a recovering punster, I don't want to puntificate. In scripts, I use them infrequently. They're harder to put across on the air than on paper. In print, word play sometimes works, but broadcasting is a different playing field. That's because many listeners usually need time to catch on, and we can't call a time-out. A gazette issued by pundits, the *New York Times's* in-house monitor, "Winners & Sinners," has set down two good rules on puns: "If in doubt, don't. If anybody nearby winces, definitely don't." The trouble with so many puns that we hear and see is that they're obvious or ham-handed, unless, of course, they're ours.

Q. You haven't mentioned pronunciation.

A. Pronunciation! I'll also mention this: Pronunciation is important in broadcasting because mistakes mean a loss in an anchor's (or reporter's) authority and credibility. The columnist Sydney J. Harris says the 10 words mispronounced most often are: *nuclear, realtor, conversant, chaise longue, harass, lingerie, frequent* (as a verb), *forte, monstrous* and *disastrous.* Three other words that I keep hearing knocked around: *covert* (the preferred pronunciation is like *cover* with a final *t*), *lambasted* (rhymes with *basted*) *onerous* (as in *honor*) and *schism* (the *sch* is pronounced like *s*) Also: *short-lived* (rhymes with *life*). *Melee*, too, is often mispronounced, although it's best not pronounced at all—unless you're writing about Malaysia.

Q. What can be done for writing blocks?

A. That question reminds me of the old-time patrolman who was taking a test for sergeant. He was asked, "What are rabies and what would you do for them?" "They're Jewish priests," he replied, "and I wouldn't do a damn thing for them."

I'd like to dispense with writing blocks that quickly, but glossing over them won't make them go away. For some newswriters, blocks are a recurring problem. I think a freelance writer sitting in his den can afford the luxury of having a writing block. But broadcast newswriters can't afford them. We have to produce a lot of copy in a fairly short time, often in desperate haste. So we can't permit ourselves any hangups. We have to develop inner strength, self-control and determination.

If you're stymied by a block and, try as you might, you can't get past it, here are several ways to deal with it: Do whatever worked for you last time. Or put your story aside—assuming you're not on deadline—and work on something else while your subconscious works on the original story. Or get up and get a cold drink. Or a hot drink. Or walk around in the newsroom. Or leave the newsroom and take a stroll. Or leave the station and take a run. Splash water on your face. Or take your meal early. Then go back to your original story and get a move on. Discipline yourself. Tell yourself, "I can do it. I will do it. I must do it." And do it. But if you're still drawing a blank, think of your paycheck, blank. If that doesn't work, lower your standards.

Q. How do you deal with the blahs?

A. Don't be blasé. It's a matter of having P.M.A. (positive mental attitude). But if newswriting becomes dull for you, if it's no longer interesting or challenging, or never was, maybe you need a change of scenery.

Q. How can I learn to write faster?

A. Write more. Speed comes with experience. Meeting deadlines is imperative, but writing fast is not necessarily a virtue. We're hired as writers, not typists. I'm suspicious of speed demons whose fingers fly across the keyboard. One of my problems is that I can't write without first thinking. Don't *they* need time to think? Don't *they* have to hunt for the right word? Don't *they* have to figure out how to say it the best way possible? (Do I sound envious?)

Q. What's the best way to avoid mistakes?

A. Do nothing. The person who makes no mistakes usually makes nothing. Mistakes are inevitable in writing in a rush in a hectic newsroom, but don't let anxiety about them spook you. Your goal should be to turn in copy with zero defects, but if writers always did that, editors would be deleted. But because writers do have someone checking their copy—be they editors, producers or anchors—writers shouldn't relax their guard against those pesky errors that try to sneak into copy.

Q. How do you deal with deadlines?

A. Dutifully. How else?

Q. Why did you call this chapter All Else?

A. What else? It's a catchall for all the odds and ends that didn't fit elsewhere, or that deserved different treatment, or that I forgot to put in earlier.

Q. How did you happen to think of All Else?

A. On the CBS Evening News with Walter Cronkite, the three writers were assigned to stories by category: International, National and

All Else. Everything that didn't fit into the first two categories—disasters, storms, space, features, plus the other writers' overflow—went into All Else. As a former All Else writer, I thought that'd be a good heading.

Q. Any afterthoughts?

A. Just one thought about "after": If you find it in one of your sentences, you're probably telling the story in the wrong sequence. So you should recast it.

Q. Anything else?

A. Do your best—or else!

7

MY LEAST WORST

If broadcast news is written on the wind, news scripts are written on Kleenex. As soon as they've done the job, they're tossed away.

Many newsrooms do hang on to scripts for reference—by insiders. But nowhere that I know of are news script files open to outsiders. So when it came time for me to get examples for this chapter, I wanted to find a newswriter willing to share his scripts with strangers and also willing to put up with their criticism and mine. Eventually, I found one: me.

I've written tens of thousands of scripts for broadcast. Once in a while, I saved a page or two, for no evident reason, perhaps in the belief that one day I'd find something to do with them. This use of my own scripts offers several advantages: With access to the writer's mind, I can probe his mental processes and get his frank comments on what he thinks went wrong. I'm also able to get his ideas on how the scripts can be improved, and he's always on hand if I have a question: I don't have to write him, phone him, visit him, or humor him.

Some of these scripts are not too bad, some, not too good. Some were written under extreme pressure with only minutes to air, and they show it. Some were written with ample time for writing and rewriting— but don't show it. And some, well, judge for yourself. Before you read *my* comment, please read the script.

So here they are, some scripts that might be called my least worst:

mb	
OSGOOD	The New York City marathon was won today by an Italian. He ran the 26 miles in two hours, 14 minutes, 53 seconds. He got a good run for his money and good money for his run. Steve Young has the story:
VTR	TRACK UP:

My lead-in would have worked just as well without the third sentence. On the other hand, it has a nice lilt to it, and it didn't do any harm.

I skipped the name of the marathon winner because the reporter used it. I specified the winner's time because the reporter did not. The reporter did note the amount of the prize, so I didn't.

I used the passive voice—"was won"—to set the scene at the outset with the combined "where" and "what" and built up to the "who." If I had used the active voice here—"An Italian won the . . . ."— I'd be giving away the high point of the story in the first breath. And listeners who hear that a foreigner has done something are probably less interested than if they hear mention of a widely known sports staple. I try to write most stories about someone's winning a prize the same way: "The Nobel Prize in Chemistry was awarded today to a lab worker in Bolivia." After you hear "was awarded today to," aren't you eager to hear who won? And don't you enjoy suspense?

mb	
PLANTE	Runner Mary Decker fell short of her goal in the Los Angeles Olympics last summer, but, as Bob McNamara reports from Eugene, Oregon, she's back on track:
VTR	TRACK UP:

It runs nine seconds. No wasted words. All one sentence: short, straight, swift.

```
mb
OSGOOD    Two Irish boys ran away
          from home in Dublin three
          days ago, hitchhiked to
          London and took an Air
          India flight to this
          country—all without a
          ticket or passport. A
          policeman at New York
          City's Kennedy airport
          became suspicious of
          them—one 10 years old,
          the other 13—and they
          fessed up. So tonight
          they're going back. If they
```

```
          could write a book on how
          they traveled free, it might
          be a runaway best-seller.
```

You had to read a long distance for a short payoff, so you might call your journey a pun-itive expedition.

```
mb
OSGOOD    The U-S boycott of the
          19-80 Moscow Olympics
          has now come full circle.
          The United States stayed
          away because of the
          Soviet invasion of
          Afghanistan. Today,
          Afghanistan said it's not
          going to take part in this
          summer's Los Angeles
          Olympics. That makes it
          eight countries, led by the
          Soviet Union, which say
          they do not choose to run.
```

This approach seems preferable to one that would start with the spot news, which is not especially exciting: "Afghanistan said today it's not going to take part in this summer's Los Angeles Olympics." Sounds like another ho-hum item. My treatment is an exercise in story-telling.

Ideally, a network newscast would carry only news that would merit display on page 1 or page 3 of an imaginary national general-interest newspaper. An exception: a newsfeature. The Afghanistan story was printed on sports pages, but I doubt that any paper carried it on page 1, except in Kabul. (And it probably got a good play there on the Kabul News Network.)

block		
CRONKITE	The young woman in the middle of the McGuire sisters' singing act was in the middle again today, this time before a federal grand jury in Chicago. The jury wanted to know about Phyllis McGuire's reputed romance with an underworld overlord, Sam Giancanna. A cameraman for station WBBM-TV filmed the courthouse comings and goings, and	Stuart Novins reports the doings:

OUTCUE: |

Until now, no listeners were aware that I misspelled "Giancana." I'm glad *he* never found out.

mb	
CRONKITE	Have you ever looked at a can of chili con carne and wondered how much of it is beans? And how much meat? Well, maybe before too long you'll be able to find out. The government said today that it's starting a revision of labeling laws so shoppers can easily tell just what's in a can—and how much of it. Richard Roth has the story in Washington:

A question lead. And a "you" lead. Rarely do I write a question lead. More often, I write a questionable lead. I think this kind of question, one that every listener can answer instantly, is acceptable.

If I had written that story straight, I probably would have started, "The government said today it's revising the law on labeling canned goods so you can easily tell what's inside—and how much of it."

Too many stories, though, start with "the government" or talk about the government. Here was a story that offered me a chance to get away from the standard governmental yawner. I don't remember whether the wire copy mentioned chili, but as a chili-eater, I'd long wondered how much is carne. Or how little. I figured that if I was curious, a lot of other people were, too. So I decided to spice up the lead by turning it into a question.

"You" grabs listeners by the collar, or by the ear. It's best used when it's almost universally applicable. That's why it sometimes makes sense to write up a postal rate increase this way: "When you mail a letter from now on, you're going to have to pay two cents more." But it makes no sense to use "you" in restrictive contexts: "You're going to have to pay more for a Rolls-Royce." Ninety-nine percent of our listeners aren't going to be buying Rollses, so they're not going to have to pay anything. Used with discrimination, though, "you" can help you.

mb		
CRONKITE	Great Britain is grim about two crises, one with the pound sterling and now one with a sterling pounder, a pounder of drums, that is, whose percussions have prompted wide repercussions. Alexander Kendrick reports:	
KENDRICK	TRACK UP	
CRONKITE	The latest medical bulletin reports the operation was a success . . . and Ringo	should be an active Starr again next month. Yeah, yeah, yeah! And that's the way it is, Wednesday, December second, 1964. This is Walter Cronkite reporting from Washington. Good Night.

Signs of strain: "pound sterling" and "sterling pounder." Not to mention "percussions" and "repercussions."

In case anyone cares, I don't know why I capitalized "n" in "night."

Yeah, if I had the power to recall scripts, this is one of those I'd want brought back to the shop for repair. Or shredding.

```
mb
CRONKITE    When it comes to shops,
            shoppers and shopping,
            there's no time like
            Christmas, no place like
            New York City and no
            observer like Charles
            Osgood:

OSGOOD      TRACK UP:
```

Another nine-second lead-in. This was a hard one to write because it was one of those annual, or biennial, excursions in search of unusual gifts or givers. Writing a lead-in to a frothy feature is hard because the feature itself, as good as it may be, often defies summarizing in several seconds, or summarizing in a way that engages listeners. And you don't want to give away the good parts of the correspondent's script.

Although I said that lead-in was hard to write, I could say almost all of them are hard. Only someone who doesn't know much about writing finds writing easy.

```
block
REASONER    There's no place like
            nowhere, but Washington
            has a tunnel that goes
            there. Martin Agronsky
            has the story:

VTR
```

Six seconds. They don't make 'em much shorter. Or shallower.

block		
CRONKITE	Humorist Irvin S. Cobb once had some fun with the name of Poet Witter Bynner. Cobb quipped: "'It's been a bitter Winter,' said Witter Bynner." But Winter was no laughing matter today in a large part of the nation. CBS News Correspondent Harry Arouh has the story:	
WBBM-RR	OUTCUE:	

If it hadn't been for Cobb and Bynner, this lead-in could have been shoved into that tunnel to nowhere.

block	
CRONKITE	Americans may think that the way British play croquet isn't cricket. But despite an ocean of difference between the two groups, they both play with English on the ball and mallets for all. Charles Collingwood reports from London:
VTR	

At least I didn't say anything about "no rest for the wicket."

mb	
CRONKITE	Ronald Reagan's positions are seen by some people as rigid, so Dan Rather compares Reagan's rhetoric and record:
RATHER	TRACK UP:

1980 Republican convention. I was churning out so many lead-ins for videotapes at the conventions, especially for "bank" pieces prepared in advance, that I don't remember whether this one was used. So this may be its première.

mb	
CRONKITE	Our country holds age in high regard in coins, wines and books—but seldom in people. So age may be an issue in November, and Andy Rooney has a new wrinkle:
ROONEY	TRACK UP:

This led into a whimsical piece prompted by a leading figure there whose face was wrinkled. And still is.

```
mb
CRONKITE        Andy Rooney has taken a
                look at—or a listen to—
                convention oratory, and,
                needless to say, finds
                most of it needless to say:


ROONEY          TRACK UP:
```

If this wasn't used at that convention, it can still be used at the next one, needless to say.

```
block
CRONKITE        Jimmy Carter may be
                accepted here with
                unanimity, but not too
                long ago he faced
                anonymity. This
                happened on "What's My
                Line" in December,
                19-73:


VTR             OUTCUE:
                "governor of the state
                of Georgia."
```

1976 Democratic convention. The videotape showed him on "What's My Line?" as a mystery guest, and—you guessed it—no one identified him.

```
mb
RATHER        Good evening.              disputants any closer
              This is the C-B-S Evening  diplomatically. We have
              News, Dan Rather          three reports; first,
              reporting. As the British
              fleet advances toward the
              disputed Falkland Islands,
              Britain and Argentina may
              be moving closer militarily.
              That's because U-S
              Secretary of State Haig
              apparently has not
              brought the two
```

This was a hodgepodge because it had to provide an umbrella for reports from three correspondents. "May" is weak, but apparently the shooting hadn't started, we had no reporters with the fleet, and whatever information we had was sketchy. Or else we'd have had a harder lead.

```
block
CRONKITE      Two tiny craft managed to   an hour. For Gemini-six's
              meet with pinpoint          astronauts, the day has
              precision in the infinite   been a strenuous one:
              depths of space . . . and
              the United States took
              another giant step today
              toward landing a man on
              the moon. Gemini-six
              rendezvoused with
              Gemini-seven high over
              the Western Pacific after
              four hours of maneuvering
              through light and darkness
              at 17-thousand, 500 miles
```

Too many numbers in the second sentence. And why an ellipsis (. . .) instead of a comma?
  "Giant step." Hmm.

block	
con'd. A	
CRONKITE	another "first"—the first American musical message from outer space. He was talked into it, in a sense, by the mission control communicator at Houston—Astronaut James McDivitt:
CRONKITE:	You can't blame him if he can't carry a tune; no room up there.

The first page of this script is missing (don't bother looking for it), but the tag may be worth a look—maybe.

block			
REASONER	Good evening. America's two astronauts both took a walk today— on the carrier Wasp as it circled off Jacksonville, Florida. James McDivitt and Edward White reviewed their four-day flight, and the space agency released spectacular film of White's walk in space. The pictures were taken		by an automatic camera mounted on the spacecraft by White himself and by another camera held by McDivitt. Charles Von Fremd reports:
		VTR	OUTCUE:

The first sentence made sense to listeners right away if they already knew that one of the astros had taken a highly publicized space walk. By that time, only isolates and anchorites wouldn't have known.

```
block
REASONER     Outer space and inner
             grace, star dust and mud.
             Eric Sevareid has a few
             thoughts on these and
             other matters:


VTR
```

This lead-in probably ran on an evening when our newscast carried a story about space, the astros' turf.

Writing an introduction to a commentary that skips around without a distinct central theme puts a writer to the test. An anchor's delivery can help him pass.

```
mb
RATHER       It may be within the letter
             of the law, but a letter
             from a member of the First
             Family has raised some
             questions—and eyebrows.
             Bill Plante has the story at
             the White House:
PLANTE       TRACK UP:
```

It's good to avoid starting a story or a lead-in—or a criticism—with an indefinite pronoun, and it's good to avoid "may," but despite these handicaps, it seems to work here.

```
mb
KURALT     At a time when the
           President is under fire,
           and the Presidency, too, it
           may be helpful to recall a
           plain-speaking, peppery
           President, a man who
           seemed to relish being on
           the firing line, a man who
           was quick to fire back or
           even fire first. And, as
           Bruce Morton recounts,
           he also was strong
           enough to hold his fire—
           or to light a fire for
           illumination and warmth:
```

I suppose I wrote so much because I thought the correspondent's script needed setting up. Whether it needed that much setting up, I don't know. The President was Truman.

```
mb
OSGOOD     Tornadoes and
           thunderstorms struck
           the southeast today and
           caused at least two
V/O        deaths. Tornadoes in
           Laurel county, Kentucky,
           in the London area,
           overturned mobile homes,
           toppled trees, battered
           buildings, peeled off
           roofs, killed cattle and
           destroyed or damaged a
           lot of other property. At
```

```
           least six people there
           were hurt.
```

If Guinness ever lists the record for the most verbs in one sentence, the second sentence would be a contender. It has seven. Seven good ones. The lead refers to the southeast, but the only place we had any footage from was Kentucky. Right at the top of the V/O, the script makes clear where the footage was shot.

```
mb
BRADLEY     Good evening.
            Hurricane Allen is gone
            with the wind—
            downgraded to a tropical
            storm.
              Its winds greatly
            reduced, the storm is now
            moving from the Texas
            coast toward Mexico.
              But when Allen swept
            ashore into Texas from
            the Gulf, it caused
            extensive damage, though
            less than feared.
```

"Gone with the wind"? Yes, I was trying for an approach that was novel.

As I re-read the last line about damage less than feared, you might be able to read between the lines: "and less than the producer had hoped for."

```
mb
OSGOOD      The weather has been so          whiteouts, visibility shrank
            severe in the Plains states,     to only several feet.
            the temperatures so low,         Across the Plains states,
            the winds so high and the        at least eight people have
            snows so deep that in            been killed. The National
            some places even highway         Guard has rescued
            snowplows have not               hundreds of stranded
            ventured out.                    motorists, but many are
V/O           Winds in Minnesota             still snowbound.
            reached 60 miles an
            hour, temperatures fell to
            16-below, and with
            snow whipped into
```

The lead-in bounces around in a sort of sing-song style, but special delivery drove it home.

As you read the V/O, you may be able to "see" the footage.

Ordinarily, eight deaths would make the lead, but I think the deaths occurred over several days. For all I can remember, there might have been no deaths that day.

This story was written for a Sunday night newscast, but it has no "today," no "tonight," no "yesterday," no "weekend." With no loss.

mb	
OSGOOD	Capitalism and communism are squaring off in a remote city in China, and it seems that capitalism has got the goods on its rival. David Jackson has the story:
VTR	TRACK UP:

The correspondent told about the emergence of private enterprise and featured busy merchants, which is why I said capitalism "has the goods." Someone made it read "has got." If I had ever used "has got" in an English class, I'd never have been able to get away with it. But in *The Careful Writer,* Theodore M. Bernstein, a language authority who was an editor at the *New York Times,* said: "To see how it adds force, compare *has to meet, must meet,* and *has got to meet.* There cannot be much doubt that *got* in this sense has simply got to win approval." And that was published in 1968. In 1980, *American Usage and Style: The Consensus* by Roy Copperud said the consensus regards "has got" as standard. For those of us who still think "has got" is redundant, maybe we've got another think coming.

mb	
SPENCER	A woman in Woodridge, Illinois, has won what she calls a victory for lefthanded people in a righthanded world: a judgment of 136-thousand dollars from a food store where she worked as a checkout clerk. She's lefthanded, but the store required her to check out groceries with her right

hand. So now the store's left holding the bag.

Although a wire service had moved the story that day, it was several days old: not fresh, but not yet stale. I did the best I could.

mb	
OSGOOD	Only a few years ago, oil was in such short supply that Washington pushed a policy of trying to squeeze oil out of rock. But, as Bob McNamara reports from Grand Junction, Colorado, some companies seem to have dug themselves into a hole:
MCNAMARA	TRACK UP:

To point up "then" and "now," I think I'd insert "now" after "companies."

mb	
SPENCER	One of the most enduring figures of the Old West is the cowboy. But many of the pioneer cowboys have been largely ignored—because they were black. Their descendents, though, have kept the campfires burning and their memories glowing. Sam Ford has the story in Boley, Oklahoma:
VTR	TRACK UP:

I could have skipped the first sentence and started with "many."

mb
OSGOOD   A new study says children
who become hooked on
television at an early age
often become teenagers
who are overweight. And
the study by two Boston
doctors reports that the
more time these teens
spend watching T-V, the
more weight they put
on—making them truly
heavy viewers.

Satisfactory.

mb
OSGOOD   Former President Carter   V/O   building on Manhattan's
arrived in New York City   Lower East Side, Mister
today to lend a hand—in   Carter, an expert
fact, both of them— to   woodworker, is going
help rebuild a burned-out   to use hammer and saw
apartment building.   to try to make the
V/O   He came by bus with   place fit again.
other volunteers from his
hometown Baptist church
in Plains, Georgia. On
arrival, they talked over
their one-week project,
sponsored by a religious
group. At the abandoned

If you've seen enough TV news, you can see the videotape covered by the
voice-over: the woodworker himself getting off the bus, people chatting,
the abandoned building. It all fits.

mb	
RATHER	Good evening.
	The greatest threat to
	economic recovery, the
	President said today, is
	high interest rates. But
	most of the interest
	during his news
	conference seemed to be
	in what was unsaid.
	Lesley Stahl has the story
	at the White House:
STAHL	TRACK UP:

Re-reading this lead-in reminds me that often a lead-in is merely a stall, playing for time, like preliminary boxing bouts occupying the gathering crowd until the main event.

mb	
CRONKITE	Although this is the main
	season for charitable
	giving, investigators have
	found that some so-called
	charities are more intent
	on taking. John Sheahan
	has the story:
SHEAHAN	TRACK UP:

The contrast between "giving" and "taking" and the emphasis on "taking" (as the last word) give this lead-in its sting.

mb

OSGOOD   This country has about 26-million military veterans, but as the two world wars fade away, more old-timers are answering their final roll call. So the largest veterans' organization, the American Legion, is using new tactics to recruit members for posts whose numbers are no longer legion. Bill Whitaker has the story:

This is the kind of story that needs perspective, as some producers like to call it, so the first sentence sets the scene and the tone. And the next may cause a groan.

block

CRONKITE   There's a new look in art, and there's more to it than meets the eye. Robert Trout reports:

CRONKITE   I suppose you could say, Op goes the easel.

First came Pop Art, then Op Art. Op, short for "optical," created the illusion of movement.

block	
CRONKITE	A flip that can launch a thousand faces: that's the ability of an amazing new machine. Nelson Benton has the story in Chicago:
VTR	
CRONKITE	Nelson, that man looks like my Walter ego.

This, too, has a tag that's better than the lead-in, but that's only mild praise. To appreciate the tag, you'd have to know that while a witness or victim described a culprit, a police technician cranked in features to produce a face on the screen. In this make-believe case, the "witness" (the reporter) carefully described the anchor, including his mustache.

I started the wrong way. The start may be catchy, but when listeners (remember them?) hear "that," they have to exert themselves to try to figure out what "that" refers to. That's why it's unsuitable to start a story by making an assertion and then adding. "That's what so-and-so says," Or "That according to. . . ." Or "That's what happened when. . . ." Or "Dead. That's what Theophilus Thackeray is."

This lead-in might be better: "A remarkable new machine provides a sketch of someone police are looking for. A technician at a lever can, with a flip, launch a thousand faces." Or something like that.

block	
CRONKITE	France long has been a haven for the strange from many lands— heretics, neurotics, the erratic and the erotic. But now France says, "Don't give me your befuddled masses." Bernard Kalb has the story:

With apologies to Emma Lazarus. Profound apologies.

```
block
REASONER    During last Sunday's          an unidentified viewer in
            inaugural demonstration        Fort Lauderdale, Florida,
            of the Earlybird               tipped police that he
            communications satellite,      recognized LeMay's face
            a Royal Canadian               as that of a man he
            Mounted Policeman              knew. LeMay, wanted for
            broadcast—to the U-S           bank robbery, was
            and Europe—a                   arrested there today
            description of a wanted         aboard his yacht. And
            man.                           once again the Royal
                                           Canadian Mounties got
VTR                                        their man, this time with
REASONER    After seeing the              the help of Earlybird—
            international broadcast,        and a birdwatcher.
```

My editor, Ed Bliss, taught me to spell out "U.S.," except when using it as an adjective, as in "the U-S Navy." I don't know why I slipped up here and how it slipped through.

In the tease before the preceding commercial, I wrote, "Earlybird catches its first worm. . . ."

```
mb
PAULEY      The outlook for wine in
            California is again—you
            might say—rosé. After a
            17-day strike, winery
            workers there have
            approved a new contract,
            and they'll start going back
            to work today—just in
            time for the peak of the
            grape harvest. They'll get a
            13 percent pay increase in
            the first year, with smaller
            increases in the next two.
```

The Today Show, Sept. 22, 1980. The editor crossed out the last sentence, apparently because he thought it would tell our viewers more than they cared to know about winery wages.

```
mb
BROKAW      The Shah of Iran has
            been flown to New York
            City for medical
            treatment. The nature of
            the Shah's illness has not
            been made public. But a
            U-S State Department
            spokesman says the Shah
            is "quite" sick. He was
            taken to New York
            Hospital—Cornell
            Medical Center. The Shah
            arrived in New York City
            on a chartered jet from
```

```
            Cuernavaca, Mexico. He
            moved to Mexico after he
            lost his throne in Iran 10
            months ago.
```

Today Show, Oct. 23, 1979. No "today" in this story. The shah landed the previous day or night, so I used the present perfect tense for this warmed-over news.

```
mb
GUIDA       Some people making news
            today:
            Actress Linda Blair: fined
            five-thousand dollars,
            sentenced to three years'
            probation and ordered to
            make 12 public
            appearances warning
            youngsters about the
            dangers of drugs. Miss
            Blair, who starred in "The
            Exorcist," had pleaded
            guilty to conspiracy to
```

```
            possess cocaine. No, she
            didn't say the devil made
            her do it.
```

"Some people making news today" was a standing head on the Today Show for a short package about prominent persons for whom we had a still photo, new or old. But the personalities we used seldom had made anything definable as news and seldom that day. But the show must go on.

Whoever deleted the last sentence in the item might have been afraid he'd be dispossessed.

---

mb

GUIDA   Some people making news today: Vladimir Horowitz plugs his ears to muffle the loud sound at a New York City disco. Apparently the pianist prefers pianissimo.

Whoever chose that item must have been at his wits' end, but every whit helps when it comes to filling a two-hour hole.

As Falstaff said about his rag-tag band of soldiers: They'll fill a pit as well as better men.

---

mb

GUIDA   Four Secretaries of State do not make a secretarial pool. But they do make an unusual group at a Washington dinner party. The current secretary, Cyrus Vance, chats with former Secretaries Henry Kissinger, William Rogers and Dean Rusk. Diplomatically, of course.

When newswriters have to think in the middle of the night, they should be forgiven their trespasses (and not deprived of their press passes).

mb

GUIDA   Athlete O-J Simpson, the
long-running star of those
rent-a-car commercials, is
not going to have the
driver's seat to himself
anymore. He's going to
share the chores with
Nancy Lopez.
Miss Lopez—a golfer—
has been chosen to
perform by herself and
with him in the rent-a-car
spots—and not just

because golfer Lopez is a
long driver.

I had to say *something*.

mb

GUIDA   British pop star Elton
John displays his new
thatch of hair. John had
been almost bald until he
started undergoing hair
transplants. He says he's
going to have two more
transplants to thicken his
thatch—although the
head of Britain is already
Thatcher.

Someone crossed out the last
clause, starting with "although."
And if anyone reading this knows
who, please write or wire me, collect.

```
mb
GUIDA        Seven persons in
             Wilmington, Delaware,
             have pointed to a man in
             court and identified him as
             the bandit who held them
             up, a Roman Catholic
             priest. But now another
             man has come forward,
             saying that he committed
             the armed robberies, not
             the priest. The judge will
             decide how to proceed
             after conferring today with
             the prosecutor, the priest
             and the penitent.
```

Once in a great while, "Some people making news" did harbor some news.

```
block
Good morning.
Oregon police are searching for a prison
escapee who was on board the United
Airlines DC-8 that crashlanded in Portland
last night. The escapee was being returned
by two guards to the Oregon state prison.
185 persons were on board the plane. In
the crash, at least 10 were killed and 45
hurt, five critically. And the escapee
apparently escaped again.
```

NBC News Update, Dec. 29, 1978. This is a second-day lead. I don't put "yesterday" in a lead, but "last night" seemed necessary here.

Why would a TV script be written across the full width of the page like a radio script? Simple. That's the way the anchor wanted it. The only thing that matters to me is the writing. Did I select the right facts, did I put them in the right order, did I use the right words, did I tell it right? I hope so.

If you think I should have written "185 *people*" instead of "persons," you may be right. I'm accustomed to using "people" for large groups or round numbers, and persons for exact numbers of small groups. I say "two persons" or "three persons," and so on, which is what I was taught in school and have never been able to unlearn. Most anchors, though, are "people" persons, and they say "two *people*." I haven't heard any say "one *people*." Yet.

It's easier to be a critic than a newswriter, but anyone who wants to be a better writer needs to be a keen critic.

"Above all else," the writer Allan W. Eckert quotes his late father as saying, "you must be your own harshest critic, your own strictest editor, your own most demanding taskmaster."

If you're honest with yourself in these respects, you will never please yourself entirely, he said, but if you keep trying to do so, you can't help pleasing others.

8

YOUR TURN

Now it's your turn. I've said most of what I know about writing, maybe even more than I know, so I'm going to give you a chance to see for yourself what you know.

You can do this by rewriting nine stories printed in this section and comparing them with my rewrites. After you've written each exercise, you can read my script, followed by my comments on why I wrote it the way I did. Then proceed to the second story and compare what you've written with what I wrote. Don't write all nine stories in a row and then compare them with my versions. Do one at a time. That way, as you go along, you may pick up a few pointers that you can put to use in your next rewrite.

This is not a test, this is not a drill. Let's call it an editorial checkup. Or a tuneup. No matter what you call it, and you needn't call it anything, it gives you an opportunity to put into play whatever know-how you've picked up in reading, or riffling, this book. At the outset, writing with speed is secondary. What's primary is getting the words right.

In these exercises—and in the newsroom—there is no one "right" version. Several versions may be "right," but they are fairly few. On the other hand, there are an infinite number of wrong ways to write a story. My version is just that: mine. It may not be the best possible, even if one could be designated "best." The version I offer is one that I think is acceptable for broadcast. By now, I should be able to write a usable story: Chances are, I've written more stories than most newswriters, have made more mistakes, have had more chances to see how to get it right, and have had more time to learn.

Here's the first piece of source copy. Your assignment: Write a 20-second story for Sunday night. Time limit: none.

94

LONDON (AP)—Smuggled letters from Soviet dissident Andrei Sakharov reveal that he has been mentally and physically tortured by Soviet secret police while in internal exile in in the closed city of Gorky, the weekly Observer reported Sunday.

The newspaper said the documents "unmask the careful plan of KGB disinformation," including postcards and telegrams carrying his wife's name, that have for nearly two years suggested Sakharov was living without problems.

Sakharov's stepdaughter, Tatyana Yankelevich, and her husband, Yefrem, received the smuggled letters and photographs in two plain envelopes mailed from an unidentified Western country to the couple in Newton, Mass., the Observer said.

It quoted Yankelevich as saying, "How they got out of the Soviet Union I cannot say, but I know the source and the source is reliable. They (the documents) have been carefully examined by the whole family and we are convinced of their authenticity."

Yankelevich, contacted in Newton by The Associated Press, confirmed that he had provided the Observer with the documents. "There were some financial arrangements, but I won't be able to discuss it," he said.

Sakharov, a physicist who led fellow scientists to produce the Soviet hydrogen bomb, has been in internal exile in Gorky, 260 miles east of Moscow, since January 1980.

He became a human rights activist in the 1960s and was ordered to Gorky after he publicly criticized the Soviets' military intervention in Afghanistan in December 1979.

The Observer said the letters, which it will publish in extract starting next week, detail the KGB's ill-treatment of Sakharov. They confirm reports that Sakharov was force-fed during two hunger strikes in 1984 and 1985 and was subjected to mental torture and physical violence while being treated at a Gorky hospital, it said.

The KGB is the Soviet security police and intelligence agency.

Sakharov spent several months on a hunger strike in an effort to get an exit visa for his wife, Yelena Bonner.

The paper said the main document is a 20-page letter
written by Sakharov in October 1984 to Dr. Anatoli
Alexandrov, president of the Soviet Academy of Sciences.
In it, Sakharov appeals for his wife to be allowed to go to
the West for medical treatment. Mrs. Bonner was granted
an exit visa late last year and she is now in Massachusetts,
where she underwent a heart bypass operation.

Sakharov also describes how he was seized by KGB
agents on May 7, 1984, and taken to Gorky's Semashko
hospital, the paper said.

Sakharov wrote that hospital authorities "kept me by
force and tormented me for four months. My attempts to
flee the hospital were always blocked by KGB men, who
were on duty round the clock to bar all means of escape,"
according to the Observer.

It said the letters "contain one of the most vivid
testimonies of human suffering ever to have emerged in
the Soviet Union."

AP-NY-02-09-86   2023EST

Here's how I wrote it.

My version is not intended for use as a template; you needn't hold
your story up against mine to make sure it corresponds in every detail. I
do think, though, that you should find that you've used most of the facts I
did and approximated my pattern. Which gives you considerable
latitude (but only 20 seconds' longitude).

> A London newspaper says letters
> smuggled from Soviet dissident Andrei
> Sakharov confirm that the secret police
> have abused him mentally and
> physically. The paper says the letters
> knock down what it calls K-G-B
> disinformation—including postcards
> and telegrams—suggesting Sakharov
> has had no problems. He and his wife
> have been in internal exile, but she's
> now in this country for medical care.

Why did I write it that way? I wouldn't assert, on my own say-so,
that Sakharov had been mistreated. Maybe he had been and maybe not.
I needed to attribute it. And I know the rule: Attribution precedes
assertion. I didn't want to name the newspaper; most listeners have never
heard of it. And those who have probably don't know whether it's

reliable. I, for one, don't know. But I do know better than to take information printed by a newspaper and report it as fact. (When I was a newspaperman, I once told a deskmate, in jest, "You can't believe what you read," and he riposted, "I don't even believe what I write.") So I started my script by attributing the Sakharov story to a London newspaper. Another drawback to naming the paper: a London observer could be a bobby.

The wire service used "tortured" in the lead, but I was leery of that. Not that I have any doubt whatsoever that the KGB is capable of torture. But how come the body of the story referred to "physical violence," not "physical torture"? Did the newspaper writer regard force-feeding as "physical violence" and "physical violence" as "torture"? Some people regard riding in an elevator with piped-in music as mental torture. And riding in a Brooklyn subway as physical violence. If the wire story had provided specifics, I might have accepted the word "tortured" without hesitation. I don't want to deviate from the facts or go beyond the facts. But what were the facts? All I knew was what the wire service rewriter told me. And all he knew, probably, was what the newspaper said had occurred. Had Sakharov himself used the word "torture," was that the translator's choice, was it the newspaper writer's characterization, or was it the wire services' contribution? I have no doubt that Sakharov has been deprived of his freedom, if it can be said anyone there has freedom, and I think he has been treated outrageously. But "torture" is another matter. If a member of my staff, someone in whom I had full confidence, told me she had learned conclusively that Sakharov had been tortured, I'd accept that. But I'm disinclined to place that much trust in a nameless wire service reporter who's rewriting a faceless newspaper reporter. So after my reasoning—please don't call it tortured—I backed off from the source copy and moderated "torture" to "abuse." It wasn't just a matter of playing safe, although better half-safe than sorry; it was a matter of my trying to get as close as possible to what was true. Or what seemed true, or at least not untrue.

To simplify the story for the listener, I used only one name, that of the central figure, Sakharov. I didn't drag in a lot of other names that'd only divert the listener's attention: his wife, Yelena Bonner; Afghanistan; Gorky; Semashko hospital; his stepdaughter, Tatyana Yankelevich, and her husband, Yefrem; the place where they live, Newton, Massachusetts. If your station is near Newton, that's another story.

Speaking of other stories—and of labored transitions—let's turn to the next story. Please write 20 seconds. Take all the time you need. Note: This story broke on a Friday but it did not move on the wires until Saturday. You're writing it for a Saturday night audience.

MINNEAPOLIS (AP)—Drinking five or more cups of coffee a day appears to increase a person's chances of developing lung cancer, according to a researcher who says his study is the first to target coffee alone.

"This is the first time that coffee has been implicated by itself" as a factor in lung cancer, Dr. Leonard Schuman, an epidemiologist at the University of Minnesota, said Friday.

He said the study also found that the effects of coffee drinking and smoking may magnify each other.

Smoking alone increases the risk of cancer tenfold, Schuman said. But men who smoked a pack or more a day and drank five or more cups of coffee had a rate of lung cancer 40 times higher than men who neither smoked nor drank coffee.

Other studies will be needed to determine if the finding represents a cause-and-effect relationship, or is just a fluke finding from one statistical study, Schuman said.

The study didn't ask people to distinguish between regular and decaffeinated coffee, so that's another question that further research might tackle, he said.

Harvard University researchers in 1981 found a statistical link between coffee drinking and pancreatic cancer, but later studies have virtually killed that theory.

Schuman and his colleagues have been studying the dietary habits of 17,818 men, all age 45 and older, and tracking their death rates over the past 18 years.

Even after smoking habits and ages were taken into consideration, those who drank five or more cups of coffee a day were seven times more likely to have died from lung cancer than the men who drank no coffee at all, Schuman said.

"On the basis of this one study, I don't think it's warranted to say 'ban coffee from your diet,'" Schuman said after the findings were reported at a Society for Epidemiologic Research meeting in Chapel Hill, N.C.

However, moderation in the amount of coffee consumed, "like moderation in many other things, might be prudent for many reasons," he added.

"Smoking is still the most important factor in lung cancer," said Schuman. He served on the U.S. surgeon general's blue-ribbon committee of experts in 1964 that concluded that smoking is a major health risk.

Schuman's colleagues in the study are Dr. Robert Gibson of the University of Minnesota-Duluth and Dr. Erik Bjelke, who now lives in Norway.

Schuman said he didn't know what chemical in coffee might be responsible for any cancer risk, but it presumably would have to enter the bloodstream to reach the lungs.

NY-06-22-85 1702EDT

Here's how I wrote it:

A medical researcher says anyone who drinks five cups of coffee a day, or more, may be increasing the chances of developing lung cancer. The University of Minnesota scientist says his study is the first to implicate coffee by itself. He also says that if someone drinks too much coffee *and* smokes, the combined effects may be far worse. But he says investigators must do more research.

That was the kind of medical story that needed attribution early and often. In fact, I started every sentence with attribution. And I avoided "yesterday." Instead, I started with the historical present tense, "says." And I'll bet that you didn't notice "says" in four sentences in a row. I didn't use the scientist's name because listeners wouldn't recognize his name; it'd only take time without shedding light. My last sentence alerted listeners to another side of the story by starting with "But." That sentence is important because it tells listeners that the findings are far from conclusive. It does weaken the story, which may be worth using only on a slow-news day, or a no-news day.

On to the next story. Make it 20 seconds, and try to write it within 35 minutes for tonight's newscast.

LOS ANGELES—More than 250 firefighters battled a stubborn, smoky fire that swept through the Central Los Angeles Library today, injuring 22 firefighters and destroying thousands of books in the downtown landmark building.

Neither Mayor Tom Bradley nor Fire Chief Donald Manning could say what caused the fire, which broke out

shortly before 11. A.M. in the book stacks. It was declared
under control six hours later, after 49 fire companies
from across the city fought the blaze.

The 60-year-old library, which had 2.3 million
volumes, was listed on the National Register of Historic
Places and was declared a historic cultural monument by
the Los Angeles Cultural Heritage Board in 1967.

But the three-story building had also been designated
as unsafe by the Los Angeles Fire Department and had a
long history of fire violations. Mayor Bradley said some
of the violations had been corrected, and library officials
said fire doors were being installed when the fire
broke out.

The interior of the library, which is situated amid a
canyon of glass skyscrapers in downtown Los Angeles,
was severely damaged. But its facade, although blackened
and scorched, remained intact, in part because it was
built of concrete, fire officials said.

"This is the most extremely difficult fire we have ever
fought," Chief Manning said. "The men could not advance
without the fire flaring up behind them."

The future of the library has been the topic of civic
debate for the last 20 years. But, while various proposals
were debated, the library began to fall into neglect,
officials said.

About two years ago, a complicated plan involving
the construction of three major buildings and the expansion of the library was worked out among private and
public officials. The library staff was scheduled to move
out next year for the expansion to begin.

Mayor Bradley, who arrived at the scene at 5 P.M.,
told reporters: "This magnificent building is something we have tried to save. We tried to get it up to
safety standards."

Until the damage can be examined, the library's
future is in doubt, the Mayor said, adding, "We will
then decide whether to try to save it or to go forward
with the remodeling."

Library officials said more than 300 employees and
visitors were evacuated within minutes of the fire alarm
sounding. Despite its landmark status, Chief Manning
said, the building had no modern sprinkler system.

According to Robert Reagan, the library's public
information director, steel fire doors were in the process

of being installed between the book stacks and the public areas when the fire broke out. About half the work had been completed, he said.

Reagan said the library, the largest in the West, was "designated unsafe by the Fire Department as early as 1979." Violations were not corrected, he said, largely because of a lack of funds and uncertainty about its future.

The major fire violations, he said, were in the stacks that contained 85 percent of the library's books. The public has no direct access to the stacks.

The building, designed by the architect Bertram Grosvenor Goodhue and dedicated in 1926, was one of the few remaining buildings with open space in what is now the city's financial district.

From balconies and plazas of the glass skyscrapers that envelop the library, hundreds of office workers spent their lunch hour watching as smoke poured from the library's windows.

Firefighters were hampered by two factors: the desire to keep water at a minimum to decrease the water damage to the books and the fact that, for several hours, they were unable to bore a hole through the library's concrete roof to let the heat and smoke escape.

"It was like walking into a solid brick oven," said Capt. Anthony Didomenico of the Los Angeles Fire Department. Most of the injuries were caused by steam burns.

By day's end, neither fire officials nor library officials could estimate the amount of damage. The rare book collection, which is kept in a fireproof vault in the building's basement, was believed to be unharmed. But the general collection of books, many of which Reagan described as "irreplaceable," were probably ruined.

"We have a great collection of books here," he said. "How can I put a price on what is a priceless collection?"

Here's how I wrote it:

A fire swept through one of the nation's biggest libraries today. The Central Los Angeles Library was damaged severely, and thousands of books were destroyed. 250 firemen fought the fire, and 22 of them were hurt. Firemen were

hampered because they tried to hold
down the use of water—to minimize
water damage to books.

Punctuation is important. It tells anchors when to pause and when to stop. I mention that because of the dash I used in the last sentence. It gives the listener a chance to consider "water" and wonder for an instant why firemen tried to hold down its use. Then the listener is promptly given the explanation. The source copy said the library was the biggest in the West, so I broadened that and made it one of the biggest in the country.

In reporting casualties, I ordinarily follow the rule "People before property." I also follow the rule "Keep like things together." I figured the reference to the books fitted better where I put it than if I had put it after the firemen. I didn't want to flit from saying the library was severely damaged to the sentence about the firemen and then go back to the destruction of books. I would have written the story differently if any firemen had been killed or severely injured. Although the source copy tells of the injured in the lead, they're not mentioned again until almost the bottom. Most of the injuries, the copy says, were caused by steam burns. In the absence of specifics, I assume none of the injuries was severe. Or severe enough to impress the reporter(s) covering the fire or the writer and editor.

Try your hand at this one, 20 seconds in 30 minutes for a Sunday night newscast:

LONDON (AP)—Smiling to a cheering crowd, Princess Diana took home from the hospital Sunday her one-day-old second son, Henry Charles Albert David.

The baby, third in line to the British throne, will be known to his family simply as Harry.

Diana, 23, wore a red coat and cradled the infant swathed in a white shawl as she left the hospital 22 hours after a routine birth. Her husband, Prince Charles, 35, accompanied Diana and their new son home to their London residence, Kensington Palace.

The princess blushed as the crowd of about 1,000 people, some of whom had waited through the night outside London's St. Mary's Hospital, waved Union Jacks and called out, "Hurrah, Harry!"

The royal couple's first child, two-year-old Prince William, visited his mother and baby brother for 15 minutes earlier.

William, looking confused by the phalanx of photo-
graphers, arrived with Charles, but left holding the hand
of his nanny, Barbara Barnes. He gave three small waves
to a delighted crowd.

The baby, taken home in a three-car motorcade at the
start of a life of wealth, privilege and constant publicity,
bears the name of England's famed Henry VIII, who
broke with Rome in 1534 because the Vatican would not
give him a divorce.

"They chose the name Henry simply because they
both like it and also because there is no other member of
the royal family at present with that name," said a Buck-
ingham Palace spokesman. "The other names all have
family connections."

Prayers of thanksgiving were offered at Sunday
church services around the country in this strongly
monarchist nation for the birth of Prince Henry, who
ranks behind Charles and William in the line of succession. He joins them as a Prince of Wales.

Bells pealed for three hours Sunday across the Glou-
cestershire village of Tetbury, where Charles and Diana
have their country residence, Highgrove House.

The palace said the royal family will call the new
prince Harry. The affectionate diminutive is in contrast
to palace instructions that William must never be
referred to as Bill, or Willy.

The new baby's second name, Charles, is both the
name of his father and of Diana's only brother, Viscount
Althorp, 21. Albert was the first name of the baby's
great-grandfather, who reigned as George VI, and of
Queen Victoria's consort.

David, a palace announcement said, was for Elizabeth
the Queen Mother's favorite brother, the late Sir David
Bowes-Lyons.

David was also one of the names of Charles' great-
uncle, Edward VIII, who abdicated in 1936 to marry a
twice-divorced American, Wallis Simpson.

"The baby is fine! My wife is even better!" Charles
shouted to the crowd outside the hospital after a three-
hour morning visit Saturday.

The speed of the announcement of the names of the
6-pound, 14-ounce baby aroused speculation the princess
knew from medical tests that it would be another boy.

William's names, William Arthur Philip Louis, were not announced until a week after his birth in the same private ward at St. Mary's on June 21, 1982.

Charles was with Diana, the daughter of Earl Spencer and a former kindergarten teacher whom he married July 29, 1981, throughout her nine-hour labor and the birth Saturday.

Queen Elizabeth II was due back in London next Friday from her Scottish residence, Balmoral, said a palace spokesman, who spoke on condition he not be identified.

The queen smiled and waved to villagers Sunday when she attended church in the nearby Scottish hamlet of Crathie. Prayers were offered for the baby, her fourth grandchild. Her only daughter, Princess Anne, 33, has two children, Peter and Zara Phillips.

The new prince pushes Charles' brothers, Andrew, 24, and Edward, 20, into fourth and fifth in the line of succession. Anne is now sixth.

AP-NY-09-16-84 1441EDT

You have to deal with a lot of facts here, and, as usual, you have to save the best and ditch the rest. Note that the story moved a day after Diana gave birth. On the day of delivery, it was reported. Most of our listeners probably knew about it already, so our story should not focus on Diana's giving birth. It should carry a second-day lead, yet inform listeners who might not have known about it or who had forgotten.

Here's how I did it:

> Princess Diana of Britain went home from a London hospital today with her day-old son, Henry Charles Albert David. The new prince will be called Harry. Mother and son were escorted home by his father, Prince Charles. The family's first-born, Prince William, is second in line to be king, and now Harry's third.

As I look back, I wonder whether I squeezed in too many facts. In my defense, in case you take the offense: I needed the baby's name and his parents' names, and I wanted to point out that Harry is not Diana's first-born. I also wanted to let listeners know why this is more than a mere birth notice, that this baby might be king one day (but not a one-day king). Yet, look at all the facts I succeeded in keeping out.

On to the next exercise. Or scrimmage. Write a 25-second story for Sunday night. This time, try to write it in less than 30 minutes. And try not to go into overtime.

WASHINGTON—Using free Washington Redskins tickets as bait, authorities arrested 100 fugitives who showed up Sunday at a pre-game brunch where police and federal marshals posed as waiters and served warrants.

U.S. marshals called it the largest mass arrest of fugitives in recent memory.

"It was like an assembly line," said Herbert M. Rutherford III, U.S. marshal for the District of Columbia. "It was party time, and they fell for it, hook, line and sinker."

"This ain't fair, this just ain't fair," said one prisoner who was led in handcuffs from one of two large buses that carried the prisoners to a local jail.

"They said they was takin' us to a football game, and that's wrong," said another man. "That's false advertising."

"I came to see Boomer, I came to see Boomer," said a third, referring to Cincinnati Bengals quarterback Boomer Esiason.

U.S. marshals, working with the Metropolitan Police Department, sent out invitations to 3,000 wanted persons. The invitations said that as a promotion for a new sports television station, Flagship International Sports Television, they were winners of two free tickets to the National Football League game Sunday between the Redskins and the Bengals.

The invitation said 10 of the "lucky winners" would receive season tickets to the Redskins' 1986 season and that a grand prize drawing would be held for an all-expenses paid trip to the upcoming Super Bowl XX in New Orleans.

The initials for the TV enterprise, F.I.S.T., also stand for the Fugitive Investigative Strike Team, a special U.S. marshals force.

About 100 fugitives responded to the invitation and appeared at the D.C. Convention Center for the special brunch. The building was decorated with signs saying, "Let's party" and "Let's all be there."

Some of the fugitives showed up wearing the bright burgundy and gold wool Redskins hats as well as Redskins buttons, while others were attired in suits and ties for the pre-game feast.

One marshal was dressed in a large yellow chicken suit with oversized red boots while another turned up as an Indian chief complete with large headdress.

Other marshals wearing tuxedos handed small name stickers to each of the fugitives.

Buses that were to take them to the game, however, took them to the police department's central cellblock several blocks away instead.

"When we verified their identity, we escorted them in small groups to a party room, where officers moved in from concealed positions and placed them under arrest," said Stanley Morris, head of the U.S. Marshals Service.

The sting netted 100 fugitives by 11 a.m., marshals said.

Arrested were two people wanted for murder, five for robbery, 15 for assault, six for burglary, 19 for bond or bail violations, 18 for narcotics violations, officials said. Others were arrested on charges of rape, arson and forgery. Two of those arrested were on the D.C. police department's ten most wanted list.

A similar scam in Hartford, Conn., in November 1984 invited people to attend a luncheon with pop singer Boy George. Fifteen were picked up by a limousine and arrested. Marshals said they used job offers as the bait to arrest about 90 people in Brooklyn last year.

"Redskin tickets are valuable. And when you're trying to get a person, you play on their greed," said Toby Roche, chief deputy U.S. marshal for Washington, who coordinated the operation.

The cost of the project was estimated to be $22,100 dollars, or about $225 dollars per arrest.

One man who got into the Convention Center before apparently being spooked by the circumstances was arrested on the street, still wearing his "Hello, my name is . . ." sticker.

APTV-12-15-85 1348EST

That's a complex story to compress, and it offers a writer many chances to fumble—and to score. Here's how I tackled it:

> Three-thousand people in the
> Washington, D.C., area were notified

they had won two free tickets to the
Redskins' football game. About 100 of
them showed up today at the
Convention Center for the tickets and a
pre-game brunch, but they were thrown
for a loss: U.S. marshals and police
sprang their trap and arrested them all
as fugitives. Some were wanted for
burglary, robbery or murder. Two of
those caught in the sting were on the
local list of Ten Most Wanted.

If mine is smoother than yours, it may be because I rewrote it for six
months. And I'm still not sure I have it right. I'm never sure.

Next case. Again 20 seconds, but this time, 25 minutes. Pretend the
story moved just before your last newscast Saturday.

OKLAHOMA CITY (AP)—A prisoner being taken by
federal marshals from Alabama to California bolted out of
a moving plane's emergency exit after landing on
Saturday and fled into the darkness, authorities said.

U.S. Marshal Stuart Earnest said the escapee, 44-year-
old Reginald D. Still, was en route from a federal hospital
in Talladega, Ala., to Sacramento, Calif., where he was
scheduled to go on trial on a charge of interstate transportation of a stolen motor vehicle.

Earnest said the plane contained 44 prisoners when
it touched down at Will Rogers World Airport. No other
prisoners tried to escape, he said.

Still wearing handcuffs and shackles, he leaped out of
the plane's emergency exit, onto a wing and then the
tarmac as the plane was braking, the marshal said.

One of eight security people on the plane jumped out
to chase the escapee, Earnest said.

Federal marshals and local, county and state authorities fanned out across the airport property, southwest of
Oklahoma City, in the search.

Prisoners are normally transported by a Boeing
727, but a backup, a Convair 580 propeller, was being
used Saturday because the jet was being repaired,
authorities said.

The U.S. marshal's service routinely transports
prisoners every other day to courts and penitentiaries
around the country. The transportation program is based

in Oklahoma City, and prisoners on overnight trips often are housed overnight at a federal correctional facility in El Reno, 30 miles west of here.
APTV-12-07-85 2251EST

Here's the way I wrote it:

> A plane with federal prisoners was taxiing at an airport near Oklahoma City this evening when a prisoner jumped off and escaped. While the plane was moving down a runway, he bolted through an emergency exit, landed on a wing, leaped to the ground and got away in the darkness, still in handcuffs and shackles. The plane had been taking him to California to stand trial for theft.

If you found that one easy, you must have done something wrong: If you start your story by saying a prisoner jumped *out* a plane or even *off* a plane, many listeners might think the plane had been aloft. I wanted to make it clear the plane was on the ground, so my story takes a few extra seconds to get to the nub.

My second sentence is long, but I think it works: It's easy to follow (certainly easier than he was), you can see the action unfold, it's energized by lively verbs, and it all flows in one direction. The last sentence in my story may seen anticlimactic after the exciting escape, but I did want to let listeners know that the fugitive is not a killer, or at least hasn't been one. I didn't use his name because he's a nonentity, and his name means nothing to listeners. I didn't use his age because I thought it wouldn't tell anyone anything; everyone has an age. I would have mentioned the lamster's age only if he were a youngster or an oldster. I did not spell out the charge against him because it takes too much time and would be unnecessary. I didn't say "*car* theft" because a "motor vehicle" could be a car, a van or a truck. I didn't tell where the flight originated or its destination because those places don't figure in the story. I didn't identify the plane because it makes no difference whether it's a Convair or an Electra, whether it's a jet or a prop plane, whether it's taking off or landing. Instead, I focused on that minute of high drama—I can see it unreel—and moved in close.

I did not report the number of inmates aboard the plane because the story was about only one. If any other prisoners had tried to escape, I would have said so. But why take time to report what didn't happen? I was pleased to learn that someone has named a "World" airport for Will Rogers, but I didn't mention it lest I run out of time.

I'd have preferred to say "tonight," but I didn't know the time of his escape, so I said "this evening." All I knew was that he fled into the darkness, but the sun sets early in mid-December. "Tonight" might have been wrong; "evening" seemed safe. The wire copy moved at almost 11 p.m., but that does not mean the story just broke. It could have been several hours old.

At a recent session of my Television Newswriting Workshop, I passed out copies of that wire story to the news staff of a TV station and asked everyone to rewrite this Saturday story into a 20-second script for use on a late Saturday newscast. Here's the most inventive lead—and keep in mind that the inmate who fled from the plane was charged with theft:

"When it comes to vehicles, Reginald Still apparently can take them or leave them." What do you think of it? Deucedly clever, eh? But what would you think if you were hearing it on the air for the first time, with no previous knowledge of the episode? The real test is: What's a listener to make of it? It's easy for insiders to get a kick out of that lead because we already knew the story. For listeners, though, this is the first exposure. So they can't savor the wordplay about "vehicles" and the inmate's being able to "take them or leave them." That sounds more like a final observation than an introduction, an epilogue rather than a prologue. Further, I wouldn't use the escapee's name so early. In fact, I didn't use it all. Why? No listener has heard of him, no listener need hear of him. (If you're his big brother, I'm just joshing.) If I heard the name of an unknown in a lead, I'd assume he's a hometowner. Also, his last name, Still, might worsen any confusion. "Still" is an adverb (*yet*), an adjective (*silent*) and common noun (*distillery*).

In case you're wondering how that inventive writer handled the rest of the story, this is his script in its entirety:

> When it comes to vehicles, Reginald Still apparently can take them or leave them. Still, an inmate being transferred from Alabama to California, tonight bolted out of a moving plane and fled into the darkness. Police said Still was wearing handcuffs and leg irons when he jumped out an emergency exit. The 44-year-old inmate was scheduled to

> stand trial on charges of stealing a
> motor vehicle.

Sounds to me as though the inmate pulled a D. B. Cooper and leaped from a plane in flight. The script doesn't say whether the plane was aloft or on the ground, just that it was moving. *Tonight* would fit better after *plane*. But one of the most important questions of all: *Where* did this happen? No matter what you might think of the lead, the lack of the *where* leaves it nowhere.

How did that writer's deskmates do with the same story? Let's take a look at some of their opening sentences and my brief comments:

> It's the stuff movies are made of. . . . a
> prisoner escape from a moving airplane
> at an Oklahoma airport.

It's not the stuff good news scripts are made of. Why "movies"? Why not name the city? Why four periods? Why not a comma or a dash? Why no strong verb, only linking verbs (*is* and *are*) and a verbal (*moving*), which does not behave like a verb? And why turn a good verb, *escape,* into a noun? Unquestionably, the lead is unsatisfactory. Here's another lead:

> Right now, the manhunt is on for a
> prisoner who, handcuffed and shackled,
> lept from a moving plane.

"Right now"? That's no way to start this story—or any story I can think of. By the time this story is broadcast, the fugitive might be recaptured, so the manhunt would be over and "right now" would be wrong now. "*The* manhunt" should be "*a* manhunt." "*Lept*"? If the writer meant "leapt," he should have shifted to the preferred past tense, "leaped." And there's no *where* there.

> Police in Oklahoma City are out chasing
> their very own Harry Houdini.

Why drag in Houdini? He was a great escape artist, but he died in 1926 and has not reappeared. His name would probably not be recognized by most listeners without a label: "The master magician Harry Houdini" or something like that. In any case, Houdini has nothing to do with this case.

Why "out"? Where else would police chase someone? If they were chasing him indoors, we'd say so. Use of "their very own" makes it sound as though the person they're chasing is a policeman. No, I'm not going to call that story a Houdunit.

> A plane left Alabama today carrying 44 prisoners to California. When it got there, it had only 43.

That script is missing more than one prisoner.

> Transporting prisoners from one place to another by jet seems to be an escape-proof method. That was until tonight.

Let's not speculate about what *seems* to be. Let's report what we know for sure, what *is*. Let's tell the news. Right now.

> Police in Oklahoma City are still looking for a prisoner who jumped out of a moving plane.

"Still looking" makes it seem the escape was reported earlier and that this is a followup story. The news is a prisoner's bold escape.

> A federal prisoner, handcuffed and shackled, managed to escape from his captors by jumping from a plane tonight.

Where? Over Alaska? "Managed to escape" = "escaped." "Captors?" A captor is someone who has captured a person or thing. If anything, the marshals are losers.

> Federal marshals are wondering tonight how their man got away . . . shackled and in handcuffs.

The writer led with reaction, not action. The news is still the escape. Or Still, the escapee.

> Federal marshals in Oklahoma City are looking for an escaped convict.

Again, reaction, not action.

> An Alabama prisoner made a daring run for it as he was being flown to California.

A running jump?

> Federal marshals in Oklahoma City are
> hunting for a prisoner who escaped on
> a wing and a prayer.

What that World War Two song, "Comin' In On a Wing and a Prayer," has to do with this story escapes me.

He didn't get away on a wing, and he probably was too busy to pray. Which might make this a good place to bail out. Of the dozen or so other scripts on the escape, one or two came close, but I won't inflict any more on you.

The writers? All I'll say, to protect the guilty, is that they work in the Lower 48 (states, not markets).

The next exercise requires you to combine two stories that moved today. Total length: 20 seconds. Time: 20 minutes.

WASHINGTON, March 18—Two United States warships heavily equipped with electronic sensors entered Soviet territorial waters in the Black Sea last week to test Soviet defenses, Pentagon officials said.

The officials said that the exercise had been ordered by the Joint Chiefs of Staff in the name of Defense Secretary Caspar W. Weinberger and that a similar exercise was planned in the Gulf of Sidra off Libya next week.

The purpose of the exercises, the officials said, is to gather intelligence, to assert the right to innocent passage and, in the case of Libya, to assert the right to sail in international waters.

The officials spoke after the Soviet Union, in a protest note, said the incident, off the southern Crimea, "was of a demonstrative, defiant nature and pursued clearly provocative aims." The naval base of Sevastopol, headquarters of the Soviet Union's Black Sea Fleet, is in the southern Crimea.

The Pentagon said in a statement that the entry of the ships into Soviet waters "was simply an exercise of the right of innocent passage."

Edward P. Djerejian, a White House spokesman, was asked whether the maneuver was provocative, in light of efforts to seek a summit meeting.

"Absolutely not," he said. "There is no intent for it to be provocative or defiant. It is simply an exercise of the right of innocent passage. This transit was, to the best of our knowledge, consistent with relevant Soviet law."

The Pentagon officials said the Black Sea maneuver and the planned exercise off Libya were also intended in part to buttress President Reagan's request for more military spending next year. They said that after past incidents in which the United States flexed its military muscle, the President's popularity jumped and his policies won renewed support in Congress.

The officials said that, in the exercise off Libya next week, three aircraft carriers—the Saratoga, the America and the Coral Sea—intended to send fighter planes into the airspace over the Gulf of Sidra. Libya considers the gulf its territorial waters; the United States does not recognize that claim.

United States warships pass through the Turkish straits from the Mediterranean Sea into the Black Sea two or three times a year, the officials said.

In the latest exercise, the guided missile cruiser Yorktown and the destroyer Caron entered the Black Sea on March 10 and left last Monday.

The Yorktown is equipped with a fire control system that can track hostile planes, ships and submarines. The Caron, which has been dispatched to gather intelligence off Central America, was loaded with additional sensors and listening devices.

Last Thursday, the officials said, the ships passed within six miles of the Crimea. The Soviet Union claims territorial waters up to 12 nautical miles. International maritime practice permits warships to pass through territorial waters in a direct line to save time and sailing distance.

No operations, such as flight or gunnery drills, are permitted during innocent passage, and Pentagon officials said none had been conducted. But they suggested that listening to Soviet transmissions or sensing radar activity would not be barred by the rules.

The American ships conducted a similar intelligence operation in December, the officials said.

Soviet ships periodically steam close to the United States, and Soviet military planes often fly along the East Coast on the way to Cuba, according to the Pengaton. Last September, Soviet warships came within 40 miles of the coast in the Gulf of Mexico, the closest since they began deploying ships in the Caribbean in 1969.

MOSCOW, March 18—The Soviet Union said today in a protest note that the American naval incursion into its territorial waters "was of a demonstrative, defiant nature and pursued clearly provocative aims."

The protest note, according to the government press agency Tass, said it "was not the first time that United States naval ships deliberately failed to comply with the laws and rules of the U.S.S.R. concerning the regime of Soviet territorial waters."

"Such violations," the note said, "can have serious consequences, the responsibility for which will be wholly on the United States."

The Soviet Union claims territorial waters 12 miles offshore, and the United States recognizes the 12-mile limit.

The Soviet Foreign Ministry spokesman, Vladimir B. Lomeiko, amplifying the protest note, said in a briefing that the American warships had entered Soviet waters up to six nautical miles and had stayed for two hours.

Lomeiko was asked about prospects for Mikhail S. Gorbachev's visit to the United States. The Russians have declined to discuss a date until progress is made in arms talks. They have also said that an American order reducing the size of Soviet missions to the United Nations did not create a favorable atmosphere.

"We believe the summit should be productive," Lomeiko said. "It should not be a meeting for the sake of a meeting. As soon as conditions are right, the Soviet Union will give its views on a date. It is the absence of the right conditions at this time that accounts for the absence of a specific date for the meeting."

My script:

> Moscow protested today that two U-S warships violated Soviet territorial waters in the Black Sea. Moscow said the ships had sailed within six miles of its coast and called their action provocative. Washington recognizes the Soviet claim to a territorial limit of 12

miles. But the Pentagon said the ships
were testing Soviet defenses and were
asserting the right to take a short cut.

By now, you probably see the way I attack a story: I go straight to
the subject, go right to a verb and then to the object, good old S-V-O.
Just the key facts, no frills.

Next exercise. Write this story for early evening, Tuesday, before
the Pope makes his first stop. Length: 20 seconds. Time: 15 minutes.

VATICAN CITY (UPI)—Pope John Paul II left Rome
Tuesday for his 32nd foreign tour, traveling to
Bangladesh, Singapore, Fiji, New Zealand, Australia and
the Seychelles on his longest and one of his most
grueling trips.

The Pontiff, who left Rome's Leonardo da Vinci
Airport 20 minutes behind schedule, will spend the night
on his jet and land early Wednesday in the Bangladesh
capital of Dhaka, where he will make 12 hours of public
appearances.

John Paul will be traveling virtually non-stop to
cover the 30,000-mile itinerary in 14 days, and is to
spend two of the first three nights sleeping aboard the
papal plane to save time.

Among the highlights of the trip are scheduled
meetings with native Fiji islanders, New Zealand Maoris
and Australian aborigines, whose numbers and culture
were nearly eliminated after European settlers arrived in
the late 18th century.

Each of the three groups is scheduled to give John
Paul a traditional welcome. In Fiji he is to receive a whale
tooth, the local version of the key to a city, and sip a
watered-down version of kava, the powerful local brew.

In New Zealand he will touch noses with a group of
Maori tribesman as a sign of trust, and in Australia,
aborigines will lead him along a traditional "meeting
path" as various tribes perform native dances and songs.

The trip—longest both in terms of distance and days
spent outside the Vatican—is the third to Asia and the
Pacific since he became pope in 1978. Half the trip will be
spent in Australia, with three days in New Zealand and
the remaining four days on brief stops in Bangladesh,
Singapore, Fiji and the Seychelles.

The Dhaka stop, during which John Paul is to ordain local priests and celebrate Mass for the country's tiny Catholic minority, could take on an unexpected inter-religious significance, a senior Vatican official said shortly before the trip.

A Moslem leader in Bangladesh recently contacted the Vatican and asked to be present at the religious services as a goodwill gesture in response to the Pope's address to Moslem youth in Casablanca in August 1985, and last month's inter-religious prayer meeting for peace in Assisi, Italy.

"This is the first time a Moslem leader has responded in such a way," the source said.

In Australia and New Zealand, church attendance has fallen off drastically in recent years and the supply of priests is fast dwindling.

Recent Australian polls show that less than 30 percent of the nation's 4 million Catholics attend Sunday Mass, while church members, as in other highly developed nations, widely ignore Rome's ban on artificial contraception.

UPI 11-18-86 01:32 PES

My script:

> Pope John Paul left Rome today for Southeast Asia on his longest trip ever. He's flying first to Dhaka, the capital of Bangladesh, a Moslem country. Other highlights: He'll meet natives in Fiji, Maoris in New Zealand, and aborigines in Australia, where he'll spend one week. His trip will take two weeks and cover 30-thousand miles.

You have plenty of facts to choose from, which in a story about John Paul you might call a potpourri. I probably chose all or almost all the essential facts; whether I put them in the right order and said what I should have said, I can't say.

The key to rewriting a story that's chock-full of facts lies in ruthlessly chucking the least important and perhaps even some of the important. We have no need to refer to him as John Paul *the second* (he can't be confused with any other living pope), we have no need to mention the Seychelles (by the seashore), the name of Rome's airport, the tardiness of his chartered plane and a host of other disposable details.

Although my version may not be creditable, it's acceptable. And I do deserve some credit for not referring to the pope as *pontiff.* (An all-news radio station went so far as to call him *peripatetic.* Ugh!)

In case you're uneasy about my second sentence, in which I have him flying, don't fret. Surely, a pope can fly if a nun can. But I certainly wouldn't refer to the pope's 32d tour; it'd sound as though he's making it in 30 seconds.

The last exercise. You're writing this for a Sunday night newscast. Length: 20 seconds. Time: 20 minutes to air—no time to err. (In the Dairy State, they say, "To err is human, to moo is bovine.")

KEYSTONE HEIGHTS, FL. (AP)—A 70-foot-wide sinkhole continued growing Sunday after swallowing one house and a carport and forcing evacuation of four homes in a retirement community, officials said.

The hole was about the size of a pickup truck when it was first discovered Saturday in this small town near Gainesville in northeastern Florida, said Mayor William Beam.

Three hours later, it had grown to 30 by 40 feet and had swallowed half of a small house owned by Keystone Heights administrator William A. Erickson.

Two hours later, the house was gone and the owners escaped only with their coats.

The carport of a second house also began slipping into the hole.

"It's still falling in, but gradual; not big hunks of stuff like (Saturday)," Clay County Public Safety director James Corbin Jr. said Sunday.

Corbin said he was not sure if other houses would follow the first house into the sinkhole. But he said the residents evacuated from four homes Saturday were moved as a safety precaution.

"We're preparing for the worst and hoping for the best," Corbin said. "What could you do?"

Clay County Administrator John Bowles estimated the hole was 45 feet deep.

A sinkhole is caused by the collapse of limestone caverns that lose water pressure that supports their roofs.

Much of Florida is susceptible to sinkholes, but central Florida and parts of northeast Florida, with limestone caverns 100 feet or more below the surface, are most vulnerable.

A celebrated sinkhole in Winter Park, near Orlando,

grew to an estimated 400 feet across in 1981 and
swallowed 250,000 cubic yards of property valued at
$2 million, five sports cars, most of two businesses, a
three-bedroom house and the deep end of an Olympic-size
swimming pool.

Florida law requires that home insurers provide
sinkhole coverage.

APTV-12-22-85 1555EST

My version:

mb		
OSGOOD	The swallows have come back to Florida. No, not the kind that flock to Capistrano but the swallows that gulp down homes.	and 45 feet deep. A sinkhole is caused when limestone caverns lose the water pressure that holds up their roofs. The most vulnerable places are in northeast and central Florida, where sinkholes most often pop up—or drop in.
V/O	The latest swallow—by a sinkhole—devoured a home at Keystone Heights, in northeast Florida. The residents escaped only with their coats. The hole is about 70 feet across	

I know: "Confidentially, it sinks." I said that just to beat you to the pun.

I could have written it as spot news or a feature; what emerged was a sort of newsfeature. Although you were asked to write 20 seconds, I wrote 30 seconds. The reason: My script had to accompany videotape that was scheduled in the lineup (or rundown) for :20. The anchor timed the lead-in at :08, so the V/O ran :22.

To give you an idea how someone else wrote this story, here's a script broadcast on network radio. It was based on wire copy that moved a couple of hours earlier than the copy reprinted above. Length: 30 seconds.

A sinkhole that's already gobbled up one home and a
carport in a Keystone Heights-Florida retirement village

is 70 feet wide . . . AND GROWING. Keystone Heights is a small town near Gainesville in northeastern Florida. The sinkhole first appeared yesterday. It was just a few feet wide but began to spread rapidly. Four families have evacuated the area. Sinkholes develop when the water pressure that supports limestone caverns drops. This happens a lot in Florida . . . especially in areas where rapid development is taking place.

What do you think of that script? If my approach to my version has any virtue, it may be its odd twist. The radio script is written as straight news, which may be just as good a way, or better, to do it. But the first fact the radio script presents—"already gobbled up one home"—is not new. The next verbs, *is,* and [is] *growing,* are unobjectionable, but it's good to remember that *is* is weak and a verb that ends with *ing* is weaker than a finite verb, one with a tense. *Village* has too many attributive nouns, used as adjectives, piled in front of it. Why repeat the name of the town? No need for *small.* Did the four families evacuate *the area* or their homes? Also: How deep was the hole?

Exercise is good for us, and I hope you've learned as much from this chapter—and this book—as I have.

9

2,002 TIPS

*This chapter introduces a collection of the author's "WordWatching"
columns—fully revised and greatly expanded. They first appeared in*
Communicator, *the magazine of the Radio-Television News Directors
Association.*

The word is out that in many newsrooms the word is in.

Words are indeed on news directors' minds: Surveys show that
almost all of them say the skill they prize most in newcomers is writing.
And news directors have told me they're paying closer attention to what's
being written. So I'm going to join them in their wordwatching and their
quest for better writing. You have my word.

As someone who lives by the word, I listen to newscasts carefully.
When I need a quick news fix, I turn to radio. For the past few days, I've
been turning it on to give New York City's top news stations a once-over.
To make sure I'd be able to quote them word for word, I taped them.
Here's some of what they broadcast:

> An ocean liner has made an unscheduled stop in the Caribbean—
> atop a coral reef.

I like that line. I traced it to the writer, Greg Johnson. He works for
The A.P. in Washington, D.C. Take a bow, Greg, but not the whole ship.

> Some residents outside Hilo, Hawaii, had to hot-foot it to safety
> after authorities told them lava was threatening their homes.

I like "hot-foot," but in the middle of the sentence it loses its kick. The
sentence would have been stronger if the writer had built up to the key
word or key idea: "Hawaii's Kilauea volcano is threatening homes near
Hilo, as lava flows closer, so some residents have had to hot-foot it away."

Today the question of aid to El Salvador became a lot more
heated because House Speaker Tip O'Neill, the ranking Democrat
in Congress, called for a full-scale investigation into whether the
War Powers Act is being violated by the Reagan administration.

Except as a transition, don't start a story with "today"; listeners
assume the news is today's. (See p. 147.) Also: questioners and questioning,
not questions, get heated. Why describe the investigation as "full-scale"? I
doubt that O'Neill or any officeholder has ever called for a half-hearted
investigation. The sentence, 40 words, is over-long. And overheated.

Mayor Koch is now a Knight of the French Legion of Honor. It
was bestowed upon him today at City Hall ceremonies. French
President François Mitterand paid Koch the visit and gave him the
award.

The item is written weakly: the first sentence lacks an action verb and
the second sentence lacks the active voice. *Is* is a linking verb, not a verb of
motion. Better: "France has made Mayor Koch a Knight of the French
Legion of Honor. President Mitterand conferred the award himself today
in City Hall." The overhaul is shorter by one-third. And stronger.

Police in Strasbourg, France, don't think the shooting of the
American consul there was a political act.

Strunk and White tell us: "Put statements in positive form." You
could improve the news item by moving "not" from before "think" to
after "was": "Police in Strasbourg, France, think the shooting of the
American consul there was *not* a political act."

[Gunmen] robbed 21 million dollars from a security vault
in Rome.

The verb should be "stole." They were robbers, but "rob" means "to
steal from." You can rob a bank, but no one robs money.

Security was tight for NATO defense ministers who began arriving in Turkey today for a ministerial-level meeting this week on
nuclear planning.

And on another newscast:

Queen Elizabeth is to arrive in Jordan today, and security is tight.

When you write, "Security is tight," your script is just about as
newsy as if you wrote, "The sun rose in the East today." If you find a
meeting of NATO defense ministers that lacks security or has lax secur-

ity, then you'd have news. If "tight security" is the most important fact that you have to write about, you probably don't have a story.

> [It] was the second hijacking in as many days.

A common error. When you start with an ordinal number, like "second," this construction requires that you follow with a cardinal number: "*two* days."

> According to the indictment, Castellano conspired in three
> murders personally.

"Personally" should be rubbed out.

> The Reagan administration is putting on the full-court press now
> on behalf of the President's aid proposals for El Salvador.

"On behalf of" should be "for." Also: overuse of "full-court press" has made it a cliché. Some writers use it to mean an all-out attack, but a "full-court press" is a basketball tactic that's defensive. (If you write about a courtroom packed by newspeople, just don't call it "a full-press court.")

> International finance is a tangled web, and it's likely to get a good
> bit more complicated as we approach the weekend and the
> threatened default by Argentina on interest payments on its mas-
> sive foreign debt.

It is a tangled web, but don't get entangled yourself, webster. Many stories *are* complex; it's our job to simplify. The broadcast sentence is too long. Imagine a newscaster reading it aloud, and imagine a listener trying to disentangle it. There's no need to tell listeners who have trouble balancing a checking account that international finance is complex.

> He's been taking a controversial position on Central America.

The *New York Times's* in-house critique, "Winners & Sinners," calls "controversial" an "empty word." W&S says it would be "hard pressed to cite a word that tells less yet appears more often."

> Jesse Jackson wasn't in New York this morning, but he'll return
> for tonight's TV debate among the three candidates.

I may be interested in where someone is or where he's going, but please don't tell me where he is not.

> With suspensions of the distribution of Girl Scout cookies
> spreading because pins and other harmful debris have been found

in a few of the cookies, the Food and Drug Administration says the F.B.I. wants to find out who planted pins and other harmful objects in some cookies.

The lead is long, crowded and underplays the core of the news: The F-B-I had entered the case. And the sentence has many other faults. It brings to mind Mark Twain's criticism of asserted defects in less than one page of *The Deerslayer:* "[James Fenimore] Cooper has scored 114 offenses against literary art out of a possible 115. It breaks the record."

Twain went on to urge that a writer "Say what he is proposing to say, not merely come near it; use the right word, not its second cousin; eschew surplusage . . .; avoid slovenliness of form; use good grammar; employ a simple and straightforward style." Amen.

The Wrong Stuff

By the time we reached Easter, I'd had it up to my keister. Not with bunnies and bonnets but with political clichés. And the worst is yet to be. With the national conventions approaching, clichés are already flying through the air like an acrobatic team, Thick and Fast.

Either we need some new clichés, as an old city editor of mine is reputed—or disreputed—to have said, or we need to try harder to resist the first cliché that comes to mind. And the second. They spring to mind because we've heard them so often they've saturated our consciousness, ready for instant retrieval. But their instantaneity and ubiquity should put us on guard.

Here are some of the political clichés that ricochet and re-echo through our minds, clichés that we should not use at the drop of a hat in the ring:

Front-runner. Put it on the back-burner. Who knows for sure which candidate—or non-candidate—is ahead until all the delegates or voters have cast ballots? As an article in the *Washington Journalism Review* said (May 1984): "Hart's New Hampshire surprise did not show that reporters need better ways to pinpoint the leader; it showed the error of trying to do so at all."

Hart attack, Hart-stopper, Hart failure. Bypass 'em. Most puns on people's names age rapidly. And most people whose names lend themselves to puns have heard them all—many times. Just don't "Kick that Block."

The last hurrah. When Edwin O'Connor's book of that title came out in 1956, the phrase was fresh. But it has long since gone stale. Like *It's all over but the shouting,* it deserves its own farewell.

An idea whose time has come. When Victor Hugo (or his translator) wrote, "Greater than the tread of mighty armies is an idea whose time has come," he expressed an idea with originality. But his line has been overused. Even the variations since it was written in 1852 have become worn out: "an idea whose time has come again," "an idea whose time has come and gone," "an idea whose time will never come." For all of them, original and variations, I think time has run out.

The right stuff. Clichés don't have it.

On the campaign trail. Too tired for *the comeback trail.*

On the hustings. Where's the hustings? It's an outdated and roundabout way of saying someone is making campaign speeches or is campaigning. (Not to be confused with the Battle of Hustings or Hustings-on-Hudson.)

On the stump. Worn to the stump. When I hear that a politician is *on the stump for votes,* I think of a peg-legged man hobbling after a truck, hoping that a bundle of ballots will tumble off.

A real horse race. Fits the definition of a cliché by Eric Partridge: "So hackneyed as to be knock-kneed and spavined."

Political warhorse. Ready for pasture.

Neck and neck. Ditto.

Won his spurs. Pack it away with the buggy whip.

Homestretch. Save it for Hialeah.

Beauty contest. Save it for Atlantic City.

Dark horse. Has been ridden into the ground, but because it packs a lot of meaning in two short words, still good for more outings. (Didja hear the one about the dark horse that won a beauty contest? A chestnut came in second. That, of course, is a color of another horse.) Other *horses* I'd stop beating: *dead, wild and Trojan.*

Political animal. A bone-weary critter ready for the glue factory.

Stormy petrel. Out of petrol.

Crossed the Rubicon. Next time it crosses your mind, ask the first five passersby what the phrase means.

Stemwinder. It may still be a favorite of politicians and political reporters, but I've never heard anyone else say it—or understand it. Its time has passed.

Political miracle. Leave miracles for ministers.

_____ *is expected to win.* Expected by whom? Don't become an expectator. As Confucius should have said, "Man who lives by crystal ball ends up eating glass."

Political powder keg. Dump it, along with *political dynamite, political bombshell, diplomatic bombshell, booby trap, time bomb,* and other duds.

Warts and all. See a dermatologist. Better yet, a dictionary or a thesaurus. What's wrong with calling an appraisal "frank" or "blunt"?

Has worn two hats, kept a high profile and *kept the political pot boiling.* They're all burned out.

Political litmus test. How many listeners know what a litmus test is? You'll see that it flunks *the acid test.*

Testing the political waters. Ready for the water closet.

Current incumbent. A redundancy. An incumbent *is* the current occupant of an office.

Margin. It's not a cliché, but it is a word that reporters covering elections and polls misuse often. If Clyde has 500,000 votes and Merrill has 400,000, some reporters say, "Clyde is leading by a five-to-four *margin.*" Wrong. He leads by a five-to-four *ratio.* A margin is the difference between two sums (100,000); a ratio is a proportion.

Open secret. If it's open, it's no longer secret.

Topic A. Passé.

Flushed with success. Use it only if you're writing about a prosperous plumber.

Once in a great while, though, a cliché is particularly apt. *Bandwagon,* for example, is one I wouldn't retire (even if it needs new tires). It works: it's not wordy; it saves many words. It sends a clear, colorful picture and it's a lot shorter and faster than, say, this definition of *bandwagon* (from William Safire's *Political Dictionary*): "a movement appealing to the herd instinct of politicians and voters to be on the winning side in any contest."

I don't want to inveigh against all clichés, but I do want to veigh in against almost all of them. When they were coined, they might well have sparkled. Their popularity, though, has been their undoing; now they're tarnished. They may be tried and true, like that cliché, but they're so trite they lack bite.

Words to the Wise

Even George Orwell himself might be at a loss for words over 1984's orgy of Orwelliana, but as a resolute wordwatcher, he still has much to tell us.

Not only did Orwell coin words that have become catchwords—doublethink, unperson, Big Brother, Newspeak—he also wrote shrewdly about using words.

After writing *Animal Farm* and before writing *1984,* he set down some rules that are still sound, equally useful for writing for print or broadcast. He knew broadcasting, having worked in radio for the BBC as a writer, producer and broadcaster.

Orwell's goal was to write plainly and clearly, to produce "prose like a window pane." His rules may not enable us to write as well as he did, but they can help:

- Never use a metaphor, simile, or other figure of speech which you are used to seeing in print. ["What a good thing Adam had," Twain said. "When he said a good thing, he knew nobody had said it before."]
- Never use a long word where a short one will do.
- If it is possible to cut a word out, always cut it out.
- Never use the passive where you can use the active.
- Never use a foreign phrase, a scientific word, or a jargon word if you can think of an everyday English equivalent.
- Break any of these rules sooner than say anything outright barbarous.

Although Orwell presented these rules in an essay in 1946, they're just as pertinent today. In the essay, "Politics and the English Language," he also offered this advice:

"A scrupulous writer, in every sentence that he writes, will ask himself at least four questions, thus: What am I trying to say? What words will express it? What image or idiom will make it clearer? Is this image fresh enough to have an effect? And he will probably ask himself two more: Could I put it more shortly? Have I said anything that is avoidably ugly?"

Orwell condemned slovenliness, vagueness and the use of ready-made phrases. And he warned against "gumming together long strips of words . . . already set in order by someone else." Once a writer falls into that habit, Orwell said, it's easier and quicker for him to say "In my opinion it is not an unjustifiable assumption that" than to say "I think."

As for the *not-un* formation, which is not uncommon, Orwell said you can cure yourself of the inclination to use it by memorizing this sentence: "A not unblack dog was chasing a not unsmall rabbit across a not ungreen field."

Orwell also pointed out the weakness of what he called "noun constructions," which rely on nouns instead of verbs. This is a noun construction: "There was a bomb explosion in City Hall." Better: "A bomb exploded in City Hall."

Noun constructions, known as "the nominal style," have been explored in *Journalism Quarterly*—and deplored. After elaborate research, Prof. Lloyd Bostian put into words and statistical tables what you may already know in your bones: "The nominal style is a poor choice for effective communication." But judging by what we hear on newscasts, too many broadcast writers do not know the nominal style is ineffective or even that it exists. Dr. Bostian, who teaches at the University of Wisconsin-Madison, wrote in *JQ* (Winter, 1983):

"Nominal prose is potentially dull because it substitutes nouns for verbs, and we know that a high noun-to-verb ratio produces dull copy. In nominal style, Latin-root nouns contain verbs, and the only verbs are weak, primarily forms of 'to be.'

"For example, this sentence is nominal: 'The identification of writing faults is his goal.' The real action of this sentence is the verb 'identify' . . .hidden in the noun 'identification.' In active form, the sentence would read, 'His goal is to identify writing faults.'"

Bostian took two research articles and rewrote each in three styles, then tested them on students. Here are his lead sentences from an article on running, written in the various styles:

Nominal—"The finding of researchers is that more and more Americans are running for the achievement of physical fitness."

Passive—"It has been found by researchers that more and more Americans are running to achieve physical fitness."

Active—"Researchers have found that more and more Americans are running to achieve physical fitness."

In his analysis of the study, Bostian refers to "readers," but his conclusions, I think, can be applied with equal, perhaps greater, force to listeners:

"Readers prefer an active style; they judge it to be more interesting, and they can read it significantly faster.

"Active voice is especially advantageous when subject matter is dull or unfamiliar.

"Nominal style is clearly the poorest choice of the three styles. The combination of unfamiliar, low-interest material and the nominal style is disastrous."

If the nominal style impairs comprehension at the university level, as it does, you can imagine what that style does to listeners. They start at a disadvantage; readers can pause to go back in a story, refer to a previous word or line, put the story aside and re-read it later. But if listeners lose the thread of a story, they'll stay lost.

One way for you and your deskmates to write more comprehensibly is to send for a paperback chock-full of useful tips on writing. The book, 140 pages, is *The Word,* subtitled *An Associated Press Guide to Good News Writing.* It was written by René J. Cappon, a general news editor. You can order it by mail from APN, Rm. 601-A, 50 Rockefeller Plaza, New York, N.Y. 10020. Price: $4, which includes postage and handling.

Cappon wrote *The Word* for print writers, but almost all of it can be extremely helpful for broadcast writers. Don't just take my word; get his.

Tips by the Score

Some of the best rules for good writing have been set down by Writer's Digest School. These 20 rules are intended for people who write for the eye, but they're just as good for people who write for the ear:

1. Prefer the plain word to the fancy.
2. Prefer the familiar word to the unfamiliar. [And use familiar words in familiar combinations.]
3. Prefer the Saxon word to the Romance.
4. Prefer nouns and verbs to adjectives and adverbs.
5. Prefer picture nouns and action verbs.
6. Never use a long word when a short one will do as well.
7. Master the simple declarative sentence.
8. Prefer the simple sentence to the complicated.
9. Vary your sentence length.
10. Put the words you want to emphasize at the beginning or end of your sentence. [The end is usually preferable.]
11. Use the active voice.
12. Put statements in a positive form.
13. Use short paragraphs.
14. Cut needless words, sentences and paragraphs.
15. Use plain, conversational English. Write like you talk.
16. Avoid imitation. Write in your natural style.
17. Write clearly.
18. Avoid gobbledygook and jargon.
19. Write to be understood, not to impress.
20. Revise and rewrite. Improvement is always possible.

A few of those rules echo *The King's English* by H.W. Fowler and F.G. Fowler. Their rules, published in 1906, are:

1. Prefer the familiar word to the far-fetched.
2. Prefer the concrete word to the abstract.
3. Prefer the single word to the locution.
4. Prefer the short word to the long.
5. Prefer the Saxon word to the Romance. [They define Romance languages as those whose grammatical structure, as well as at least part of their vocabulary, is directly descended from Latin.]

"Anyone who wishes to become a good writer," the Fowlers say, "should endeavour, before he allows himself to be tempted by the more showy qualities, to be direct, simple, brief, vigorous and lucid." (*The King's English?* Yes, and so's the Queen.)

Simple & Direct by Jacques Barzun also lists sensible rules. Here are several:

— Weed out the jargon.
— Have a point and make it by means of the best word.
— Look for *all* fancy wordings and get rid of them.
— For a plain style, avoid everything that can be called roundabout—in idea, in linking, or in expression.
— To be plain and straight-forward, resist equally the appeal of old finery and the temptation of smart novelties.
— The mark of a plain tone is combined lucidity and force.
— Read and revise, reread and revise. . . .

The only general rule for good writing is "the search for complete adequacy," Barzun later wrote in *The Modern Researcher* (with Henry F. Graff): "Try to find out what you mean . . . and put it down without frills or apologies."

Some especially useful rules are offered by John R. Trimble in his *Writing with Style:*

— Write with the assumption that your reader [think *listener*] is a companionable friend with a warm sense of humor and an appreciation of straightforwardness.
— Write as if you were actually talking to that friend, but talking with enough leisure to frame your thoughts concisely and interestingly.

— Use the fewest words possible and the simplest words possible.

— Read your prose aloud. *Always* read your prose aloud. If it sounds as if it came out of a machine . . . , spare your reader [again, think *listener*] and rewrite it.

— If you've written a paragraph that sounds heavy and tortured, put down your pencil and ask yourself: "If I were actually speaking these thoughts to a friend, how would I probably say them?" Then go ahead and talk them *out loud,* and when you've finished, write down as nearly as you can recall what you said.

Other helpful rules have been set down by Theodore A. Rees Cheney in his *Getting the Words Right: How to Revise, Edit & Rewrite:*

— Concentrate on the subject and eliminate digressions.

— Be sensitive to rhythm and sound. . . .

— Avoid ambiguity.

— Avoid things that kill emphasis: . . . passive verbs, abstract or indirect language, intensifiers, clichés. . . .

— Put important things anywhere but the middle.

— Bring emphasis by careful word choice and positioning.

Still more good rules, these from M. L. Stein's *Write Clearly— Speak Effectively:*

— Keep your sentences generally short, with one idea to a sentence.

— Get attention in your opening sentence by producing something interesting for the reader or listener.

— Be objective and impersonal so you can see facts and issues in proper perspective.

— Try [to] rid yourself of many of the bromides, truisms and platitudes that find their way into so much writing and speaking. Put your brain to work on new ways of saying things.

— Edit, edit, edit.

Have you noticed that most of these experts are singing the same tune? In some places, they're singing in unison; in a few places, they differ on the lyrics. But, by and large, it's the same song. Another member of the chorus, Robert Gunning, set down what he called Ten

Principles of Clear Writing in *The Technique of Clear Writing:*

— Keep sentences short.

— Prefer the simple to the complex.

— Prefer the familiar word.

— Avoid unnecessary words.

— Put action in your verbs.

— Write like you talk. [He says the use of *as* instead of *like,* as many grammarians insist on, would make the sentence ambiguous.]

— Use terms your reader can picture. [Think *listener.*]

— Tie in with your reader's experience.

— Make full use of variety. [He says, "You need a wide knowledge of the flexibility and variety of the language."]

— Write to express, not impress.

Another expert, Jefferson D. Bates, also lays down 10 principles in *Writing with Precision:*

— Prefer the active voice.

— Don't make nouns out of good, strong "working verbs."

— Be concise.

— Be specific.

— Keep related sentence elements together.

— Avoid unnecessary shifts [of number, tense, subject].

— Prefer the simple word.

— Don't repeat a word or words unnecessarily.

— Make sentence elements parallel.

— Arrange your material logically.

One of the country's leading authorities on writing, Roy Peter Clark, an associate director of the Poynter Institute for Media Studies in St. Petersburg, Florida, has listed some steps in writing that he says work well when used wisely. Although he's addressing print writers, what he says applies to us, and though he refers to "techniques," we would do well to consider them rules. Among them, including some of his commentary:

— Envision a general audience. A journalist who writes for a general audience will find the language becoming purer and clearer. When I am struggling to make something clear, even to a general audience, I fantasize a conversation with my mother. If she asked me, "What did you learn at city council today?" I would not respond: "The city council agreed by a one-vote margin Friday to apply for federal matching funds to permit them to support a project to aid small businesses in the black community by giving them lower interest loans." I might be more inclined to say, "Well, Ma, black business people are struggling, and the city council thinks it has found a way to help them out." Sometimes, when you imagine telling a story to a single human being, your voice changes and your language becomes more simple and direct.

— Slow down the pace of information. Too much writing on difficult subjects is of the "dense-pack" variety: information stuffed into tight, dense paragraphs and conveyed at a rate that takes the breath away.

— Don't clutter leads with confusing statistics, technical information or bureaucratic names.

— Remember that numbers can be numbing.

— Translate jargon.

— Consider the impact.

— Eliminate unnecessary information.*

The record for the number of writer's rules between two covers probably should go to Gary Provost for his *100 Ways to Improve Your Writing*. Here are 15:

— Write a strong lead.

— Don't explain when you don't have to.

— Write complete sentences.

— Keep related words together.

— Respect the rules of grammar.

— Prefer good writing to good grammar.

— Use dense words. [A "dense" word, he says, is one that crams a lot of meaning into a small space. For example, "once a month" can be reduced to "monthly." And "people they didn't know" = "strangers."]

— Use short words.

— Use active verbs.

*Roy Peter Clark, "Making Hard Facts Easy Reading: 14 Steps to Clarity," *Washington Journalism Review,* Jan./Feb., 1984, 24-27.

— Use strong verbs.

— Use specific nouns.

— Use the active voice—most of the time.

— Say things in a positive way—most of the time.

— Put emphatic words at the end.

— Stop writing when you get to the end.

Some of the soundest rules were set down by Douglas Southall Freeman, and he put them to good use: He won the Pulitzer Prize twice. His 20 rules:

— Above all, be clear.

— Therefore, use simple English.

— To that end, write short sentences.

— Do not change the subject in the middle of the sentence unless there is (a) definite antithesis or (b) no possible way of changing the subject. If you must change subject, always insert a comma at the end of the clause that precedes the one in which you make the change.

— Do not end sentences with participial phrases. Beware of such construction as "The mayor refused to discuss the subject, *saying* it was one for the consideration of the council."

— Do not change the voice of a verb in the middle of a sentence. If you start with an active verb, keep it active. It is sloppy to say: He went to Hopewell and was met by. . . ."

— Seek to leave the meaning of the sentence incomplete until the last word. Add nothing after the meaning is complete. Start a new sentence then.

— Avoid loose construction. Try never to begin sentences with *And* or *But* [But in broadcast writing, they're O.K.]

— Never use vague or unusual words that divert the reader's attention from what you are reporting.

— Make every antecedent plain: Never permit "it" or "that" or any similar word to refer to different things in the same sentence.

— Where you write a clause beginning with *which,* do not follow it with one that begins *and which.* Never write a sentence such as "The ordinance which was considered by the finance committee *and which* was recommended to the council. . . ."

— Avoid successive sentences that begin with the same word, unless emphasis is desired. Especially, in quoting a man, never have one sentence begin "*He* said" and then have the next sentence start "*He* stated."

— In sentences where several nouns, phrases or clauses depend on the same verb, put the longer phrase or clause last. For instance, do not say, "He addressed the general assembly, the members of the corporation commission, and the governor." [As he suggested, the example should be rewritten to go from short to long: "the governor, the general assembly and the members of the corporation commission." That rule has given us "life, liberty and the pursuit of happiness."]

— If you are compelled, for condensation, to use many long sentences, relieve them by employing very short sentences at intervals.

— In conditional sentences, seek to put the conditional clause before the principal clause. An *if* clause at the beginning of a sentence is better placed than at the end, unless the whole point of the sentence lies in the *if*.

— Be accurate in the use of synonyms and avoid overloading a sentence with a long phrase employed as a synonym. You will do well to buy and keep on your desk a copy of [*Roget's Thesaurus*]. . . .

— Avoid successive sentences with the same form and conjunction. One of the surest ways to kill interest and to make a story dull is to use a succession of compound sentences, the clauses of which are connected by *and.* Change the conjunction and the form of the sentences as often as possible.

— Shun the employment of nouns as adjectives; it is the lowest form of careless English. There always are better ways to condense than to pile up nouns before a noun and to pretend they are adjectives.

— Avoid successive words that begin or end with the same syllables, for instance *re* or *ex* at the beginning of words and *ly* or *ing* as the final syllable.

— Try to end every story with a strong, and, if possible, a short sentence.

Freeman wrote the rules in the 1920s, but they're just as applicable today—and just as useful for us. He was then a newspaper editor in Richmond, Virginia. He called them "The *News Leader's* Twenty Fundamental Rules of News Writing." And he applied them in his Pulitzer-winning biographies of Robert E. Lee and Washington.

A later editor of the *News Leader,* the columnist James J. Kilpatrick, has also laid down some rules:

— We ought to master our tools. [He's alluding to *words*.]
— We ought to pay more attention to cadence. [He quotes Barbara Tuchman: "An essential element for good writing is a good ear: One must listen to the sound of one's prose."]
— We ought to pay closer attention to the arrangement of our words and clauses.
— We ought to keep in mind that words have nuances; words carry connotations, and words that may be appropriate in one context may not be appropriate for another. We ought constantly to search for the right word.
— We must copy-edit, copy-edit, copy-edit!

Kilpatrick also has listed some "ought nots":

— We ought not to use clichés.
— We ought never to fall into gobbledegook.
— We ought not to mangle our sentences.
— As a general rule, we ought not to use euphemisms.
— We ought not to pile up nouns as adjectives.
— We ought not to coin words wantonly.
— We must not break the rules of grammar.
— We ought not to be redundant.
— We ought not to use words that have double meanings. [He's talking about ambiguity, not suggestive remarks.]
— We ought not to write portmanteau sentences. [He refers to a sentence in which a writer "tried to pack everything he owned into a single traveling bag, and he left ties, socks and shirttails sticking out."]

In *The Writer's Art* (published by Andrews, McMeel & Parker of Fairway, Kansas, at $8.95), Kilpatrick elaborates on these and other rules, provides examples of usage (and abusage), and offers insights that can help good writers become better.

If Douglas Southall Freeman had expanded on his rule about the sequence of words in a sentence, he might have added that elements in a series should be listed, where suitable, in ascending order of importance or impact. That gives the last-named element the most emphasis: "I came, I saw, I conquered." Exceptions: A series shouldn't deviate from any chronological—or logical—need. And you can't set up a series in the order of climax if the elements are unrelated or unimportant: "He bought milk, tea and wood."

A newscaster recently said, for example, terrorists had singled out Americans for "threats, taunting and terror." The sequence should have started with the mildest misdeed, "taunts" (a noun, not "taunting," a gerund). The series should have stepped up to the next more serious offense, "threats," and peaked, as it did, with the strongest word, "terror." (I disagree with the writer who says, "No one needs to know what a gerund is, except people taking a test that asks: 'What's a gerund?'")

When you don't build up to the strongest word in a series like that, your sentence stumbles. That happened to Chicago's late Mayor Richard J. Daley in his lament about critics: "They have vilified me, they have crucified me, yes, they have even criticized me."

Man cannot live by rules alone, but they can help..

10

WHO SAYS SO?

The 11 p.m. newscast on my TV the other night began:

> Good evening. The United States and Iran . . . locked in aerial
> combat over the Persian Gulf . . .with oil prices skyrocketing and
> Western economies sagging.

Jolted by that ominous opening, I strained to catch every word as
the co-anchor picked it up:

> That's the fear tonight . . . in the wake of a series of air attacks
> on oil tankers in the Persian Gulf. . . .

What? The newscast starts with a rock-'em, sock-'em, riveting lead,
boldly describing U.S.-Iranian combat, then retreats by saying it's just a
fear. But nowhere in the long package does anyone—other than an
anchor—express such a fear.

The script—and I quote from it exactly, including ellipsis points—
goes on to say that at the State Department, "concern over the Persian
Gulf was evident." But the script did not say the "concern" extended to
combat. And "concern" is not "fear."

The effect of that scary lead is that it alarms listeners. Many, after
hearing only the first few seconds of the newscast, might have started
talking or shouting to other people about the "news" of U.S. combat. In
the hubbub of the household, they might not have heard the next
anchor's saying it was only a fear. And they might not have listened to the
rest of the story carefully and realized that "fear" of combat was
expressed only by the anchor. Many listeners—and half-listeners—who
caught the mention of "fear" were probably left concerned and confused.
Some might have even become fearful themselves. All of them were
misinformed.

What bothers me is the apparent willingness of the anchors, pro-
ducer(s) and writer(s) of the newscast to ignore one of the basic questions
that a reporter should ask: "Who says so?" If they had paused to ask,
"Just who is it who says he fears U.S.-Iranian combat?" they would have
seen that their imaginative lead was merely imaginary. If they did ask—
and answer—that question and decided to go ahead anyway with the
fabrication, they ignored their obligations to their news director and to
their public.

They also could have tested the validity of their approach by applying a basic rule of broadcast newswriting: Start the lead with the source
of the assertion that someone fears the entry of this country into the
fighting. The information the newsroom had available, probably wire
service stories, apparently didn't point to anyone who had made known
such a fear, so by that time they should have realized that their hard-
hitting lead was hollow. And they should have shot it down.

Few leads are so misleading as that one, but I do hear many that are
unsatisfactory because they make startling, controversial or questionable
assertions without first saying who's doing the asserting.

Or some leads start with quotations, without first saying who's
being quoted. The offense is compounded when the quotation contains a
"you" or an "I" or both, as in this broadcast script:

> "If you don't come here this year when I want you to, I won't go
> there next year." So says President Reagan to President Mikhail
> Gorbachev. Reagan doesn't want Gorbachev here in September.
> He says it's too close to the Congressional election in November.

Besides starting with a quotation, this story, reprinted in its entirety,
has several problems. It does not name the country Gorbachev heads. He
is not president. We usually don't have time for propriety, but because of
my upbringing at CBS News, I think it's desirable to grant the President
of this country, on second reference, the courtesy title of Mr.

On first hearing this item—and there's no second chance—a listener
would wonder who "you" is—or are. And he'd wonder who "I" is. And
where "here" is. After the listener hears "So says President Reagan," the
listener has to try to go back in his mind and fill in the pieces in the puzzle
and, at the same time, keep up with the rest of the story. Also: The writer
probably intended "he" to refer to Mr. Reagan, but it doesn't.

When we converse, we invariably put the source first: "He told
me. . . ."; "She told him. . . ."; "I told them. . . ." People are attuned to
this pattern of conversation, which is why it makes sense for broadcast
newswriters to stick to this pattern and write the way people talk.

Writers for print routinely place attribution at the end of a sentence, frequently with "according to." Or they tag the tail of a 25-word sentence with "he said." Broadcast writers, though, must keep in mind that they're not writing for the eye but for a much different receiver, the ear. But they shouldn't overdo attribution. Not every story, let alone every sentence, needs attribution. When you have a story where the facts are indisputable—say, two cars collided on Main Street—you probably need not attribute the story to police. But if police say one driver had been drinking, or police affix blame, you'd better attribute that assertion to police.

When attribution is essential, it should precede the assertion. Experts, seldom unanimous, agree on this principle, which I've reduced to three words: Attribution precedes assertion. Here's what they say in their books:

"You put attribution at the head of the sentence."

> EDWARD BLISS JR. and JOHN M. PATTERSON
> *Writing News for Broadcast*

"When attribution is needed, name the source at the beginning of the sentence if possible, and never any later than the middle."

> E. JOSEPH BROUSSARD and JACK F. HOLGATE
> *Writing & Reporting Broadcast News*

"The attribution should always come at the beginning of the sentence."

> IRVING E. FANG
> *Television News, Radio News*

"Never lead with a quotation. Always give the source of the information before you give the information."

> DANIEL E. GARVEY and WILLIAM L. RIVERS
> *Newswriting for the Electronic Media*

"Because of the characteristics of the broadcast medium, it is confusing for the listener to hear the source for a statement at the end of that statement."

> MARK W. HALL
> *Broadcast Journalism*

"Put the attribution high in the story so your audience will not have to wait to figure out where the report came from. And put the attribution at the head of the sentence rather than at the end as is done in newspapers."

> PHILLIP O. KEIRSTEAD
> *Journalist's Notebook of Live Radio-TV News*

"You say who said it before you relate what he said."

CAROLYN DIANA LEWIS
Reporting for Television

"Begin sentences with a source, with the attribution."

MELVIN MENCHER
News Reporting and Writing

"*Never*, under any circumstances, start a sentence with a direct quote and tack the source at the end. . . . This method. . . . violates a fundamental rule of good broadcast writing."

The Associated Press Radio-Television News Style Book (1962)

"Attribution always should precede the quotation. . . . attribution must always precede the indirect quote."

THE MISSOURI GROUP: BRIAN S. BROOKS,
GEORGE KENNEDY, DARYL R. MOEN and DON RANLY
News Reporting and Writing

"Broadcast stories usually *sound* more natural if you name the source at the beginning of the sentence."

FREDERICK SHOOK and DAN LATTIMORE
The Broadcast News Process

"The best way to avoid . . . confusion is to lead with the source attribution."

G. PAUL SMEYAK
Broadcast News Writing

"Sentences are clearest when the attribution is placed at the start of the sentence."

MITCHELL STEPHENS
Broadcast News

"In placing the source first, the radio writer again aligns himself with the conversationalist and departs from newspaper style, which in itself was a departure from the earlier oral style."

CARL WARREN
Radio News Writing and Editing

"It is best to let the listener-viewers know who is talking before you tell them what is being said. This means the writer begins with an attribution."

J. CLARK WEAVER
Broadcast Newswriting as Process

"Attribution in broadcast copy is always at the beginning, never at the end, of a sentence."

> TED WHITE, ADRIAN J. MEPPEN and STEVE YOUNG
> *Broadcast News Writing, Reporting and Production*

"Name the source at the beginning of a sentence if this can be done without awkwardness. And it generally can be."

> ARTHUR WIMER and DALE BRIX
> *Workbook for Radio and TV News Editing and Writing*

"We ALWAYS report attribution at the beginning of a sentence, because that's the way we report it in our everyday conversations."

> K. TIM WULFEMEYER
> *Broadcast Newswriting*

"The source belongs at the beginning of the sentence."

> *The United Press International Broadcast Stylebook*

"Getting attribution into your copy early on in the story is a cardinal rule that almost never should be violated."

> *The Associated Press Broadcast News Style Book* (1976)

(Yes, the A.P. and U.P.I. had different styles for "stylebook.")

This rule was stated even more forcefully in a book, *Television News Reporting* by the Staff of CBS News, published in 1958:

> When writing for television, always say *who* before you say *what* someone said or did. . . . The viewer is entitled to know the authority for a statement or action first so that he can gauge what importance to attach to it as the newscaster relates it. . . .
> Do not make the mistake of leading a story with an interesting quote and then identifying the speaker in the second sentence. Almost inevitably, some viewers will miss the connection and will accept the quote as the newscaster's own opinion.

In other words: Attribution precedes assertion.

Quote, Unquote

Quoth a network newscaster:

> Gorbachev delivered his sharpest attack yet against President Reagan's "Star Wars" plan, warning of, quote, "rough times ahead" if President Reagan and his aides, quote, "continue along the perilous path they have laid." Unquote.

To "quote" or not to "quote"? That is the question: whether 'tis nobler in the mind to "quote" or take another tack to avoid a sea of troubles.

That and other quotidian questions about quotations vex many a writer, so let's see what experts say:

"Thoughtless use of such hackneyed terms as 'quote' and 'end quote' tend to interrupt the listener's thought. They have a barking, staccato sound no matter how softly they are spoken. They call attention to themselves and detract from the story."

The observation comes from one of the first books on broadcast newswriting, *A Manual of Radio News Writing* by Burton L. Hotaling. It was published in 1947.

Another expert on the same wavelength was the first news director of CBS, Paul W. White. He wrote in *News on the Air,* also published in 1947:

"Remember that since the word 'quote' is foreign to the ear as far as ordinary conversation is concerned, it probably always is disturbing to the listener. . . . Please, please don't use 'unquote.'"

"Such phrases as 'and I quote' and 'end quote' are . . . shunned by skillful writers," Mitchell V. Charnley said in *News by Radio,* published in 1948. "The need for them can be avoided in most cases by careful use of the more conversational devices." (These hard-to-find books are held by the library at Northwestern's Medill School of Journalism, but my recent delight in locating them imploded when I learned that the collection is being disbanded. Until 1947, Charnley said, published material on handling radio news was scant: apparently only two mimeographed handbooks put together before World War II and two pamphlets printed by news agencies during the war.)

The same disdain for "quote" and "unquote" is also expressed in the newest textbook I've seen, *Broadcast News,* 2d ed., published in 1986: "This heavy-handed device [*quote*] has become antiquated," according to the author, Mitchell Stephens. He suggests the use of "more subtle and less formal alternatives." These attributing phrases inform listeners in a conversational way that they're about to hear a direct quotation:

He put it this way. . . .
She used these words. . . .
The governor's exact words were. . . .
As he put it. . . .
. . .what she called. . . .

These are the union leader's words. . . .
As she expressed it. . . .
To use his words. . . .
In the words of. . . .

In other words, there are many other words. Even so, some writers use "quote" and "unquote" so often you'd think they're trying to fill a quota. Maybe they need to consider a few more quotations:

"Avoid the words 'quote,' 'unquote' and 'end quote. . . .' This style has become trite and stilted."

> BASKETT MOSSE
> *Radio News Handbook*, 1947

"It is old-fashioned to say 'quote' and 'unquote.'"

> U.S. DEFENSE INFORMATION SCHOOL
> *Broadcast Writing Style Guide*, 1967

"The oldtime use of quote-unquote has long gone by the boards . . . ."

> *The Associated Press Broadcast News Style Book*, 1976

"It is not necessary to start and end a quotation with the verbal quotation marks *quote* and *unquote*. Usually a quotation can be identified by inflection of the voice or [by attributing phrases]."

> EDWARD BLISS JR. and JOHN M. PATTERSON
> *Writing News for Broadcast*, 1978

"Don't use the hackneyed QUOTE-UNQUOTE."

> JOSEPH BROUSSARD and JACK F. HOLGATE
> *Writing and Reporting Broadcast News*, 1982

"Never use the words *quote, unquote* and *quotation*."

> FREDERICK SHOOK and DAN LATTIMORE
> *The Broadcast News Process*, 1982

"NEVER use the old 'quote, unquote' method."

> K. TIM WULFEMEYER
> *Broadcast Newswriting*, 1983

"The use of the terms 'quote' and 'unquote' is cumbersome and lacks finesse."

> J. CLARK WEAVER
> *Broadcast Newswriting as Process*, 1984

"You should avoid using the expression 'quote . . . unquote.'
> TED WHITE, ADRIAN J. MEPPEN and STEVE YOUNG
> *Broadcast News Writing, Reporting, and Production,* 1984

"Many (though by no means all) writers find the words 'quote' and 'unquote' and 'end quote' to be awkward and not suited to a conversational writing style."
> RICHARD D. YOAKAM and CHARLES F. CREMER
> *ENG: Television News and the New Technology,* 1985

When should a writer use a direct quotation? "Only when it's neat, compact and the wording is exceptional," says Mitch Stephens. "Otherwise, paraphrase." Exception: "President Nixon said—quote—'I am not a crook'—unquote." If you wrote, "President Nixon says he's not a crook," you'd drain the remark of its tang.

Using direct quotations in stories is, more often than not, "lazy writing," according to the A.P. 1972 Style Book.

"In most cases," writes Tim Wulfemeyer, "paraphrasing allows us to condense a source's words, and we can often make his or her points more understandable."

So let's rewrite what the newscaster said at the outset. With good delivery, punctuated by pitch, pace and pause, this version is better: "Gorbachev made his sharpest attack yet on President Reagan's 'Star Wars' plan. He warned of 'rough times ahead' if President Reagan and his aides continue on what Gorbachev called their 'perilous path.'"

And now if you need help to quash "quote-unquote" in your newsroom, you can quote our quorum.

Non-Starters

There is a quick, easy way to start a story or a column: "There is. . . ." That's why so many writers often start stories that way:

> There's a big fire near City Hall.
> There's a shooting at the Courthouse.
> There has been a train collision near Dullsville.

Now let's dump the wordy, murky *there is* and go straight to the news with a vigorous verb:

> A big fire has broken out near City Hall.
> A lawyer has been shot in the Courthouse.
> Two trains have collided near Dullsville.

These revised sentences are much stronger than the originals because they do away with the indefinite, indirect, indolent *there is* and start with the subject of the sentence. And instead of relying on the static *is*, they move the action along with energetic verbs. If you have a nail to hit, David Lambuth said, hit it on the head.

"Both [*there is* and *there are*] are dead phrases and should be used as a last resort," says John R. Trimble in *Writing with Style* (Prentice-Hall). "Eliminating them through recasting," he suggests, "usually results in sentences that are more vivid, concrete and terse. There are many exceptions, though, and this sentence is one of them."

A simple explanation for the weakness of *there is* is offered by Lambuth in *The Golden Book on Writing:* "The habit of beginning statements with the impersonal and usually vague *there is* or *there are* shoves the really significant verb into subordinate place instead of letting it stand vigorously on its own feet. In place of saying *A brick house stands on the corner,* you find yourself lazily falling into *There is a brick house which stands on the corner.* In the latter sentence, the attention is first drawn to *there is,* and from that to *stands,* which ought to have the whole emphasis, because it is the one definite statement in the sentence." (Lambuth's book, now in paperback, was first published more than 60 years ago, which may explain why *house* is followed by *which* instead of the now-preferred *that.*)

"*There* itself is not bad," says Theodore A. Rees Cheney, "it's the company it keeps that gets it in trouble. *There* usually hangs out innocently on the corner with other idlers, verbs like *is, was, are, have been, had been,* and other weak verbs of being." In *Getting the Words Right: How to Revise, Edit & Rewrite,* he says, "These colorless verbs merely indicate that something exists, nothing about how it exists, how it behaves . . . nothing to pique our interest."

Equally wasteful in starting a story—or sentence—is *It is.* So experts advise against it. (To be exact, against *it is;* it's also a good idea usually not to start with an indefinite pronoun like *it.*)

When *there* is used with *is* or any form of *to be* to introduce a sentence, *there* is called an expletive. So is *it* when coupled with a form of *to be,* as in *it is.* The wordiness—and unworthiness—of this kind of beginning can be seen in the Latin origin of *expletive:* "added merely to fill up." So the best rule for newswriters is: Make sure your scripts have their expletives deleted.

Newswriters should also be alert to other weaknesses in their scripts. "Be especially ready to revise a sentence," Frederick Crews writes in *The Random House Handbook,* if you notice that its main assertion:

1. has as its verb a form of the colorless, inert *to be* (*is, are, was, were, had been,* etc.);

2. conveys action through a noun rather than a verb (*there was a meeting* instead of *they met*);

3. has its verb in the passive voice;

4. begins with one of the delaying formulas—*it is, it was,* etc.;

5. contains one or more *that* or *what* clauses, suggesting a displacement of your main idea to a grammatically minor part of the assertion; or

6. seems to go on and on without interruption, requiring an effort of memory to keep it together. (*It is what she recalled from childhood about the begonia gardens that were cultivated in Capitola that drew her to return to that part of the coastline one summer after another.*)

Of these six danger signals, Crews says, the last one *always* calls for revision. The other five are just warning flags: "When you have made an indistinct assertion, it will probably show more than one of the features we have named; and you can make your assertion more distinct simply by replacing those features."

"Give" and "Take"

What do you think of this lead—by a networker in New York City?

> An American airlift advance team has arrived to help bring food to millions of Ethiopians dying from famine.

Please don't say it's strictly from hunger. Surely, though, it needs help. First, people die *of* an ailment, not *from.* Second, famine is not something that anyone dies of. People die *in* a famine. Further, the sentence confuses *bring* and *take. Bring* implies movement toward the speaker (*Bring it* here to me); *take* implies movement away from the speaker. (*Take it* there). You ask someone to *take* your letter to the post office; you ask him to *bring* back stamps. A reporter at the airfield where the advance team landed would have been justified in using *bring,* but the newscaster in New York City should have used *take* or *deliver.*

In the impromptu give-and-take between co-anchors or between an anchor and a reporter, there are far more chances for lapses than in a written script. That's why written words are, with exceptions, preferred. Recently, an anchor ad-libbed about some new electronic devices:

> Actually, I have heard that some of our correspondents actually will carry these on stories.

One sentence, 15 words, two of them *actually!* When you delete *actually,* you'll see that the sentence means the same thing without *actually.* In 95 cases in 100, *actually* adds nothing. Usually, it detracts. Used twice in one sentence, it distracts.

A good rule to bear in mind is one that writers can apply to every word in a sentence: "If it's not necessary to put it in, it is necessary to leave it out."

Misuse of words in newscasts is hardly news, but this jarred me the other day. In a story about the stock market, a reporter said:

> Add to this the possibility of a disappointing Christmas for retailers, the lingering problem of the Federal deficit and the uncertain tax outlook, and you see why some analysts say the rally could *run amuck* by next week.

He probably wanted to say the rally could run out of steam, or stumble; *run amuck* means to be in a frenzy to kill. But even Wall Street's high muckamucks mustn't run amuck, especially if they want to make a killing.

"Today"

Today, wordwatchers, let's look at *today.*

It's a daily irritant for writers who wonder where in a story to insert *today* and whether to use it at all. It also annoys listeners who dislike having *today, today, today* tapping a tattoo on their eardrums.

"In the broadcasting business," Allan Jackson of CBS News once wrote, "the customers (your listeners) assume you're talking about what happened today; in fact, by the very nature of the medium, they assume you're talking about what is happening not only today but, to a large extent, right now." Allan died about 10 years ago, but his advice is just as timely today.

The first editor of the "CBS Evening News with Walter Cronkite," Ed Bliss, told me the other day that his chief chore in scrutinizing the scripts of the three writers was deleting *today.* Although Ed was jesting, he made it clear that the overuse of *today* is nothing to wink at.

Using *today* in the first story of a newscast seems reasonable, maybe in the first two stories. But Ed advises in his *Writing News for Broadcast,* "Avoid a succession of leads containing the word *today,* especially in news summaries when repetition of the word becomes painful."

"It is a mark of the amateur to use *today* in every story you write," according to another textbook, *Broadcast News Writing, Reporting and*

Production by Ted White, Adrian J. Meppen and Steve Young. "Your listeners," they write, "assume that your stories deal with events that are taking place today without your reminding them every 20 seconds."

On evening newscasts, *this evening* or *tonight* in a story may make it seem newsier. Some stations, though, in an effort to make their late newscasts seem different from their evening news and seem up-to-the-minute put *tonight* in every story. Even if every story is fresh or has a new angle, this approach is palling.

For example, an anchor on a late newscast reported, "A British researcher said tonight . . . ." For me, that was a first, the first time I ever heard of a researcher who made public his findings in the middle of the night, as it was in Britain. We can't rule out the possibility that he called a news conference for 0100 Greenwich, but that's a mean time.

When we talk about times and *today* and *tonight,* we should use our local time. Occasionally, a writer will see a story from Moscow that says *Pravda* said something *tonight.* The time there might have been 6 p.m. But in Washington, D.C., that's mid-morning. Yet, a few newscasters will go on the air at 6 p.m. or later and say, "Moscow said *tonight.* . . ." I'd say the person who writes it that way is either unthinking or careless with the truth. (*Pravda,* by the way, is the Russian word for truth; *Izvestia* is Russian for news. That prompted wags to say, "There's no pravda in Izvestia and no izvestia in Pravda.") So if a writer is careful, he'll write, "Moscow said *today* . . . ." But in most cases, chances are, the writer could skip the time element and use the present tense: "Moscow *says.* . . ." The illogicality of using any but local time is apparent in this imaginary lead: "A top Soviet official said *tomorrow.* . . ." Only rarely is it necessary to say that it's tomorrow in Moscow and that something occurred at dawn there.

If a story—or a producer—does cry out for a *today* or a *tonight,* where in a sentence do we put the pesky adverb? If you have the urge to use *today* or *tonight* in the first sentence, try to use it after the verb. I see no sense in using *today* before the verb, before we even tell listeners what the action is. We often hear stories that start, "The White House today said. . . ." The use of *today* near the top delays listeners from learning why they should keep listening. If you must use *today* in a story like that, you can make it, "The White House said today. . . ." *Today* is one of those words so commonplace in newscasts that they can easily induce a yawn, according to Mitchell Stephens in *Broadcast News.* "They are best kept out of the lead," he writes, "or at least out of the first few words of the lead—what might be called the 'lead's lead.' News is what is special about a story, not what is common to every story."

Avoid putting *today* at the end of the first sentence unless it's especially short. Putting *today* at the end can be awkward and can make the story wrong. Recently, I heard this on a network newscast. "Another Lebanese died of injuries received in that terrorist bombing of the U.S. embassy today." Sounds like the bomb went off today; in fact, the Lebanese *died* today.

As for starting a story with *today* or *tonight,* don't, unless it's intended as a transition from a related story with a different time element. Another possible exception: to draw a sharp contrast, perhaps something like this: "Today, Mayor Meyer passed a tough physical. Tonight, he dropped dead." But I'd probably write it this way: "Mayor Meyer is dead. He died tonight of. . . ." Another angle on *today* comes from Jerry Bohnen, assistant news director, KTOK-AM, Oklahoma City, who says his shop tries to avoid *today*. He says *today* is too broad and covers too great a time span. Instead, he prefers to "narrow the time frame" for the listener. Rather than say, "A judge will decide *today,"* Jerry favors saying, "A judge will decide *this afternoon." * Although that's longer than a simple *today,* it is more specific and more immediate. If you have time, his approach may be appropriate occasionally. On an evening newscast, though, I wouldn't say that something happened *this morning.* That's wordy, too long ago and immaterial. Nor, on an evening newscast, would I say that something happened *this afternoon.* It's wordy and immaterial. In most cases, it's unimportant whether the mayor said something at 11:30 a.m. or 3:30 p.m. If the story just broke and the news is significant, I might consider featuring the time element: "Mayor Trumbull says he's resigning. He said *a few minutes ago* that his doctor advised him to move promptly to a warmer climate." Or: "Mayor Trumbull is planning to resign *within the hour."* Or "Mayor Trumbull and Governor Graham are meeting *at this hour."* I think those phrases, where appropriate, heighten the now-ness of news.

Using *yesterday* or *last night* in a lead is foolish; listeners want to know what went on today and, better yet, what's going on right now. If you're dealing with a yesterday story, write a second-day lead, starting with the *today* angle. If it's a *yesterday* story that has just come to light, focus on today's disclosure or use the present perfect tense: "A man *has been* shot dead. . . ." If you must use *yesterday* or *last night* to avoid misleading listeners, use it in the second or third sentence.

Whatever you do, don't put two time elements in the same sentence. This network example presents the worst of times:

> The Chinese Air Force pilot who crash-landed his twin-engine bomber in South Korea *last night today* asked for political asylum in Taiwan.

Better: "The Chinese Air Force pilot who landed his bomber in South Korea has asked for political asylum in Taiwan." Or ". . . is now asking for. . . ."

Another lead that causes a listener's mind to swivel:

> And in the news *this morning,* in New York City, four men armed with handguns *last night* made off with a Wells Fargo truck containing 50-million dollars.

There's no need to say "in the news" in a newscast, and there was no need to say *this morning;* listeners can be expected to know that. The writer can get to the heart of the story sooner by not using the company's name in the first sentence. The story is about the robbery; whether it was Wells Fargo or Purolator or Brinks is secondary. Better: "Gunmen in New York City have stolen an armored truck with 50-million dollars."

Speaking of Brinks, here's a lead broadcast recently: "Correspondent _____ _____ begins our coverage of President Reagan on the brink of the summit." *Brink* of the summit? A brink is the edge at the top of a steep or vertical slope. A canyon or a chasm has a brink or two. And *brink* also can be used figuratively to mean "verge": "on the brink of bankruptcy," "brink of tears," "brink of war," "brink of day." But "*brink* of the summit" is faulty—logically and geologically.

The launching of the latest space shuttle reminds me of another problem: some newscasters' reliance on clichés. They describe launchings as "picture-perfect," "letter-perfect," or "textbook-perfect." For most of us, a simple "perfect" is sufficiently perfect. And when a shuttle is aloft, some of them say the crew has "a mixed bag" of assignments, or "a laundry list" of tasks, or "a shopping list." Even when writers string clichés together like beads, we can usually figure out what they're trying to say, but this lead left me dazed:

> Like the sailing ship she is named after, the new shuttle Discovery will begin its first mission of exploration tomorrow.

Did the writer mean that Henry Hudson's ship, *for* which the shuttle was named, would be sailing into space? Don't look for an answer in this space.

When a U.S. balloonist reached Europe recently, a network newscaster reported he had crossed the Atlantic "successfully." That's like the news item we've heard—more than once—that someone has climbed Mount Everest "successfully." But I still haven't heard of anyone who has reached the top "unsuccessfully." Or swum the English Channel "unsuccessfully."

Another network story that didn't succeed:

> Hurricane Diana is on a collision course with the coast of North Carolina.

For objects to collide or to be on a collision course, they must both be moving. To make that story correct, North Carolina would have to be coasting.

Tonight

A new blight is blanketing the land: *Tonight* Shows, featuring *tonight: tonight* this, *tonight* that, *tonight* the world.

Night after night, newscasters start stories with *tonight* and punctuate them with *tonight,* story after story.

So many *tonights* are sprinkled in newscasts you'd think some stations are slyly plugging a new product named Tonite. Intended as a stimulant, it's now a depressant.

The writers' intentions are good: They want to make their late newscasts differ from their early 'casts. To do that, some take the trouble to try to find out what's new, if anything; some merely reword the early scripts. But many who update early stories figure that the best way to go is to insert *tonight,* the sooner the better.

Some newscasters go through such contortions to stress *tonight* that they twist their sentences out of shape. And by injecting *tonight* into certain stories, they also twist the truth.

Let's look at several broadcast examples:

> In DeKalb County tonight, just outside the town of Somonauk, the search goes on tonight for a seven-year-old girl.

This was the lead story, so one *tonight* might be all right, but two in one sentence? After all, listeners know that *are still searching* has to be *now, right now, at this very moment,* and they also know that when it's 10 p.m., and it's dark outside, they're engulfed by night. And they don't need to be reminded repeatedly, like clockwork.

Those first four words of the story hold no attraction, and starting with *In* is pointless. Nor is there any point in turning a good verb, *search,* into a noun. There's no need for *the town of; outside* can be reduced to *near.*

Better: "Police and volunteers in DeKalb County are still searching near Somonauk for a seven-year-old girl."

> Actor Stacy Keach is a free man tonight. Keach was released from a prison in England this morning after serving six months of a nine-month sentence for smuggling cocaine.

On a 10 p.m. or 11 p.m. newscast, why mention *this morning* unless the time element is significant? If you're trying to avoid *today* in the first sentence in the belief that *today* sounds too long ago, use the present perfect tense. It shows an action has been perfected, or completed, at the time of writing or speaking but is still pertinent; it can also show that an action is continuing into the present. Use of the present perfect tense also enables you to avoid that dirty word *yesterday* in the lead.

It's true that Keach "*is* free tonight," but *is* is weak. Better: "Actor Stacy Keach has been freed from prison. He was released in England today after doing six months for smuggling cocaine." The length of his sentence is immaterial unless you can say why he didn't serve the full term. Maybe the facts warrant your writing, "Because of good behavior, Keach was freed three months early." That way, you're doing the math for the listener and simplifying the sentence—yours.

> Two top school officials in Du Page County tonight are pleading not guilty to charges they used school funds to pay for activities at sex clubs.

Where are they pleading, in night court? They almost certainly entered their plea that day, not at night. So the use of the present progressive tense, *are pleading,* which stresses the continuity of the action, is suspect. Further, the adverb *tonight* (or *today*) is best placed after the verb. The broadcast sentence could have been strengthened by making it "*their* activities." I assume they were spending the school's money on their own activities, not squandering it on other people's.

> Tonight, all is right in the world. The swallows have returned to San Juan Capistrano.

After the first sentence, listeners may wonder whether all's right with their hearing. After all, they've been hearing a steady stream of what's wrong in the world, so that sentence may throw them. The anchor's delivery, though, *might* make it acceptable. But if the writer's going to use that line, he probably should use it the way it's most widely known: "All's right *with* the world." There's nothing wrong with saying "All is right *in* the world," but listeners familiar with Browning's line might think the anchor is misquoting it. The broadcast lead-in could work if the writer had reversed the order of the two sentences and said: "The swallows have returned to San Juan Capistrano, and all's right with the world." They've been returning there for more than 200 years, so you might wonder what makes this story news, what makes it different tonight? The answer: videotape, today's.

> In New York City tonight, school authorities are defending a
> decision to open a separate high school just for students who are
> homosexual.

At 11 p.m., school officials there aren't defending decisions or anything else at that late hour, except their lives.

> In Chicago politics tonight, the mayor and his City Council
> opponents are locking horns once again. Aldermen from the
> council's majority bloc forced adjournment of today's council
> meeting, just 23 minutes after it began.

If the meeting broke up hours ago, during the day, how could their horns still be locked *tonight?* And if you pepper your scripts with *tonight,* how do you point up the immediacy of a story that broke tonight?

The "In" lead is weak, the word *politics* a waste. (Who'd start a story about the President by saying, "In national government tonight, . . ."?)

Locked horns should be consigned to the cliché closet, unless you're writing about trombonists at a jam session. Or about moose or elk. As for that unnatural *tonight,* let's respect our listeners' intelligence and not try to hornswoggle them.

11

QUESTIONS OR ANSWERS?

What do you think of question leads? And of these broadcast examples?

> The Achille Lauro is docked safely in Port Said this morning. But where are the hijackers? Have they already gone free?

You're asking *us?* We tuned in to find out.

> First, amazement. Then, outrage. Tonight, above all, confusion. Who, if anyone, has custody of the four Achille Lauro hijack murderers who took partly paralyzed 69-year-old Leon Klinghoffer from his wheelchair, shot him, killed him and tossed him overboard? Who, if anyone, will bring the murderers to justice?

Why the time-consuming hard sell—"amazement," "outrage" and "confusion"? And who's going to stop asking us questions and start telling us what's new?

> What do Coca-Cola, Caterpillar and General Electric have in common? They're just a few of the American companies represented in Moscow at a round of talks on increasing U.S.— Soviet trade.

How do writers hatch so many question leads that are inane? Questions that no listener could answer, guess at, or even care about? If the story is worth telling, why not go ahead and tell it?

> Did Ponce De Leon ever find the fountain of youth he was seeking in Florida? A Philadelphia man says he ran into the 500-year-old Spanish conquistador back in 1973, and he looked *marvelous*—not a day over 23.

You don't think I could make that up, do you?

What went wrong? That question tonight confronted doctors
after a sharp reversal in the condition of a man being kept alive
by the only mechanical heart of its kind.

When a listener hears that question before he hears what happened,
does he have the slightest idea what the anchor's talking about? Better:
"The first man with the so-called Penn State heart has taken a bad turn,
and his doctors are trying to find out what went wrong."

Now, what did the United States know during the hijack in
progress and when? How did this affect what Egypt ended up
doing and what the United States may have been planning to do?

Who needs rhetorical questions?

When did NASA know about problems with the shuttle's rocket
boosters, and what did the agency do about it?

Why not skip the questions and go straight to the news? Better: "The
commission on the Challenger explosion will try to find out today when
NASA learned about problems with the shuttle's rocket boosters. And
what the agency did about them."

Question: What did the French president and the prime minister
know and when did they know it?

Dear anchor, don't you think listeners can recognize a question by
the word order and the rising inflection? And can do it without being told
they're about to be asked a question? Isn't there a better way to start this
story than with a question, a question that echoes one first asked during
Watergate, one that through overuse has become waterlogged? Another
usage that has become soggy: "Smith's throwing arm is the big *question
mark.*"

Should a nurse be paid as much as a prison guard? That's the
contention of the American Nurses Association. . . .

Should a writer be paid for turning out that *non sequitur?* How can
anyone contend a question?

Here's a riddle: What totally American art form has been
overhauled by some people in Argentina who want to bring it
back home to America right after they market-test it in France?

A riddle? "Market-test" or "test-market"? (Do you "drive-test" a car
or "test-drive" it?)

Of course, they play the same courses, they use basically the same equipment, but how different is women's golf, that is, big-time women's golf from men's golf? We're going to be putting that question to two of the very best women on the golf tour in just a few minutes.

Didn't the anchor consider the peril of a premature pronoun (*they*), one that precedes the subject? In this case, the peril is more pronounced because the anchor never does say who *they* are. And the opening *of course* is way off course. That's no way to start a story or an intro. As for the question, if I were to ask an audience, that isn't the way I'd put it—or putt it.

What looks like a large potato and travels at high speeds?

A promo for "M*A*S*H"? The newscaster's answer to his half-baked question: Halley's comet.

Is it good news or bad news: the falling dollar and the rising yen?

True or false: The newscaster was writing under the influence of Sam Goldwyn, who reportedly said, "For your information, I would like to ask a question."

What's wrong with question leads? When was the last time you started a conversation with a question? (Except for "How are you?") And when was the last time you bought a newspaper to read its questions? Or turned on a newscast to catch the latest questions?

Any other reasons those leads are objectionable? Yes; question leads sound like commercials or quiz shows, trivialize the news, may be hard to deliver, don't inform and don't get to the point pronto.

So why do writers persist in whipping up question leads? Is it because they don't know the answers? Or because it's easier to ask a question than to burrow through a jumble of facts and think through a newsy lead?

Is a question lead ever acceptable? Perhaps, if the anchor is not playing games with the listener and the question is either one that a listener *can* answer, almost instantly, or one that provokes thought—but not too much thought, lest the listener lose the thread. In almost all cases, though, answers beat questions. No question about it.

Questions for Yourself

The art of writing, as an editor somewhere says every seven seconds, lies in rewriting what you've already rewritten. True, broadcast writers barely have enough time to write, let alone rewrite. But when they do have time, or can make time, rewriting usually improves scripts. Which is why the text for today's sermon is itself a rewrite: "Writers of the world, repent—and rewrite."

How can writers find time to rewrite? One way is to start writing earlier. Or rearrange or trim other activities. Another way is to avoid dawdling.

Before we rewrite, we should examine our scripts for signs of sloppy—and sleepy—writing. In the pressure-cooker atmosphere of a newsroom, we often put down the first words that come to mind and lapse into constructions and locutions that are wordy and weak. But if we read—and reread, and rethink—our scripts carefully, we can often see the soft spots. Some need to be cut out, others need to be reworded. Writers should ask themselves at least three questions before turning in copy, according to René J. Cappon, author of *The Word: An Associated Press Guide to Good Writing:*

> Have I said what I meant to say?
> Have I put it as concisely as possible?
> Have I put things as simply as possible?

One of the most common problems in scripts is wordiness. In a medium where time is precious and communication should be clear, direct and fast, a good writer makes every word count. Generally, the fewer words a writer uses to tell a story, the stronger the communication. If you ever discover a fire, shout, "A conflagration is consuming the premises." If no one responds, make it short and simple: "Fire!"

The first words to look for when you review a script are words that don't count—except in adding to the word-count. "Stretchers" is what Sheridan Baker calls them. "*To be,* itself," he says, "frequently ought not to be." In *The Complete Stylist and Handbook,* Prof. Baker offers examples of sentences where the original *to be* should be deleted: "He seems [to be] upset about something," "She considers him [to be] perfect," "This appears [to be] difficult."

"Above all," he writes, "keep your sentences awake by not putting them into these favorite stretchers of the passivists, *There is . . . which, It is . . . that,* and the like." And he advises: "Cut every *it* not referring to something, if you can. Some *it's* and *there's* are immutably idiomatic, of course: *It is raining. There is nothing to do.* But you can cut most of them for a real gain.

"Next to activating your passive verbs, and cutting the passive *there is's* and *it is's*, perhaps nothing so improves your prose as to go through it systematically also deleting every *to be,* every *which, that, who,* and *whom* not needed for utter clarity or for spacing out a thought. All your sentences will feel better." And sound better.

Also watch out for signs of what Baker calls "the of-and-which disease": "The passive sentence also breaks out in a rash of *of's* and *which's,* and even the active sentence can suffer. Diagnosis: something like sleeping sickness. *With's, in's, to's* and *by's* also inflamed. Surgery imperative."

The skills of a surgeon—or a rewriter—were needed on a recent network newscast that was slowed and sapped by a slew of stretchers, several in one segment:

> Elsewhere in the country, in Clinton County, Missouri, today, there was a violent protest against the forced sale of a family farm. About 300 people from an agriculture protest group . . . tried to keep officials from carrying out the sale. They failed. The sale went on. There were a few arrests, and there were no injuries.

Now let's take a second look: No need to start a story with "Elsewhere" or "Elsewhere in the country." Almost every story comes from somewhere else. Although I wouldn't start with "Elsewhere," I wouldn't start with "In [place-name]." One of my first broadcast editors, Bob Siller, told me not to do it, that it's a lazy man's way of starting a story. After his instruction sank in, I realized that a writer could, without thought or effort, start any story that way: "In Katmandu, Nepal, an avalanche killed. . . ."; "In Timbuktu, Mali, rebels massacred hundreds of. . . ."; "In Tippecanoe, Indiana, a man broke into a bank and stole. . . ." (But no man can do what Katmandu.)

A place-name is not news. What *happened* is news. So for me, *In* is out. It's best to go ahead and tell the story as interestingly as possible. But the writer should try to put the place-name near the top, not at the end of a long first sentence. If the writer delays the place-name too long, the listener might assume the news occurred in his or her area.

Starting a story with *in* is acceptable, even desirable, in specific circumstances. In a series of fast reactions or developments, it makes sense to use an *in* after an umbrella lead: "The United Nations called on all members today to. . . . In Washington, the President promptly said. . . . In London, the prime minister said. . . . In Paris, the French president said. . . ."

As for the broadcast about the forced sale of a farm, not many people are going to turn up the sound when they hear an item that starts out talking about a county in a distant place. This would be better: "Protesters [at least this word holds promise of action] in Clinton County, Missouri, tried to block officials from selling a family farm."

I'm not sure how to rewrite the next sentence in the script because I don't know what an "agriculture protest group" is. Does it protest agriculture? Does it protest the use of "agriculture" instead of "farming"? Or the use of "agricultural implement" instead of "farm tool"?

As for the two *there were*'s in the story's last sentence, let's recast the sentence: "Police [or sheriff's deputies, or lawmen] arrested a few people [protestors? farmers? members of the family?]." I wouldn't take time to write that no one was hurt. It's news that no one was hurt only when the story is about an event in which someone might have been expected to be hurt, but, remarkably, no one was hurt.

And *why,* dear anchor, was the family forced to sell its farm?

Starting a sentence with *There were* or *There is* brings to mind Gertrude Stein's complaint about her hometown, Oakland, California: "There's no there there." Experts have remarked that *There is* lacks substance, that it delays the action in a sentence and shoves the significant verb into a subordinate place. They say it's a dead phrase and should be used only as a last resort.

I hesitate to say that after two *there were*'s in one sentence, the anchor was dragging. But he was, and he began the next item the same way:

There is a report of poisoned water today, water that may have been poisoned by toxic waste. The Interior Department has ordered the closing of. . . .

Better: "The government has ordered the closing of a California wildlife refuge because its water may be poisoned. The cause is said to be toxic waste. . . ." If the refuge had already been closed, I'd write, "The government has closed a. . . ." Whatever strength that news had was leached out of it by the anchor's first words, *There is.* Also: When the anchor said there's a "report," did he mean a reporter has turned in a story about the purported poisoning? Or did the anchor say "report" because it was only a rumor? The script probably was based on wire copy, but news services aren't in the business of circulating rumors, so his use of "report" probably was thoughtless.

As they say euphemistically about a new show trying out for Broadway but found wanting, the script "needs work." That means reworking. Which means rethinking and rewriting.

Hit List

Some sportswriters work so hard at trying to reach listeners that they must think a metaphor is something you shout through.

Occasionally, a figure of speech, like a metaphor or simile, can make copy come alive if it's fresh or at least not stale. Too often, though, writers fall back on a device so worn out that its fizz has fizzled.

Although no central registry keeps track of every use of a metaphor (an implied comparison) or simile (explicit comparison), even half-listeners might sense that "war of words" is one of newscasters' most overworked metaphors. A word doctor would pronounce it a dead metaphor. If it's only overworked, it needs a rest; if it's dead, it needs burial. Yet a network anchor recently reported that someone had "triggered a war of words."

The first use of "war of words" is attributed to Alexander Pope (not to be confused with Pope Alexander). According to *The Oxford English Dictionary,* the English poet used "war of words" in 1725. That makes the metaphor more than 260 years old. Even Milton Berle wouldn't take material that old—not even from a Youngman. As for "trigger," it's so overused, I avoid it unless I'm writing about Roy Rogers' horse.

"Metaphor" comes from the Greek word for transference, and Pope has been praised for his ability to transfer the fury of fighting to talking. For the first recorded use of this comparison, he certainly deserves credit. And so does the first wordwatcher who recognized Pope's imaginative phrase and used it himself (with or without credit). But over two-and-a-half centuries, it has become a warhorse, trotted out so often by so many writers that it has become worn out.

Instead of striving for originality and shunning clichés, unthinking writers turn every clothesline quarrel, as we used to call a backyard shouting match, into a "war of words."

These overkillers should be reminded of Strunk and White's advice in *The Elements of Style:* "Use figures of speech sparingly." Orwell put it more sternly: "Never use a metaphor, simile or other figure of speech which you are used to seeing in print."

Some that Orwell would have put the kibosh on are included by Harold Evans in *Newsman's English.* Here are several from his three-page list of what he calls "stale expressions":

armed to the teeth	bitter end
beat a hasty retreat	brutal reminder
bewildering variety	built-in safeguard

burning issue
checkered career
cherished belief
city fathers
conspicuous by its absence
cool as a cucumber
coveted trophy
crack troops
daring daylight robbery
deafening crash
doctors fought
dramatic new move
fly in the ointment
finishing touches
foregone conclusion
given the green light
goes without saying
hook or by crook
in full swing
in the nick of time
lashed out
last but not least
leaps and bounds

left up in the air
lending a helping hand
long arm of the law
matter of life and death
move into high gear
none the worse for wear
not to be outdone
over and above
pros and cons
proud heritage
psychological moment
red faces
red-letter day
reduced to matchwood
64,000-dollar question
spearheading the campaign
speculation was rife
spirited debate
spotlight the need
storm of protest
upset the apple cart
voiced approval
wealth of information

"They [clichés] are so smooth from wear," says *The Written Word*, "that they slip off the tongue or pen with great ease, and that can be the undoing of an unwary writer or speaker. . . . The temptation [to use them] is great merely because many of the expressions in question are catchy (or once were), and to an untrained user of language their surface appeal and never-ending appearance may seem a recommendation in itself . . . *Do one's thing, bite the bullet* and *keep a low profile* suggest that such expressions seem to age very fast through relentless use."

The guide carries a five-page list of clichés. Here are some:

agonizing reappraisal
agree to disagree
as a matter of fact
as luck would have it
brave the elements
bright and early
by the same token
calm before the storm
can't see the forest for the
    trees
dead as a doornail

easier said than done
fall on deaf ears
few and far between
go over the top
handwriting on the wall
hit the nail on the head
hit the spot
hue and cry
if the truth be told
in no uncertain terms
it stands to reason

land-office business
long arm of coincidence
none the worse for wear
on cloud nine
part and parcel
point with pride
rain cats and dogs
separate the men from the
   boys
separate the sheep from the
   goats
sick and tired
silver lining in the cloud
stagger the imagination
sweet smell of success
take a dim view of
that's for sure

truth is stranger than fiction
uncharted seas
understatement of
   the _____
view with alarm
what with one thing or
   another
when all is said and done
   [more is said than done]
when you come down to it
wide-open spaces
you can say that again
you win some, you lose some
you're damned if you do,
   you're damned if you don't
your guess is as good
   as _____

My most memorable teacher, Curtis D. MacDougall, offered some figures of speech (in *Interpretative Reporting*) that he said "are whiskered with age and mark their innocent user as callow":

ax to grind
blessing in disguise
clutches of the law
hail of bullets
in the limelight
police combing the city

slow as molasses in January
the crying need
threw a monkey wrench into
watery grave
worked like Trojans

MacDougall's book also lists what he calls "shopworn personifications":

Dame Fashion
Dan Cupid
Father Time
G.I. Joe
Jack Frost

John Q. Public
Lady Luck
Man in the Street
Mother Nature
Mr. Average Citizen

Some metaphors and clichés can be classed as "journalese," the superficial style of writing said to be characteristic of many newspapers and magazines. Dr. MacDougall's list of words that have lost their effectiveness through repetition includes:

brutally murdered
death car
feeling ran high

gruesome find
gumshoes
infuriated mob

mystery surrounds   sleuths
police dragnets   swoop down

Other words in that category are provided by E.L. Callihan in *Grammar for Journalists:*

grilled [unless your're writing   fusillade of bullets
   about a barbecue]   a shot rang out
reign of terror   miraculous escape
pitched battle   caught red-handed
pool of blood   shrouded in mystery
hail of bullets

Still more trite expressions are listed by Richard D. Mallery in *Grammar, Rhetoric and Composition:*

as luck would have it   looking for all the world like
clear as crystal   method in his madness
deadly earnest   powers that be
doomed to disappointment   psychological moment
dull thud   riot of color
grim reaper   venture a suggestion
irony of fate

The editorial consultant Albert Toner has listed hundreds of once-bright words and phrases that have lost their luster and become clichés. "How many of these tranquilizers," he asks, "do you mistake for stimulants?"

back-to-back   psychic income
close encounters of any kind   says it all
collision course   single most
comparing apples and   slippery slope
   oranges   smoking gun
conventional wisdom   state of the art
cutting edge   tell it like it is
fast lane   very private person
fat city   wall-to-wall
game plan   where it's at
hard ball   back to basics or square one
hit the ground running   or the drawing board
interestingly enough   beautiful people
name of the game   can of worms
nation that can go to the moon   couldn't agree more/care less
Operation Whatever   cutting-room floor
Project Anything   different drummer

doing something right
down the tubes
extra mile
eyeball to eyeball
father figure
forget it
game of inches
garbage in, garbage out
goes with the territory
hearts and minds
like gangbusters
mind-boggling

moment of truth
one-on-one
only game in town
pecking order
reinventing the wheel
rubber chicken circuit
since sliced bread
smart money
tip of the iceberg
up for grabs
won't fly/wash

As far as exhausted expressions go, that's not *the whole kit and caboodle, not by a long shot,* but those samples provide enough *food for thought* to help writers think more about what they write—which is, after all, *the bottom line.*

One of the most fertile fields for clichés is the athletic field. Sportswriters, says Callihan, must learn to avoid words and expressions like these:

pill
apple
horsehide
pellet
pigskin
hoghide
tangle with

rifled the ball
battled furiously
charity toss
chalked up a victory
in the shadow of their own
 goal posts

Some sportswriters seem to think that writing in simple English might cause them to be benched, so they do their double-barreled damnedest. They say a batter has *belted a four-bagger, clouted one for the circuit, poked one out of the park,* or hit a *roundtripper, a tater, a goner, a dinger, a grand slam,* even a *grand salami.* They'll go to any lengths—even *the length of two football fields*—to sidestep simplicity. The sports producer William Weinbaum tells of a few formulas they rely on to avoid that dreaded word, *homer.* "You can hang a star on that baby," "It's see ya later time," and "That dog will hunt." Intent on grandstanding, they ignore the easiest—and best—way to say it: "He hit a home run." After some of the offenders condescend to write "hit," I recommend they learn to say "win"—as a verb. I keep hearing about teams that *triumphed, grabbed a win, rolled up a victory,* or *handed a defeat to.* I'd like to hear more about teams that just *won.*

Now that we've disposed of that "mixed bag of leftovers," a term recently minted by a newscaster (a mixed metaphor like that is what Theodore Bernstein calls a "mixaphor"), let's look at another case of wrongdoing, one that was broadcast not long ago:

> New York City detectives today will pick up self-admitted subway vigilante Bernhard Goetz, who waived extradition at a court appearance in Concord, New Hampshire.

Obviously—except to the writer who wrote the copy, the editor who edited it, the producer who produced it and the anchor who delivered it—no one can admit anything but oneself. So "self-admitted" is tautological. A logical thought would have prompted someone to delete "self"; it should have been self-evident.

After a second look at the broadcast sentence, I'd rewrite it and try to place "today" (as I always do if I use it) after the verb: "New York City police are going to bring back the so-called subway vigilante, Bernhard Goetz, today from New Hampshire. He waived extradition at a hearing in Concord." I substituted "police" for "detectives"; it's shorter, and, besides, they didn't have to do any detecting.

A network newscaster just reported that indictments against a mess of mobsters had been "handed down." Delete "down" and make it "up." A grand jury hands *up* indictments to a judge. And a judge hands *down* rulings. That's today's final decision.

Once is Enough

Do you ever hear a newscaster speak of an *acute* crisis? Or hear him say *new* record, *controversial* issue or *final* outcome?

If so, you've heard a redundancy, something said superfluously. Using too many words to express an idea or repeating needlessly is objectionable—unless you're talking about Duran Duran, Sirhan Sirhan, Pago Pago or Walla Walla.

I've been nudged into writing about redundancies by a suggestion from a western wordwatcher, Mike Berriochoa, N.D. of KONA-AM and FM, Tri-Cities, Washington. He offers a few redundancies that he has come across: a forest fire that's *fully* surrounded, a burning home that's *completely* engulfed, then *totally* destroyed.

Other redundancies—in italics—that we should guard against:

all-time record	*new* recruit
new bride	build a *new* jail

circle *around*
square-*shaped*
green-*colored*
large-*size*
friendly *in nature*
short *in stature*
few *in number*
wide variety
head honcho
state of Ohio
capital *city*
sworn affidavit
funeral *service*
self-confessed
asphyxiated *to death*
smothered *to death*
strangled *to death*
originally established
first began
first built
first discovered
first *and foremost*
disappeared *from view*
invisible *to the eye*
major breakthrough
major milestone
mental attitude
temporarily suspended
while *at the same time*
widow of *the late*
advance planning
positively identify
grocery *store*
invited guests
fall *down*
pay *out*
continue *on*
canceled *out*
lift *up*
up above
down below
if, *as and when*
unless *and until*
exact same
necessary requirements
repeat *again*
serious danger

private industry
old adage
grateful thanks
basic fundamentals
usual custom
customary practice
still remains
component parts
appointed *to the position of*
commute to *and from*
shuttle *back and forth*
join *together*
eliminate *entirely*
so *consequently*
cirrhosis *of the liver*
put to death by *lethal*
  injection
strictly prohibited
surrounding circumstances
depreciate *in value*
opening gambit
undergraduate *student*
fellow classmate
doctor *by profession*
true facts
over-exaggerate
exact address
value judgment
violent explosion
vitally necessary
local resident
nodded *her head*
shrugged *her shoulders*
a smile *on her face*
Easter *Sunday*
Christmas *Day*
legal contract
personal friend
personal opinion
personal vendetta
official business
as a *general* rule
general public
general consensus
consensus *of opinion*
total extinction
total monopoly

totally annihilate	in three months' *time*
flaming inferno	it's raining *outside*
passing fad	*joint* cooperation
ten acres *of land*	*mutual* cooperation
a distance of five miles	*previous* police record
seems *to be*	*previous* experience
appeared *on the scene*	*past* history
they're *both* alike	puppy *dog*
definite decision	glance *briefly*
ever since	reason *why*
awkward predicament	each *and every*
hired mercenary	*completely* full
pair *of* twins	*patently* obvious
grand jury indictment	*close* proximity
county coroner	*close* scrutiny
at *the corner of* Oak and Polk	*intents and* purposes
for *the purpose of*	*ways and* means
future outlook	compromise *solution*
future prospects	*eye*witness
minor quibble	*ultimate* goal
noon luncheon	*ultimate* outcome
may *possibly*	*end* result
short *space of* time	*final* climax
in *a period of* 90 days	*final* completion
	complete stop

Some redundancies show up in ads, repeatedly: *advance* reservations, *pre*-reserved seating, *free* gift, *full* quart, *hot* water heater, *new* innovation, *extra* bonus, and kills bugs *dead*.

When we're chatting, we often lapse into careless speech, which is harmless *enough*. "A man who never said an unnecessary word," Bergen Evans observed, "would say very little during a long life and would not be pleasant company."

Anyone who was in my company might have heard me order a tuna *fish* sandwich. No more. Since a friend pointed out my offense, I've tried to economize by cutting back just to tuna—and hold the *fish*.

In newscasts, economy in language is not merely desirable, it's essential. Redundancies waste time, blur meaning and lessen impact: the fewer words you use to tell a broadcast news story, the clearer and more forceful the communication. Flab weakens communication and crowds out other news. With leaner stories, you can fit more stories into a newscast and make your newscast newsier.

An anchor who says tuna *fish* should not be canned. But we must guard against wasting words. Air time is precious. The battle cry of

Strunk and White in their venerable *Elements of Style:* "Omit needless words."

One of Strunk and White's reminders is, "Avoid foreign languages. . . . Write in English." I recalled it when the space shuttle Discovery was poised for launching the day after its first liftoff was postponed. When the crew boarded the second time, a newscaster said the astronauts must have "a feeling of déjà vu. . . ." What he meant, I suppose, was that they felt a sense of having endured this pre-launch wait before. But that common use of "déjà vu" is wrong. "Déjà vu" is the *illusion* of having already experienced something that is, in fact, being experienced for the first time. Often, when newscasters use a foreign word, they misuse it or mispronounce it. Even when they get it right, most listeners misunderstand it or don't understand it. After all, how many listeners know French? ("Déjà vu" is not to be confused with deejay view or what the comedian George Carlin calls "vuja dé," which he defines, roughly, as "Where the bleep is this and what the bleep am I doing here?") Even if a newscaster knows how to use "déjà vu" correctly, he shouldn't use it at all. Next time you hear it, and you will, you may recall what Yogi Berra said (or is said to have said): "It's déjà vu all over again."

Far more important than knowing a few foreign words, writers should know the meaning of English words and how to use them correctly. Yet we often hear mistakes that writers could catch merely by checking a dictionary. Recently, I heard a newsman report on the murder of a Denver talk-show host: "Someone fired a salvo of bullets from a high-caliber gun. . . ." According to the Naval Terms Dictionary, a salvo is one or more shots fired simultaneously by the same battery (set of big guns) at the same target. So the gunman in Denver could not have fired a salvo, no matter what his caliber.

While I'm talking about gunfire, I might as well note that I think some newscasters overdo the word "war." I prefer to save it for armed conflict between nations, even gangs. But when I keep hearing of "the war against scofflaws," "the war against jaywalkers," "the war against crabgrass," I get war-weary. What prompts me to start a campaign (no, I don't declare war) against the spread of "war" is the use I heard the other day. A newscaster said the President's chief economic adviser had often "warred" with the Reagan Administration. Not "disagreed with," "argued with," or "stood up to," but "warred." I'd call it overkill. Or *over*shrill. (When *I* commit a redundancy, I call it reinforcement.)

Just as bad, sometimes, is underkill. I heard a case of that recently on a network newscast in the lead of a story:

There were no surprises at Wimbledon today.

Reminds me of a newspaper banner that reads: NO ONE HURT IN NO PLANE CRASH. The tennis lead has several faults: It starts with "There were," a weak way to write a lead, and it says nothing. Although the tennis results may come as no surprise to the newscaster, the average listener would regard it as news. Better: "Tennis star Martina Navratilova was favored to win at Wimbledon today—and she did. She won her fifth singles title there, her third straight."

Another fault with the broadcast lead: it's negative. Strunk and White urge: "Put statements in a positive form. Make definite assertions. Avoid tame, colorless, hesitating, noncommittal language. . . . Consciously or unconsciously, the reader is dissatisfied with being told what is not; he wishes to be told what is."

After a recent column of mine quoted George Orwell on the clumsiness of the *not-un* formation. I heard this on the air:

A post-convention boomlet is not unexpected and certainly not unwelcome for the vacationing Mondale. . . .

This construction, expressing an affirmative by negating its opposite, is hard for a listener to sort out, and two double negatives in a row, as in that sentence, leave me out of sorts. And might well leave Orwell unwell.

Writers in broadcast newsrooms often work in a hubbub, and, under the stress of fighting a deadline, they sometimes turn in copy that's not so strong as it could be. For example, here's a lead sentence I heard on the air recently:

A prominent international bridge player told today how she was threatened with death by kidnappers in Washington, DC.

It could be strengthened by building up to the strongest words, "threatened with death," not burying them in the middle of the sentence. Also, it's undesirable to put the place-name last. Better: "A prominent international bridge player told today how kidnappers in Washington, D.C., threatened her with death."

If the writer of the first version had re-read his script just one more time, he would have spotted the weaknesses before he heard them on the air. I ought to know. I was the writer—and still am. Or am I being redundant?

12

BAD NEWS

"We start with some bad news," the anchor said somberly the other morning on his network newscast.

I had been only half-listening, but that gloomy opening hit me like a batch of ice cubes—still in a freezer tray. The news certainly sounded worrisome. Was it an assassination? A terrorist bombing? A disaster?

The anchor went on grimly to report the news: The actor James Mason was dead. I couldn't help wondering, for whom was that news bad? Presumably, family, friends and fans. But the death of one person, even a personage, is generally accepted by listeners as just another news item. After all, they've become accustomed to a cascade of calamities, catastrophes and cataclysms. As good an actor as Mason had been, he was no longer a big, big name on moviegoers' mental marquees.

Opening the newscast with a story on Mason's death would have been acceptable if the newscaster had reported it straight—without telegraphing us that he was going to deliver "bad news."

Whenever I have to write an obituary or any story, I'm still guided by a rule I learned in school: Don't label news as good or bad. What may be bad for some listeners may be good for others. Heavy rain can be bad for pedestrians, motorists and sunbathers. But it can be good for farmers, taxi drivers and umbrella vendors.

"Good news" abounds on broadcasts when the prime rate drops. But for listeners, a drop in the prime has both positive and negative sides. Anyone who takes out a home improvement loan, for example, will benefit right away. And if other borrowing costs start to fall again, consumers could save interest on adjustable rate home mortgages and similar borrowings.

But for many listeners, lower rates are "bad news." Many consumers like high interest rates because it enables them to earn strong returns on their investments, like money market funds and U.S. Government securities.

I also was taught not to tell an audience that a story is distressing, or interesting, or amusing; let *listeners* decide. The best policy is to stick to the facts and just tell the news.

If the "good news" or "bad news" is tied to a specific person or group, characterizing the news may be valid. For example: "Mayor Murphy received good news today from his doctor." Or "The I.R.S. has bad news for taxpayers." Otherwise, a newscaster should let listeners, if they wish, decide whether it's good or bad. Or good *and* bad.

Anchors should also avoid "good news-bad news" leads, such as "Governor Graham has good news and bad news for farmers. The good news is. . . ." I think the "good news-bad news" approach is suitable for Johnny Carson, but some newscasters have used it so much and for so long that it has lost whatever appeal it had—and has become bad news.

In fact, the "good news-bad news" gimmick has been traced back to Biblical times. When Moses came down from Mount Sinai with the Commandments, he reportedly told his people, "I have good news and bad news. The good news is that I got them down from 40 to 10. The bad news is that adultery is still in."

I said "reportedly" because a news director who reads that may muse, "If a minicam wasn't there to shoot it, did it really happen?"

This I heard myself: A network newscaster said British and Chinese diplomats had worked out an agreement on the future of Hong Kong and had "initialized" it. *Initialized?* I was traumatized, though not so severely as the Padres were Trammeltized.

The suffix *ize* long has been fused onto nouns and adjectives to turn them into verbs: apologize, burglarize, computerize, hospitalize, jeopardize, legalize, pasteurize, polarize, synthesize, even decriminalize. I won't itemize them, but writers should realize they can't slap on an *ize* indiscriminately, especially if an existing verb does the job. "Initialize" is unneeded because an established verb already means "to sign one's initials": it's *initial.*

Another verb that strikes me as misbegotten is *finalize.* It has the ring, or thud, of bureaucratic jargon, and we already have ways to convey the action intended by *finalize:* "end," "make final," "put in final form," "finish," "complete," "wrap up."

Under *finalize,* the *American Heritage Dictionary* (1982) says the verb was unacceptable to the vast majority of its Usage Panel. The panel comprises leading writers, editors and grammarians, about 150 in all. That edition does not report the panel's votes on questionable words, but the 1969 edition reported *finalize* was found unacceptable by 90 percent of the panel.

A local newscaster recently spoke of "unionized" teachers. This usage seems strange; it made me think of teachers who had been processed in some way. Sounds like something that might have been done to people lacking polish: *Simonized.*

Another problem I don't sympathize with or temporize about: what some grammarians call "stacking." That's the practice of piling adjectives and nouns-as-adjectives in front of nouns. One of the most horrendous examples was uncorked recently by a network newscaster who spoke of "a new and improved revised-downward federal budget deficit forecast."

Rather than try to punctuate it, I'll try to puncture it. When the anchor finally reaches the first noun, "budget," the average listener probably thinks that's the subject of the sentence. But it's quickly followed by another noun, "deficit," so he realigns his train of thought, if he can, and surmises that the story is about a budget deficit. Wrong. All those adjectives and nouns modify what it's really all about: a forecast.

A listener can catch a couple of adjectives before a noun, but seven are far too many, especially those seven. What makes it even tougher to untangle is that two of them *(budget, deficit)* are nouns pressed into service as adjectives. The sentence should be rewritten—and the writer sentenced.

A newspaper reader might be able to thread his way through that thicket of words because he'd first see a headline, read the sentence at his own pace, re-read whatever isn't clear and perhaps rip it out of the paper for review. And any story written that heavy-handedly ought to be ripped out. But a listener who wanted to figure out that sentence as it was spoken would have to be a Champollion, the French Egyptologist who deciphered the Rosetta stone. Or he'd have to have total recall—with instant replay.

The problem with that writing is that a listener can't grasp it instantly; the problem with the writer was not that he wasn't trying but that he was trying too hard. Maybe he wanted to make himself heard by hammering out a slam-bang sentence, one that would put a dent in the listener's mind. But no one will remember it, and children will never recite it.

That's my *un*revised downward forecast.

Wasting Time

Many newscasters fritter away time by talking too much about time. Example:

Space shuttle Challenger will be landing later today.

"Later" is unneeded. As soon as we hear "will be," we know that the shuttle has not landed yet, is not landing now, but that it *will be.* Because it *will be,* the landing will have to take place in the future (and, we hope, not in the pasture). Everything that happens after the anchor or reporter speaks must be *later.* It's inevitable. So if an event will take place today after the newscast, there's no need to say *later.*

We hear morning newscasts say the President will meet with his advisers *"later* today." If he's going to be meeting today, it must be *later* (not *later on*). Later, we hear stories telling us he met with advisers *"earlier* today." If he *met* with them, the meeting is already past-tensed. So whatever happened before the newscaster spoke that sentence *had* to be earlier. So why say *earlier?* Sometimes we hear a story like this:

The Union Carbide Company says it will resume production of the deadly chemical . . . at its plant in Institute, West Virginia, *some time* today.

If the writer had spent some time thinking, he might have realized that everything occurs at *some time.* Perhaps he wanted to put across the idea that the time of the resumption is unknown or indefinite. So what? Even if he knew at noon that it'd resume at 2 p.m. or 3:30 p.m., he needn't take time—his time and our time—to tell us the precise moment. What is important is that the factory *will* resume production today. If a newscaster is reporting an impending community event, like a town meeting, mention of the time may be essential. But in 99 stories in 100, it's a waste of time.

Are there any exceptions to the advice against writing *earlier today* and *later today?* Yes. Almost every bit of advice or rule is subject to exception. Example: "The President will meet with his cabinet this afternoon and will confer *later today* with his National Security Council."

Sooner or later, we have to deal with other words that add nothing to a sentence. And if they don't add, they detract. Here's a Washington correspondent's recent opening line:

Well, needless to say, they were not encouraged here by Nabih Berri's comments.

For openers: If something *is* needless to say, there's no need to say it—and to say it's *needless to say*. And we have no need to hear it. If the story is worth reporting but the reporter doesn't think much of it, he shouldn't dismiss it on air by introducing it with a put-down.

Obviously. That's another wasted word. If something is obvious, why say so? A fact may be obvious to the reporter and to some listeners, but not all. Of course not. Aha, another superfluity: *of course.* Here's an example from a network newscast:

> Today is Good Friday, *of course,* the day when Christians
> around the world. . . . And, *of course,* at sundown tonight Jews
> begin the celebration of Passover.

The curse of *of course* is that it sounds apologetic and condescending. It sounds as though the newscaster is sorry he has to say something that everyone knows. On another level, it sounds as though his message is: "You undoubtedly know this already, *of course;* you know you do, but I'm going ahead because not everyone knows as much as you and I do." Or it might sound as though he means, "*I* know this, *of course,* but I had better inform you." Listeners who didn't know about today's religious holidays might well resent the *of course* because they'd think it implies they should have known. Often, the information that a writer couples with *of course* is not widely known or obvious.

Even when a writer deals with a widely known fact, it's best to skip the *of course* and tell the story straightaway. Better: "Today is Good Friday, the day when Christians. . . ." Or: "Christians are observing Good Friday." The use of the present tense tells that it's going on at this very moment, so there's no need for *today.* One way for a writer to deal with a widely known fact that many people may not be mindful of is to mention it only in passing, not as the news itself: "The celebration of Good Friday by Christians today coincides with the start of the Jewish Passover. The two holidays coincide that way only once every. . . ." Thus, the coincidence becomes the news, yet the listener learns—or is reminded—that today is Good Friday and the start of Passover. In my book, but not in the Good Book, the *news* value of the two holidays has—through the millenia—slipped.

Of course is a short form for another phrase that popped up in a network story about the airlines' frequent flyer programs:

> But, *as we all know,* you can't get something for nothing
> forever. The I.R.S. is now pondering whether frequent flyers
> should pay income tax on all those trips.

Sounds as though the reporter knows she's going to dispense an obvious truth, so she wants to assure the listener that she's no fool, that she knows that what she's about to say is clear to everyone. The truism that you can't get something for nothing is about as profound, informative, and newsy as saying, "Nothing lasts forever." Or as many a Wall Street sage says when a stock falters, "No tree grows to the sky." Even the frequent flyer programs aren't giving away anything; they're exacting a price for what seems like a bonus. That you can't get something for nothing (at least in my experience) *goes without saying.* And if it goes without saying, why say it?

Another waste of words, not to mention an assault on reason, is the lead that goes like this—and, in fact, went like this:

> Everyone this morning's talking about the big fight last
> night. . . .

Not everyone was talking about it. I, for one, didn't even know there had been a fight. And not even everyone who knew it was still talking about it. Or, at that hour, even talking.

Any assertion that brooks no exception or qualification is an assertion that bears scrutiny. It is safe to say that *everyone* is mortal, but any sentence—or at least any sentence that I can think of right now—that uses *everyone* is risking an implosion. Another network example, this about the stock market's steady advances early this year:

> Everyone is looking for an even bigger winning streak.

If everyone on Wall Street—and elsewhere—were of one mind, the market might stand stock-still.

Another recent broadcast generalization:

> All of Britain is talking about a royal scandal. . . .

Whatever the scandal, I can't imagine that everyone there was talking about it. Or even knew about it. Or cared about it. The "royal scandal" dealt with a member of the royal family, through marriage, who confirmed that her father had been a member of the Nazi S.S. She herself was not a Nazi, and her father was long dead, so who was scandalized? Was *everyone* in Britain talking about it? In a nation with so many subjects?

The flip side of *everyone* is *no one.* One of my favorites—but not everyone's—appears in stories about escapees: "*No one* knows where he is." In fact, he himself knows, and his whereabouts might also be known by a friend, a relative, someone harboring him, or by someone sheltering him without knowing he's on the lam. If police knew where to find him, he wouldn't be a fugitive. By definition, that's someone whose whereabouts is unknown. When he escapes, he doesn't broadcast his breakout. *Needless to say,* he goes without saying.

Empty Words

Quick: Name anyone in public life who's not "controversial." Or anything in public life, from abortion to zip codes. Even if Mother Teresa went on a newscast and said, "God bless America," some people would complain. Switchboard operators know listeners complain about every blessed thing.

Almost everything in the news is controversial, meaning that it's subject to or marked by controversy—"a dispute, especially a lengthy and public one, between sides holding opposing views." And in some minds, "controversial" has come to mean "disapproved of" or "causing criticism."

Whatever writers mean when they add "controversial," many of them seem to think it's a flavor enhancer, bound to spice up a script. Take this example, please:

> Senator Edward Kennedy's controversial tour of South Africa
> has ended on a controversial note.

What made Kennedy's tour "controversial"? Most Americans probably didn't even know about it, and of those who did, probably few cared. Or at least care enough to create a controversy. And how did his tour end on a "controversial" note? According to the network newscast, about 100 black demonstrators prevented him from making a final speech in the black township of Soweto. Is the stifling of speech "controversial"? True, there was a ruckus, but the relatively small group heckling Kennedy hardly caused a controversy; listeners in this country hadn't even known about the dustup.

In any case, nothing justified the writer's use of "controversial" twice in one short sentence. The writer used the word probably because it popped into her head without effort, and she figured it'd add punch to the story. Instead, she should have taken time to construct a strong sentence, relying on nouns and verbs, not mindless clichés.

The *New York Times's* in-house monitor, *Winners & Sinners,* said, "*W & S* would be hard pressed to cite a word that tells less, yet appears more often, than *controversial.*" *W & S* said (11/29/82) that during a lull on night rewrite, two reporters tapped the *Times's* Information Bank computer to see what the staff had been calling "controversial." They found that in two recent weeks, "controversial" had been applied more than 30 times—to Robert S. McNamara, McGeorge Bundy, the suffragist Lucy Stone, a fumble by a football player, pet projects of legislators, a U.S. stamp honoring the memory of St. Francis of Assisi, banks' alliances with brokerages, an endorsement by N.O.W., a new building in Portland, Oregon, an umpire's home-run call, Linda Ronstadt's "new wave" album, remedies for the rising cost of health care and, among others, the N.C.A.A.

No wonder *W & S* called "controversial" an empty word. Not only has overuse caused its meaning to be drained, but "controversial" has become a sort of cliché, constantly on call to try to prop up a story. But its emptiness has left it impotent. And no longer is its worth even controversial.

Listeners are showered by empty words, the latest outpouring inspired by the inauguration. Take "pomp and circumstance." In his *Dictionary of Clichés*, Eric Partridge defines "p. and c." as "splendour of the whole and magnificence of the details." The average listener, though, doesn't know what "circumstance" means, even circumstantially. Here's an example of its recent use on a newscast:

> Soviet Defense Minister Dmitri Ustinov is being buried in
> Moscow's Red Square today with the full pomp and circumstance
> that his motherland can offer.

What does "circumstance" add to that sentence? Color? Detail? For me, it adds only pomposity. And prolixity. When I hear "pomp and circumstance," I think of Sir Edward Elgar's march. Shakespeareans might think of the line from *Othello:* "pride, pomp and circumstance of glorious war." In that time, "circumstance" meant any formal show or ceremony. But William and Mary Morris say in their *Dictionary of Word and Phrase Origins* that meaning—in case you want a second opinion—is archaic.

The sentence about Ustinov's burial has a problem: Instead of saying "the *full* p. and c. *that* his motherland can offer," it should say "*all* the p. and c. his motherland can offer." While we're at it, let's look at another flaw: Ustinov received all the p. and c. that Moscow did offer, not all that it could have offered.

Editors should also keep an eye out for old proverbs served up as fresh dressing for what's supposed to be news. Here's how a network anchor recently began a story:

Haste makes waste, as the saying goes. . . .

Haste does make waste, and it also makes for reliance on clichés. Hundreds of years ago, that line was good, so good that it became popular. And its popularity is what has turned it into a cliché. Air time is too valuable to squander on clichés. As the saying goes, *"Time is money."*

The writer who relied on "Haste makes waste" might not even regard that as a cliché. Differences of opinion on what constitutes a cliché are the subject of a verse printed by Roy Copperud in his *American Usage and Style: The Consensus:*

> If you scorn what is trite
> I warn you, go slow
> For one man's cliché
> Is another's *bon mot.*

With the approach of April 15, dedicated wordwatchers had better keep a sharp watch for clichés that tax us all. One that's recycled annually is T. S. Eliot's line from *The Waste Land:* "April is the cruelest month." Even as you read this advisory from WordWatching Central, a newscaster somewhere is probably delivering that line as though it were newly born. Instead, at the age of 65, after a life of overwork, it deserves retirement, not with a bang but a whimper (another Eliot line that deserves a long rest). So do variations: "For the Chicago Cubs, September has become the cruelest month."

Another certainty with the advent of April is that many newscasters will work into a story or a lead-in Ben Franklin's wrinkled adage: "Nothing is certain but death and taxes." Not to mention clichés. But as Prof. Ted Peterson wrote to me recently: "If you must perpetrate a cliché, rework it for freshness. For instance: When a veterinarian removed the bladder from a cat, he remarked, 'Just a case of letting the bag out of the cat.' Get the idea?"

Gotcha.

Ms. Guidance

At the risk of being ex*Communicator*ed, at least from this issue on women and minorities, I want to say that I'm what you might call a *Ms.*ogynist: I don't like "Ms." I don't mean I dislike Mss. (or whatever they call themselves) personally. I just dislike the courtesy title "Ms.": I don't write it, I don't say it, I don't hear it. Network newscasters use it rarely, perhaps, in part, because of misgivings over the buzz-saw sound: "Miz." In workshops and classrooms, though, I'm often asked about

"Ms." In reply, I can do no better than quote Trevor Fishlock who wrote about "Ms." in the *Times* of London:

"It is artificial, ugly, silly, means nothing and is rotten English. It is a faddish, middle-class plaything, and far from disguising the marital status of women, as is claimed, it draws attention to it. It is a vanity." Fishlock ended his 1980 essay by saying, "There is an important battle to be fought for all women, not just a tiny elite." But, he said, "Ms. is one of the excesses of the revolution and should be junked." The *Times* of London *has* junked it. And many U.S. publications also have junked it. The author Willard R. Espy says "Ms." will probably last longer in junk mail than anywhere else.

According to a recent survey of copy chiefs of the top U.S. newspapers and magazines, "Ms." is on its—or her—way out. Three years ago, the annual survey found that "Ms." was acceptable to 57.3 percent of those surveyed. But the new survey says only 28.4 percent of the 200 respondents would let it stand in copy; 76.1 percent would change or omit it. The survey, conducted by Richard L. Tobin, who teaches journalism at Indiana University, was published in the April, 1985 issue of *Quill*.

The A.P. and U.P.I. stylebooks advise using "Ms." only if the woman prefers it. The *New York Times Manual of Style and Usage,* published in 1976, was more restrictive: "As an honorific, use it only in quoted matter, in letters to the editor and in news articles, in passages discussing the term itself."

But the *New York Times* recently reversed itself. An Editors' Note in mid-1986 said: "Beginning today, The *New York Times* will use 'Ms.' as an honorific in its news and editorial columns. Until now, 'Ms.' had not been used because of the belief that it had not passed sufficiently into the language to be accepted as common usage. The *Times* now believes that 'Ms.' has become a part of the language and is changing its policy. The *Times* will continue to use 'Miss' or 'Mrs.' when it knows the marital status of a woman in the news, unless she prefers 'Ms.' 'Ms.' will also be used when a woman's marital status is not known, or when a married woman wishes to use it with her prior name in professional or private life." That prompted Gloria Steinem to express gratitude that she'd no longer be referred to as "Miss Steinem of Ms. magazine." Whatever the policy of publications, few people use "Ms." as a spoken form of address. Or say it at all.

Some of the copy chiefs who replied to the survey quoted in *Quill* said their newsrooms had dropped all courtesy titles, including "Mr.,"

"Mrs." and "Miss," except for certain types of stories, like obits and engagements. In writing for broadcast, I use "Mr." in a second or subsequent reference to the U.S. President. In a second mention of a woman in a story, I use her title, if any, or I refer to her as "Miss" or "Mrs."

I'm confused by a word I've been reading and hearing more often: "arguably." When the attempted murder trial of Claus von Bülow was moved to Providence, R.I., a network correspondent said, "Newport has lost what is arguably the socialite trial of the century." A leading dictionary, *Webster's New World,* gives only one definition for "arguably": "as can be supported by argument." My favorite desk dictionary, *American Heritage,* defines "arguable" as "open to argument." The newsman probably used "arguably" to mean, "I think this may be 'the' trial of the century, but I can't say so with certainty." He certainly doesn't have the time or resources to pin it down; in fact, it's an assertion not susceptible of proof, so no one can pin it down. For a casual listener, the newsman *is* calling it "the" trial of the century. I surmise that few listeners catch the "arguably," and fewer still realize it's used as an escape hatch.

The correspondent's assertion also gets another argument: Is the von Bülow trial "bigger" than the sensational trial of Harry K. Thaw, the socialite who murdered architect Stanford White because of his affair with Thaw's wife, Evelyn Nesbitt Thaw (made into a movie, "Girl in the Red Velvet Swing")? "Bigger" than Gloria Vanderbilt's scandalous custody trial? "Bigger" than the stock fraud trial of socialite Richard Whitney, a former president of the New York Stock Exchange sent to Sing Sing? Anyway, even if the von Bülow trial is not the "biggest," whatever that might mean, it's big enough. And the correspondent needn't embroider it.

As Einstein put it, "If you are out to describe the truth, leave elegance to the tailor."

World's Biggest Snow Cone

Some newspapers run children's pages with a picture-puzzle that asks, "How many mistakes can you find?" So we're going to challenge grown-ups with a faulty word picture: How many mistakes can *you* find?

> Five years ago today, with unprecedented fury, Mount Saint
> Helens erupted, decimating 150 square miles of lush green forest.

That's the lead of a story broadcast recently by a TV network reporter. She didn't sign an organ donor card to allow this recital, but she should be pleased that she's contributing to the advancement of newswriting.

We can't tell from her lead whether she meant that the fury was unprecedented for Mount St. Helens or for all volcanoes everywhere. In either case, she was wrong.

The eruption that was most destructive in recent times was that of Krakatoa in 1883. The volcano, in Indonesia, generated tidal waves that killed 36,000 people. "The enormous discharge threw into the air nearly five cubic miles of rock fragments," says the *Encyclopaedia Britannica,* "and the fine dust [caused] spectacular red sunsets all over the world through the following year."

But the biggest blowup in modern times was that of Tambora, also in Indonesia. Its eruption in 1815 disgorged more than seven cubic miles of material, according to the U.S. Geological Survey; Mount St. Helens spewed less than one cubic mile. And the USGS says the 1980 eruption was not even Mount St. Helens' biggest.

The reporter would have been on safe ground if she had just told her story without straining, if she had not tried to punch it up with *unprecedented.* When an editor sees that word, it should set off a mental alarm. So should other absolutes and superlatives: *first, biggest, oldest, fastest, slowest, richest* and other *est* words. An editor should ask: How do we know this is the *first?* How do we know this is the world's *biggest* snow cone? And even if we're satisfied that it is, does its *first*-ness make it worth reporting? If we can't confirm it on our own, are we attributing it properly?

And how do we know this is the world's *thickest* waffle? Or this is the *first* time anyone has hijacked a bandwagon? Is there a central registry that has been keeping track of everything everywhere forever—accurately? (One of the exceptions: sports, where statisticians seem to record even the glove size of batboys.)

A reporter on the scene could not know or easily obtain the history of volcanoes (unless he's a closet volcanologist). Even the people I spoke with at the Geological Survey had to dig it out and call me back. But a prudent reporter will not trot out *unique, unprecedented, unparalleled, unsurpassed,* or any other such word without knowing that it's true—*and* worth mentioning.

Another problem with the reporter's lead: She misused "decimate." It originally meant to kill every tenth person but now is sometimes used to mean the destruction of a large part of a group. But even a volcano cannot "decimate" trees, only people. The reporter might have meant "devastate." (I've also heard a newscaster tell of a building in Beirut that had been "decimated." And a network correspondent spoke of an effort in Washington to "decimate" a plan.)

By starting the volcano story with "Five years ago today," the reporter deprived the anchor of the anniversary angle for the lead-in. A correspondent in the field (or forest) should ordinarily start a story with what will become the second sentence. She does that by picking up from—or playing off—the anchor's lead-in. That might seem like quite a trick, because the anchor's lead-in is usually written only after the correspondent's piece has been put into the lineup.

One way to see to it that the lead-in and the script dovetail, says Norman Glubok, a CBS News producer, is for the correspondent to submit, with her script, a proposed anchor lead-in. Once the correspondent thinks through what her story is all about, she'll have an idea for the lead-in. That'll give her a head start on writing her script. However the correspondent starts, she should leave some key material for the anchor to introduce the piece. If the story is about the governor, a correspondent can expect the anchor to mention "Governor Bennett" in the lead-in. So the correspondent can start her script with "the governor," skipping his name. The correspondent should take care that she leave the anchor a strong fact or two for the lead-in. In most cases, she should omit them from her script. Otherwise, when the piece is broadcast, she'll be the one who'll sound repetitious.

For the volcano story, my suggested anchor lead-in—based on hearing the whole story—would be: "Mount Saint Helens erupted five years ago today, but nearby residents are, in a sense, still feeling aftershocks. Jane Jones has the story in Washington state."

Another point: The first sentence in the script that was broadcast could have been improved by changing the participle *decimating* to a finite verb, one with a tense, and by using only one adjective: "The volcano blew up with great fury—and destroyed 150 square miles of forest." That's shorter, sharper, stronger.

Speaking of blowups (and if you like that transition, you'd better try to raise your standards), news director Dick Nelson of WLOS-TV, Asheville, N.C., has written to ask about my reference to a story on the blowup by the so-called subway vigilante Bernhard Goetz. Dick wants to know whether it's acceptable to call Goetz a vigilante.

"Vigilante" was first used more than 100 years ago to refer to a member of a "vigilance committee." The committees were formed, mostly in the South and West, to see that criminals were punished. Often, punishment was inflicted by members themselves, occasionally on suspects who were blameless. One case of frontier justice administered by vigilantes was reported in Denver's *Rocky Mountain News* on May 31, 1862: "The vigys pointed to an empty saddle and gave him just 10 minutes to skedaddle." *A Dictionary of Americanisms* by Mitford M. Mathews also offers examples showing "vigilante" has been used in this century. And in recent years I've seen it used to describe people who take the law into their hands.

I'm not keen about writing *subway vigilante* (when I used it in a column, I was only quoting someone), but I think it's acceptable for our purposes—at least in this case. The term has been widely applied to him, so people know in an instant who he is and what he did. It's not as though we were declaring him guilty; he acknowledges being a vigilante. I'd precede that label with *so-called* to avoid using a label that some people regard as negative, the kind that we shouldn't be fastening onto anyone. By using the shorthand device *subway vigilante,* we can capture an event that would otherwise take many words to describe. Let's try it without the short cut: "The man who shot four teenagers in a New York City subway train, Bernhard Goetz, was arraigned today and pleaded not guilty. He says the teens were threatening him." Now, availing ourselves of our shorthand, let's set the scene swiftly: "The so-called subway vigilante, Bernhard Goetz, has pleaded not guilty."

I myself have been insufficiently vigilant. Alan Cohn of WFAS-AM and FM, White Plains, N.Y., has pointed out my incorrect reference to Claus von Bülow's "murder trial." Von Bülow was tried for *attempted* murder. I plead guilty.

13

BLOOPERS AND BLUNDERS, BITS AND BITES

Some newspeople have clearly shown they deserve network recognition on prime time—for their bloopers and blunders:

> In the Bronx this morning, a guilty conviction.

WordWatcher's verdict: guilty of aggravated redundancy.

> This fellow . . .did the exact same work in the exact same shop. . . .

Verdict: the same.

> Police say the fireman was knocked from an aerial ladder oy a hose when he fell to the ground.

Huh?

> Pan Am will continue to service its other routes.

Correct: "Pan Am will still *serve* its other routes." A mechanic *services* a plane; a boar *services* a sow.

Reporting from Geneva on the arms control talks several hours after Chernenko's death, a correspondent said:

> The new negotiations are expected to last for years. In any event, Chernenko would have been unlikely to live to see the end.

Unlikely? He didn't even live till the newscast. At least, the newsman didn't say Chernenko's death was a turning point in his life.

> Communist forces entered the city from six different directions.

All directions are different, so *different* is superfluous. In another newscast:

> They make speeches in seven different languages.

Same problem. And this:

> Four explosions in three different parts of Belgium. . . .

No different.

> For the second time in the past four days, federal authorities are landing a knockout blow on a local outlaw motorcycle gang.

If the first blow had been a knockout, there'd be no need for another knockout. Further, the opening phrase—"For the second time in the past four days"—delays the action and diminishes its newsiness. If the writer had room, he might have said later, "It was the second raid in four days." The writer also mentioned "four *separate* indictments." No, he didn't say the feds arrested "13 separate people."

> The rock group Wham! [has started] their history-making tour of China.

First, the collective noun "group" takes the singular, so "their" should be "its." No one, not even Wham!, enters history books by whim. News-writers do not determine who "makes history"; historians do. (So do commissars—in loose-leaf history books.) I don't want to slam Wham!, but I doubt that it'll make even a footnote, except in a history of rock or a history of hype.

> [Edgar Degas] will be 150 years old this year.

No matter what the anchor meant to say, that sentence would make the French painter the oldest master. The anchor was wrong on two counts. Degas was born in 1834, so 1985 was the 151st anniversary of his birth. He died in 1917, so he could not be 151—or 150.

> There was even a new American record established in Potsdam today.

A record set today *is* new, so *new record* is redundant.

> Firemen tonight called to the scene of. . . .

By omitting *were* before *called,* this incomplete sentence sounds as though firemen responded to the fire by phone. Delete *the scene of.*

> It's May 29th, if you're just getting up.

If I've been up for an hour, what's the date?

> A 44-year-old mother and nurse was found stabbed to death by
> her daughter.

Did the daughter commit the crime or discover it? Sharp-eyed Emerson
Stone has found another ambiguity (*triguity*?) in *by*, which means "next
to"; he asks whether the writer meant mother and daughter were found
side by side. In fact, the daughter found the body. The lead should not
have compounded the confusion by identifying the victim as both
mother and nurse. Nor should her age have preceded what happened to
her. Age is not more important than everything else in the story. Age is
not exciting; everyone has an age. I'd use her age but later. Better: "A
nurse has been found stabbed to death in her home. Her daughter found
the body. . . ."

> Emotions run so high in these games, where hopes soar one
> minute and are dashed the next. _____ _____ has been
> on this emotional roller coaster with the Villanova fans. What's
> the mood in Lexington, _____ , or need I ask?

The whole lead-in is questionable. Is the anchor sure that's Lexington?
The only place I know of that's awash in so much emotion is Clichéville.

A story about the arrest of a suspect in a fire that killed seven persons:

> His name is 18-year-old Walter Craig.

Imagine squeezing all that onto a nameplate.

> It happened last night at 13th and Locust in City Center, Phila-
> delphia. A fight between a pair of transvestites ended in death for
> one and arrest for the other.

Transvestites may pair up, but they don't come in pairs. Besides, the lead
is weak. Avoid starting a story with the indefinite pronoun "it." I'm not
saying "never." (Almost never do I say "never.") And I wouldn't use "last
night" or "yesterday" in a first sentence. Another fault: The only verb in
the second sentence is "ended," a poor choice in dealing with a killing. A
transvestite is someone who dresses in the garb of the opposite sex, so in a
story like this, the sex must be specified. Better: "Two male transvestites
started quarreling in City Center, Philadelphia, and one of them was
stabbed to death. The other one has been charged with murder. The fight
occurred last night at 13th and Locust. . . ."

In a story about the President's impending visit to Bitburg, West Germany, a newscaster said a certain development had "reawakened the furor." For all we could tell, he might have spelled it. "Führer." If the writer had read his copy aloud carefully before he broadcast it, he might have caught the unfortunate ambiguity. Another newsman recently referred to a high-powered broadcaster as a "broadcasting magnate." That made me think of a magnet used in a speaker. These cases of hearing something other than what the newscaster meant should remind us of the risk in using homophones, words that sound the same but whose meanings differ. Other words to watch for—and listen for—in broadcast copy:

aides/aids/AIDS	heroin/heroine
bare/bear	hoard/horde
brake/break	mass of/massive
breadth/breath	miner/minor
cache/cash	passed/past
cite/sight/site	plain/plane
complement/compliment	rain/reign/rein
council/consul/counsel	raise/raze
deceased/diseased	road/rode/rowed
defuse/diffuse	symbol/cymbal
farewell/ fare well	their/there/they're
for/fore/four	threw/through
formally/formerly	to/too/two
hear/here	wholly/holy/holey

Those are just a few of the many homophones lurking in our keyboards, but they're enough to remind us of all the double meanings we have to guard against. Not that we can't use any of those words; we have to. We just have to keep in mind that what makes sense to the eye can cause double trouble for the ear. An amusing example of the confusion caused by homophones occurs in a skit by the comic Benny Hill. Two workmen drag sacks of telephones into a room and put them on a table. Hill, performing with a small band, snaps impatiently, "I told you, two *sax*ophones!"

And please don't call Liberace "a magnetic Pole."

Whether we're dodging homophones or striving for unambiguous clarity in putting words together, we can benefit from a rule offered by Richard D. Yoakam and Charles F. Cremer in their book, *ENG: Television News and the New Technology:*

> You should write not only so that the news item can be understood, but also so that the item cannot be misunderstood.

Searching for Lightning

"An unemployed poet," an anchor said on the air recently, "held a two-hour siege at the altar of St. Patrick's Cathedral in New York last night."

An *un*employed poet? Have you ever heard of anyone employed at writing poetry? (As the poet Robert Graves once told a banker, "There's no money in poetry—and no poetry in money.") And have you ever heard of one man, particularly a poet, laying siege to anything, especially when he's on the inside?

A siege, according to any old dictionary, or any new one, is "the surrounding and blocking of a town or fortress by an army bent on capturing it." By extension, police can lay siege to a building. The intruder in the cathedral, pretending to have a bomb, did take control of the altar and hold off police. But no matter what he did, he did not lay siege to the altar or the cathedral. And he certainly didn't "hold" a siege. One can hold a grudge, or an audience, or a winning hand, but no number of people, even an army, can "hold" a siege. Police probably had *besieged* him (and *beseeched* him), so, chances are, he himself was *under* siege. Whatever was happening, he was too occupied to commit any new rhymes.

If only the anchor or someone on the script assembly line had checked a dictionary for *siege,* he would have seen that the word in the script was being misused.

Handy thing, a dictionary. If we just take a moment to use it, it can often keep us out of trouble. I usually turn first to my *American Heritage* (first edition). It's liftable and occasionally uplifting. Its Usage Panel of writers, editors and educators provides guidance in notes on hundreds of words. Among them, for example, is a note on "behalf." When should we say "*in* behalf of someone"? And when "*on* behalf"? The dictionary also carries synonyms for many words, spelling out nuances of words that may seem similar; for instance, *continual, continuous, constant, ceaseless, incessant, perpetual, eternal, perennial, interminable.*

For a larger collection of synonyms, newsrooms need a good thesaurus. The one I find most helpful is *Roget's International* (Harper & Row). Other thesauruses named Roget are not so good; likewise, *Webster's New International*—the 2nd edition is best—is not to be confused with any Webster's, a name available to anyone.

Another reference book that I find valuable is *American Usage and Style: The Consensus* (Van Nostrand Reinhold) by Roy Copperud. An expert himself, he offers comments of other experts on disputed points and gives his own views.

When I can't find what I'm looking for in Copperud's book, or if I want a second—or third—opinion, or if I can't find anyone who agrees with me, I turn to one of the other leading guides on usage. (See list in Appendix A.)

The *Hotline Handbook* is based on a phone-in grammar service sponsored by the University of Arkansas at Little Rock. This campus doesn't have a football team, but a member of the English faculty will tackle any question on usage, free. All you have to do is phone (501) 569-3162. An expert is on hand from 8 a.m. to noon, Central time, sometimes all day, Monday through Friday.

One hotline that's easy to remember is at York College in Queens, N.Y.: (718) REWRITE. Someone there fields questions from 1 p.m. to 4 p.m., Eastern time, Monday through Friday.

A West Coast hotline is staffed near Los Angeles by Moorpark College: (805) 529-2321, 8 a.m. to noon, Pacific time, Monday through Friday, September through June. The founder of the hotline, Michael Strumpf, has written a book (with Auriel Douglas), *Painless, Perfect Grammar: Tips from the Grammar Hotline.*

The hotbed of hotlines, with three grammar services, is Cincinnati. More than 25 other grammar hotlines—listed in the back of the book—have sprung up across this country and Canada. And one of the services even accepts collect calls. (See Appendix B.)

A writer can't pick up a phone every time he's stumped, but he can pick up a usage book. The thinnest work on usage I've run across is the *Goof/Proofer*. It runs 44 pages, and its pages are small enough (3½″ x 5½″) to fit in a shirt pocket. It focuses on two dozen of the most common goofs, some we all hear: misuses of *I, me, myself* and other personal pronouns; misuse of *like;* confusion of *good* and *well;* misuse of *and* after *try* [as in "I'll try and go"]; confusion of *fewer* and *less;* confusion of *can* and *may;* use of verbs and pronouns that don't agree in number with their subjects. The introduction recommends that the reader concentrate on getting rid of just one of these goofs every week.

Goof/Proofer also lists more than 300 homonyms. Most homonyms are also homophones, words that sound the same but have different meanings; homophones are also *spelled* differently. Any broadcaster can benefit from a reminder that when he delivers one word, a listener may hear another word.

A copy of *Goof/Proofer,* prepared by Stephen J. Manhard, can be obtained for $2 postpaid from SPELL (Society for the Preservation of English Language and Literature), 365 First St., Los Altos, Calif. 94022. Anyone who joins the non-profit organization can get a copy free. And anyone who reads this far is entitled to a small reward, an observation by Mark Twain:

> The difference between the almost right word and the right word is really a large matter—'tis the difference between the lightning bug and the lightning.

One of the not-at-all-right words for the first sentence of a story is *continues.* The reason: It tells the listener that something that was going on is still going on, certainly not a newsy, interesting, inviting way to start a story. *Continues* lacks motion, which is especially desirable for the start of a story. Action verbs make sentences move, but *continues* is unmoving. Recently, I heard this lifeless lead on the air:

> The stalemate in Beirut *continues.* Shiite terrorists *continue* to hold some 40 American hostages, and the terrorists *continue* to demand freedom for some 700 Moslems held in northern Israel. . . .

Three *continues* in seven seconds! Dull, duller, dullissimo. The writer should have searched for the latest development or taken a new approach and led with that. Almost any verb would be preferable to *continues.* For a subsequent sentence, *continues* may, just may, be acceptable, but for the crucial first sentence, it's inapt. So let offenders be warned about their thoughtless habit: It should be discontinued.

And for those who've made it this far, we're offering another bonus, more of what Twain said about "the right word":

"A powerful agent is the right word; it lights the reader's way and makes it plain. A close approximation to it will answer, and much traveling is done in a well-enough fashion by its help, but we do not welcome it and rejoice in it as we do when *the* right word blazes out on us. Whenever we come upon one of these intensely right words in a book or a newspaper, the resulting effect is physical as well as spiritual, and electrically prompt. It tingles exquisitely around through the walls of the mouth and tastes as tart and crisp and good as the autumn butter that creams the sumac berry."

Not by the Numbers

Odds and ends, dribs and drabs, bits and bites from broadcasts:

Indeed, Europe is said to have larger banks but fewer of them.
We have more banks but they are smaller than those in Europe.

That second sentence is a funhouse mirror of the first, which indicates a lack of due reflection. The item is reminiscent of a parody of T.S. Eliot: "As we get older, we do not get any younger."

As for "we," whenever I hear a newscaster use it, I wonder whether he's referring to himself, his station or his nation. The only people with the right to use "we," according to Mark Twain, are presidents, editors and people with tapeworms. (And perhaps pregnant women.)

Twenty-seven people are dead, 43 injured, the result of a bus accident in Mexico. Police say the crowded bus blew a tire and went spinning off a highway 150 miles west of Mexico City. The bus crashed at the bottom of a gorge.

Stories like this that start with numbers leave me numb. Before I hear the final score, my mind needs a warm-up. Further, any form of *to be* is weak, so saying people *are* dead is lifeless. The accident was dramatic, but the only verb in the first sentence, *are*, lacks ardor. Also, by putting the place-name last, the writer leaves the listener wondering whether the accident occurred in his area or in his country; he doesn't find out until the sentence ends. That's too late.

Another drawback: After the newscaster gave us the outcome in his first breath, the sentence rolled downhill. A writer can create a strong sentence by building up to the most important point, not down from it. This rewrite is better: "A bus in Mexico blew a tire, spun off a highway and plunged into a gorge. Twenty-seven people were killed. Forty-three were hurt."

More than 40 people were injured today when a couple of bombs exploded aboard a truck transporting military explosives through Oklahoma. _____ _____ reports it could have been much worse.

Like the previous story, this anchor lead-in starts with a number and proceeds in reverse chronological order. Then it tells us what caused the casualties and where. Also undesirable: He talks about *explosives* that *exploded.* The story would convey more impact by starting with the most vivid aspect and using a vigorous verb: "A truck carrying military explosives in Oklahoma blew up today, and more than 40 people were hurt."

The newscaster's intro to the correspondent says *it could have been much worse,* which is inane, obvious and adds nothing. After just about any accident, someone could write that it might have been much worse. Or, as a newscaster said recently after another accident, it "did not have to happen."

Another newscaster took this approach to the same explosion:

> There's now a crater 30 feet wide and 18 feet deep on a highway near the town of Checotah in eastern Oklahoma. It was created today when a car going the wrong way on an entrance ramp hit a military truck carrying ten bombs. Some of them detonated. . . .

Detonated, mind you, not *blew up.* Maybe that newscaster likes Latin-root words because he was once an altar boy. Almost any lead that starts with *There is* or *It is,* both dead phrases, should be altered. Further, the writer backed into the story. But it could have been worse, but not much.

> According to court documents, Whitworth relayed his information to Walker in Hong Kong when the carrier pulled in for a port visit.

The most important element in the sentence is the circumstances of the alleged transfer. But in the middle of the sentence, "Hong Kong" is passed over quickly, so it lacks importance. The key facts in the news item could have been highlighted by progressing chronologically and building up to the main idea: "According to court documents, Whitworth gave Walker the information when the carrier visited Hong Kong." (With Walker now convicted of running a spy ring for Moscow, will he be labeled *Johnnie Walker, Red?*)

> There's new concern this week about an old air-safety problem, near-misses in the sky.

If two planes nearly miss but don't miss, they collide. If they nearly collide, they've had a near-collision, not a "near-miss." Besides steering clear of "near-miss," I also avoid "mid-air." If you write that two planes collided over the Grand Canyon, the *over* conveys the idea that the collision occurred in the air, not on the ground. I also keep away from the murky "near-panic" and "near-riot." The law says a riot is a violent disturbance by three or more persons. Is a "near-riot" a ruckus caused by *two* persons? As for "near-miss," isn't that a bride who was almost jilted?

Have you ever been bothered by airline people's use of English? When I make a flight reservation and the agent recaps my itinerary, she often tells me I'll be "arriving *into*" a certain airport. Sounds scary. When I board a plane, a flight attendant often says the plane will be taking off "momentarily." Where I come from, "momentarily" means "for a moment," not "in a moment." And the attendant explains the safety features, demonstrates the oxygen mask and points out the elastic tabs "on either side." That, too, is disquieting, because "either" means "one or the other," not "both." Mary P. Clunis says she was sitting in a plane when the pilot said over the P.A. that this would be his last flight. Gulp! I'm also a bit troubled when I hear a flight attendant say, "We'll be on the ground shortly." (It reminds me of a sailor who, in a storm, offers mock reassurance to his shipmates: "We're only two miles from land—straight down.") And I also heard a attendant say recently, "If you're terminating in Chicago. . . ." Many terminators have populated Chicago (or de-populated it), but should airlines be encouraging that sort of thing? Maybe they could ease my anxiety by brushing up on their English. As the columnist William Safire says, rephrasing Lord Nelson at Trafalgar, "English expects all of us to do our duty."

And why do airline personnel use such fancy language? This I heard the other day: "The fasten-seatbelt sign is still *illuminated*"? Five syllables when one would do the job: *on.*

You can see another example of airlinespeak on signs at Nashville airport:

> The airlines have implemented enhanced security procedures designed for the protection of customers and employees. We regret any inconvenience you may experience as a result of increased security surveillance.

That high-flown jargon can easily be brought down to earth: "We're taking stronger steps to protect you. If you're inconvenienced, we're sorry." This revision may not be worthy of chiseling in marble, but at least it's only 12 words; the original is 29 words. Halving the word-count and simplifying the language helps to make the message clearer, crisper and comprehensible.

Another airline abomination but one that can't be shortened: "de-plane," as in "Passengers will de-plane through the front exit."

> United Airlines had better luck getting planes into the air today than it did yesterday. . . .

That story about the pilots' strike troubles me because it suggests that the airline puts planes into the sky through luck.

> Today begins a special time for Polish-Americans, a time to cele-brate their culture as part of Polish-American Heritage Month.

Today begins? The *event* begins. Today the beguine can begin, and the beguine can begin the day, but *today* can't begin anything. Let's hope the writer doesn't think "Voice-check" is General Jaruzelski's first name.

14

WRITING THAT NEEDS RIGHTING

"Don't knock the weather; nine-tenths of the people couldn't start
a conversation if it didn't change once in a while."

FRANK MC KINNEY (KIN) HUBBARD

Start a *conversation?* If it weren't for the weather, I couldn't even start
this column. So I don't knock the weather, certainly not in the weather
issue; that leaves me with a few extra knocks for weathercasters and
newscasters. But Ed Bliss says an editor should be hard on copy, not on
people, so I'll edit myself and say the knocks are for weather *copy.*

The worse the weather, it often seems, the worse the copy. Instead of
telling a dramatic story in a simple, sober style, too many writers shift
their typewriters into overwrite.But he who overwrites, undermines. In
contrast, read the powerful but simple account of the biggest story ever.
Here's how one of the first Hebrew rewritemen handled the lead: "In the
beginning, God created the heaven(s) and the earth." Period. Great
event, simple words, short sentence, strong impact.

One of the most objectionable aspects of much weather coverage is
what the 19th century British critic John Ruskin called the "pathetic
fallacy." When a writer ascribes human characteristics, motivation, or
behavior to inanimate objects, animals or natural phenomena, Ruskin
said he commits a "pathetic fallacy." Some poets have made this
approach, known as anthropomorphism, work—*the cruel sea, smiling
skies, laughing waters*—but in broadcast scripts, it's usually inappro-
priate or overdone. Here are some recent broadcast examples:

Residents are also waiting, waiting for the fickle but dangerous
Hurricane Elena to make up her mind.

"Fickle"? "Make up her *mind*"? Nonsense. No storm, even one with a
name, has a mind to make up, so it can't be fickle. Also: in "fickle but

dangerous," *but* is wrong; Elena's changeability helps make it dangerous. So *but* should be *and*. And "fickle" should be canned.

> Hurricane Nele has apparently decided not to visit Hawaii.

If that Nele had any sense, she would have parked between a pineapple plantation and a macadamia grove.

> Hurricane Gloria is still 550 miles out in the Atlantic, but already it's drawing a bead on the Outer Banks of North Carolina.

"Drawing a bead"? Glorioski.

> Hurricane Gloria first dropped anchor and came ashore overnight across the unprotected Outer Bank islands of North Carolina, almost a worst-possible-case scenario.

When a ship drops anchor, it can't sail away without weighing anchor. So how could a storm "drop anchor" and keep on going? "Worst-possible-case scenario" seems to be an effort to pump up "worst-case scenario," which is bureaucratic jargon. But the sly "almost" says it's not the worst. The weather-beaten "scenario" is best left for Washington and Hollywood.

> Her 130-mile-an-hour winds are on a collision course with the nation's most populated corridor, on the Eastern seaboard.

A car can hit a tree, but they can't collide. Only moving objects collide.

> A mammoth hurricane in size and scope, but not the killer hurricane forecasters feared it might become.

"Mammoth" describes its size, so using "size" adds nothing. If the writer used "scope" to mean "the area covered by an activity," as the dictionary defines it, then "mammoth" should cover it. Better: "The hurricane is mammoth but not so mighty as forecasters had feared."

> Her threat was more menacing than her power.

"Threat" = "menace," so the sentence is windy double-talk.

> Those killer tornadoes, reminders that just because records are set doesn't mean the news is good.

Who needs to be reminded that a record might relate to news that's bad? But the writer needs to be reminded that there's no such thing as a "killer tornado." Or a "killer cyclone" (though sci-fi has "killer clones."). No storm ever set out with malice aforethought or a hit list. Storms have the means to kill, but no minds, no motives. Storms do kill, but that doesn't make them "killer storms." Likewise, there is no such thing as a "killer wind," "killer hurricane," "killer typhoon" or, as a network newscaster said, a "killer volcano." Just killjoys, killer whales and Kilkenny cats.

> Vice President Bush will visit the strickened area to let the people of this state know the Administration's concern for their plight.

"Strickened"?

> Officials along the Mississippi and Alabama coasts are trying to convince residents in the danger area to leave their homes.

The writer has mistaken "convince" for "persuade." You *convince* someone *that* he should leave or *convince* him *of* the need to leave. But you *persuade* him *to* leave.

> As we said earlier, many people, thousands, have been evacu-ated, and, as we said earlier, the hotels also have been closed down. Now this is the first time in the history of Atlantic City that something like that has happened. Many schools are closed today, and, as we said. . . .

If you've already said it, why say you've said it? And why keep saying you've said it? Why, why, why?

> "The path that it's taking now is reminiscent of the storms that go way back in time to 1938 or so, the one that would affect central Long Island and southern New England. If it had gone maybe farther east, it would have missed some of those areas. But it's just hugging the coast now until it does that."

That's what the man said, but what did he say?

> "Those kind of rains can be moving all the way up to northern New England."

Make it *kinds.*

"Words still count with me," the writer E. B. White often said. And his recent death recalls words of his that still count with writers, particularly those in Strunk and White's *The Elements of Style.* Even a quick rundown of the handbook's topic headings is refreshing:

   — Use the active voice

   — Put statements in positive form

— Use definite, specific, concrete language
— Avoid a succession of loose sentences
— Express co-ordinate ideas in similar form
— Keep related words together
— Place the emphatic words of a sentence at the end
— Place yourself in the background
— Write in a way that comes naturally
— Write with nouns and verbs
— Revise and rewrite
— Avoid the use of qualifiers
— Avoid fancy words
— Do not inject opinion
— Use figures of speech sparingly
— Do not take short cuts at the cost of clarity
— Avoid foreign languages
— Prefer the standard to the offbeat

And four topic headings that are especially apt for the broadcasters quoted in this column:

— Be clear
— Do not overwrite
— Do not overstate
— Omit needless words

Once we grasp those points, we'll have the elements of style.

Going Overboard

We often write too fast, think too slow, or know too little. How else could some of these snippets find their way onto the air?

He's a Soviet seaman who twice jumped ship near New Orleans.

He jumped overboard, so the best way to put it is, "He jumped *off* his ship." *Jump ship* is slang for "desert." It also means to go ashore without permission. Some sailors, though, go ashore *with* permission, then *jump ship.*

Ridge Shannon of Shawnee Mission, Kansas, tells me he heard one news report that the Soviet seaman had "*literally* jumped ship." In almost all cases, *literally* adds nothing to a sentence—except length. And *literally* should not be confused with *figuratively*. F'rinstance: "He *literally* hit the ceiling." He hit it *figuratively*, unless you're writing about Michael Jordan or Michelangelo.

How about *virtually?* Ridge asks. Many people use it to mean *almost*, but some careful writers use it only to mean "in effect although not in fact." An assistant news director filling in for his boss, who's on indefinite leave, is *virtually* the N.D.

> The American Museum of Folk Art is actually holding a contest for the best quilt in America. . . .

Without *actually*, the sentence means the same. *Literally.*

> The devastation was so widespread and communications so bad that only tonight did it become clear that this is a very major disaster. . . .

"*Very* major" is a solecism; an intensifier (*very*) cannot be used with a comparative. Writers should use intensifiers—reinforcing terms like *very, absolutely, certainly, definitely, quite*—seldom. If you choose the right adjectives and adverbs, you don't need intensifiers. *Disaster* implies large-scale destruction and death. Has there ever been a *minor* disaster?

On the very day the *New York Times* was reporting a major initiative, a major undertaking, a major speech, two major changes, a major operation and a major cause, according to Bill Bryson in *The Penguin Dictionary of Troublesome Words,* the *Times* of London was reporting a major scandal, a major change, two major improvements, two major steps, a major proposal, a major source of profits and a major refurbishment. Bryson, a *Times* of London editor—born and educated in Iowa—says:

> *Major,* it seems, has become a major word. Generally imprecise, frequently fatuous and always grossly overworked, it is in almost every instance better replaced by a more expressive term.

As far as I'm concerned, and I *am* concerned, that's a major pronounce-ment. *Really.*

> It is only possible to understand the enormity of what happened here by taking one case, one heartbreaking case at a time.

Enormity = great wickedness. The writer meant *enormousness;* he could have used *scope, extent,* or perhaps *immensity.*

Hospitals were filled to capacity.

A redundancy. Fortunately, the writer didn't say some patients were "in guarded condition." *Guarded* = cautious; the hospital's forecast can be *guarded*. A patient can be in guarded condition only when he's a prisoner.

Another term we shouldn't borrow, one used by police reporters after an accident: "The two boys were *treated and released.*" If they had been hospitalized, we would say so. I've never heard of anyone's being "treated and hospitalized." If you say the boys were treated, that implies they were released. (The comedian George Carlin complains that whenever he's treated, he's detained.)

> The *final completion* of I-95 to the airport is a major step in making Philadelphia a modern city.

Do you think the perpetrator of that redundancy should be finalized?

> The three armed gunmen who have been holding court officials as hostages left the building and are at a nearby airport.

Armed gunmen should be *dis*armed.

> The F.B.I. says that he's been given a safe haven in Cuba, along with a part of the stolen loot.

Loot = stolen goods. A keen wordwatcher, Emerson Stone of CBS News, recalls another odd redundancy, a superfluous suffix. A computer expert told him that her company had simplified its computer's keyboard, and she added: "We wanted to eliminate jargonese."

> The stock market's been flying higher for months, breaking one new record after another and racking up profits for investors big and small of 201 billion dollars.

New record is an old redundancy. The total value of all Big Board stocks traded last year was 970 billion, but only an investor himself knows whether his sale of stock is profitable. If he sells for less than he paid, he's not racking up profits. The reporter did not specify how many days were needed to reach that "201 billion," a sum that strikes me as counterfeit.

> He said his personal secretary and her cohorts have left the Rajneesh organization 55 million dollars in debt.

A *cohort* is not a consort or crony; a cohort, originally a large unit of Roman soldiers, may be used to classify a group with the same characteristic(s), say, the cohort of people born in 1955.

> After months of wrangling over which oxes should be gored on
> the horns of tax reform, the House Ways and Means Committee,
> after voting down a G.O.P. alternative, approved a Democratic
> rewrite of the nation's tax code.

Oxes should be *oxen,* and they should be gored no more, especially on
the "horns of tax reform"—whatever that is, or they are.

> Each player admitted that Strong was not the only source of their
> drugs and that their cocaine use had been extensive.

Each is singular, so *their* should be changed to *his.* Drop the second *their.*
Also: Someone can admit his own wrongdoing, but he can't *admit*
anyone else's.

> A devastating fire early this morning swept through a stable at
> the famed Belmont race track. . . .

Scratch *famed.* It's a headline word, not a conversational word. *Famous*
is conversational, but it's a good word to avoid in newswriting. *Famous*
means "widely known." If a place is indeed widely known, it needn't be
called *famous.* Besides, if a listener never heard of a place, calling it
famous won't help him or the story. Is Belmont more *famous* than any
other track? The story is not about the celebrity or obscurity of Belmont.
It's about the 45 horses that were killed in the fire.

> Something of a royal sendoff today for Prince Charles and Princess
> Diana as they left swanky Palm Beach, Florida, for London.

Something in me not fond of an incomplete sentence. Something not
fond of *something of a.* Something else: please, no *swanky*-panky.
Swanky smacks of gushy gossip columnists. In the same breathless bag:
posh, pricey, deluxe, ritzy, glitzy, glittery and *glamorous.* Also: *chi-chi*
(sounds like a panda).

A Canadian news director, John McFadyen of CKFM-FM,
Toronto, told me, with a wink (I think), that Americans should use
"royal sendoff" only when writing about the Boston Tea Party or the
American Revolution.

> Police in New York City are looking for a trio of thieves who
> robbed a subway token booth early this morning.

They were not a *trio,* even though they did act in concert. Imagine a
newscaster's distress if three thieves had robbed the actress Helen
Twelvetrees.

A pair of U.S. warships is on patrol in the Gulf of Oman, monitoring radio frequencies, ready to escort any cargo vessel that calls for help.

The Navy does have pairs: binoculars, semaphore flags and Shore Patrol. But ships don't come by the pair.

Last week in Congress, a surprise upset for President Reagan.

An incomplete sentence or sentence fragment is something that sometimes works, but not this one. *Surprise upset* is redundant; an upset *is* a surprise. Also: Did the President score an upset or did someone upset him? If the writer had said "an upset *by*," instead of "an upset *for*," the meaning would have been unambiguous.

Almost 500 alleged Mafioso are on trial.

The plural is *Mafiosi.* Get it right, Buster!

Ups and Downs

A TV network correspondent reported the other night that a nationally known candidate was "mired down." But the newsman mucked it up. Someone who's mired *is* down—stuck or sunk in mud. Although the use of a superfluous adverb, such as *down,* is not on the up and up, it seems to be popping up more and more.

So this month's watchword for wordwatchers is: Tighten copy. (If you tighten it *up,* you may not wind up a titan.) Some verbs— occasionally called merged verbs—do take an adverb or preposition: cave *in,* look *over,* sound *off,* and perhaps what that correspondent had in mind, *bog down.*

We often hear newscasters talk about factories that have been closed *down* or opened *up,* and in those cases, *down* and *up* should be offed. In *The Careful Writer,* Theodore M. Bernstein calls these adverbs and prepositions "verb tails." He puts them in three categories: necessary (bottle *up,* break *in,* burn *down*); usually unnecessary (check *over,* head *up,* hide *out*), and unnecessary but idiomatic (visit *with,* slow *down,* hurry *up*). When a reporter is unsure whether a certain verb needs a tail, he can look it up in a good dictionary.

No newsroom should be without a good dictionary. Better: Every newsroom should have a good dictionary. The second sentence is easier to understand and more emphatic. That's why writers should put their sentences in a positive form.

Recently, I heard a story open in slo-mo, then slip into no-mo:

> A package of military aid for El Salvador has been the subject of much debate in Congress lately. Today is no exception. House Speaker Thomas O'Neill predicts. . . .

The first sentence is not news. Someone might try to justify it by calling it background, but I think it should not be thrust into the foreground. Also, that sentence is constructed flimsily. The first verb, "has been," is a form of "to be"; like other linking verbs, it's anemic. It links but doesn't move. And the script's second sentence says feebly, "Today is no exception." Unfortunately, we often have to write stories about the unexceptional, but we don't ballyhoo their banality. Instead, we try to pump life into stories that are dead, dying or dormant. If we put aside news value, we could improve the lead yet follow that writer's pattern: "Congress has been debating military aid for El Salvador, and today House Speaker Thomas O'Neill predicted. . . ." But I think it's important to start a story, whenever possible, by telling listeners something they don't know already. Using only the facts available in that script, I'd try to strengthen the lead by starting with a today angle: "Congress resumed debate today on military aid for El Salvador."

Another broadcast item began wimpishly:

> The diplomatic chill continues between the superpowers.

That's not news; it's olds. If something continues, it has been going on and is still going on, so it is not new or news.

News generally reflects change. Except for a siege, a strike, a fast, a drought or other long-running story, no change means no news. So the "continues" in the script is static. It doesn't advance the story, such as it might be. And it doesn't arrest the listener's attention. Even if a newscaster is dealing with a story that changes only by millimeters, like that of hijackers holding a plane on a runway, he should search for a new angle or a new approach, then use vigorous verbs. "Continues," as I say continually, is as unappealing as gulag goulash.

Having a good dictionary in a newsroom is not enough. Writers should be encouraged to consult it. One way to arouse their interest may be to post a sign at the dictionary stand that warns: Do Not Open This Book! My experience in newsrooms—broadcast and print, network and local, man and boy—is that the best writers go to dictionaries most. And that writers most in need of dictionaries go least. This philosophizing is inspired by a lead I recently heard:

> Power and influence win their magic in many different ways.

I wasn't sure whether the newscaster had said "*win* their magic" or "*wend* their magic." If only someone in the newsroom assembly line had wondered about "*win* [or *wend*] their magic," and wended his way to the dictionary, the newscaster might have been able to *work* his magic.

Another writer who should have checked his dictionary (but not at the door) said that at the national convention in Dallas (I won't identify the political party or the offending party), "the crescendo rose." A crescendo is a gradual increase in the volume of sound, so it's the business of crescendos to rise. And of diminuendos to fall. A more common error was committed at the convention by a correspondent who said,

> But they come to Dallas . . . to bake in the 106-degree heat. . . .

Whatever they might have been cooking up, they didn't go to Dallas to bake. They did bake, but their goal was to stay cool.

One last note: Some newswriters have too many ironies in their fire. In fact, they often have no ironies at all, but they're quick to describe various occurrences as ironic. Irony is the use of words to convey the opposite of their literal meaning; an irony is also an incongruity between what might be expected and what does occur. Yet here's what a reporter broadcast after an Amtrak train ran off the tracks:

> More than half those on Train Number 60 were from a group ironically called Adventures Unlimited.

Apparently, the members were looking for a new adventure, and they found one. Their name is not ironic, and their being thrown by an iron horse is not ironic.

I myself was irenic until I received a postal card from Ridge Shannon of Shawnee Mission, Kansas. He said my use of "refer back" two months ago was redundant. He's right, and I'm contrite.

"Out of" Abounds

If there's anything some writers never run out of, it's *out of:*

> A story *out of* the White House tonight that. . . .
> A report *out of* London today. . . .
> News *out of* Hollywood. . . .

Out of? News comes *from* somewhere. I've never heard anyone else use *out of* that way, except sheriffs in Westerns: "The word outta Fort Dodge is that them varmints is back to their old tricks."

Although some newswriters have made *out of* common, that doesn't make it acceptable. As the columnist William Safire has said: "Common usage excuses; good usage demands."

But even with the substitution of *from,* those leads need to be rewritten. Instead of telling the news, they start by saying they're *going* to be telling the news. People tune in newscasts expecting to hear newscasters deliver news, so an anchor shouldn't start by talking *about* news but start *with* news.

Newscasts consist of stories, so there's no need to start with the word *story.* The lead that told of a "report out of. . . ." has another flaw. The noun *report* has two meanings: one, a factual account; the other, a rumor. So when we hear of a "*report* from" somewhere, we have no idea whether it's well-grounded or unfounded.

We also hear sportscasters describe an athlete as "*out of* Milwaukee." Milwaukee is not something you run out of. And certainly nothing you can run out and get more of. No matter where you're *from.*

More writing that needs righting:

> Qaddafi also denied that Palestinian terrorist Abu Nidal lives and operates out of Libya.

The writer meant ". . . lives *in* Libya and operates out of Libya." This use of *out of*—after a verb like *operates*—is standard, but *from* is faster. The broadcast sentence has a past-tense denial of present-tense action; it makes more sense to start with the historical present tense: "Qadaffi also *denies* . . ."

> The Census Bureau *is out* tonight *with* word of a baby boomlet gone bust. . . .

Is out with seems to be getting into more newscasts, but it's blander than bean curd. Like other forms of *to be, is* conveys no motion, no action. It's inert. Better: "The Census Bureau *says* the baby boomlet has gone bust." Not good, but better. Let's take up a new battle cry: "Out, damned *out with!*"

> Police said the exact number and extent of their injuries was not immediately available.

The sentence has what an ad for zippers used to call "gaposis." The gap should be filled by making the sentence read: "Police said the exact number *of injured.* . . ." (And the verb *was* should have been *were.*) But even after closing the gap, we still have a sentence that lacks zip. Better:

"Police say they don't know how many people were hurt—or how badly."

> People came from as far as Chicago and Oregon to catch one
> furtive, faraway glimpse of the future queen.

Furtive = stealthy. The correspondent should have sneaked a look in a dictionary. Maybe he meant *fleeting*. The people he spoke of didn't travel that far to catch a *glimpse;* they traveled that far to get a close look, but they wound up far away. (His kind of construction pops up often: "He returned home *to* find his wife shot." Should be: "He returned home *and* found his wife shot.") The people who traveled to Springfield, Virginia, from Oregon came from a lot farther than Chicago, so the correspondent has no need to mention Chicago. Further, cities and states should not be mixed. If it had been desirable to mention a half-way place, he should have changed "Chicago" to "Illinois."

His mention of "the future queen" refers to Diana, Princess of Wales. But she may or may not become queen—and definitely not "*the* queen.*" If Diana were to die while Elizabeth is still queen or if Prince Charles dies, Diana won't become queen. And if they're divorced, or if he renounces the throne, she won't become queen. And John McFadyen, N.D. of CKFM-FM, Toronto, says that if Charles does become king, Diana will not necessarily become queen. She would become queen only if Charles exercises his royal prerogative to have her named queen. His mother, Queen Elizabeth, whose royal birth makes her *the* queen, has not chosen to have her husband, Prince Philip, elevated to king. So calling Diana "the future queen" is presumptuous.

> A murder today is sending shock waves through a quiet Abington
> neighborhood. The body of a woman was discovered at about
> three-thirty this afternoon in the basement of her home in the
> 21-hundred block of Rush Road. Police say 44-year-old Marge
> McAndrews was stabbed to death. Her body was found by her
> 18-year-old daughter. Police aren't sure what happened, but it
> appears that the woman surprised a burglar. The search is on for
> her killer.

Like too many first-day leads, that one focuses on reaction, not action. The writer should zero in on the murder, not on "shock waves"—whatever they are. The time when the body was found is irrelevant. If the writer wanted to let listeners know of the recency, perhaps he could have said "this afternoon" or "in mid-afternoon." Or "within the past hour" or "a short time ago." The hour and minute add nothing; everything happens at one time or another. Who was she? Occupation? Family? Was it one of her knives? Rather than write "Police aren't sure," I'd write, "Police say they think Mrs. [?] McAndrews surprised a burglar."

The story's last sentence, about the search for the killer, is not worth mentioning. Nothing unusual about searching for a killer. When a Boy Scout helps an old woman cross the street, that's not unusual. But if he trips her, we have news. So if police *refuse* to search, that's news.

> The Soviet Union shot two astronauts into space. . . .

As soon as I heard *shot two astronauts,* I was startled: Was it a shoot-'em-up?

Ing Spots

If you keep hearing an *ing*-ing in your ears, it may be because some newscasts carry more *ings* than buses in Beijing:*

> *Raising* clenched fists and *singing* freedom songs, 20-thousand blacks are *gathering* for a mass funeral in a segregated South African township. Police are out in force, but there has been no trouble. 29 victims of racial unrest are *being* buried . . . .

That network story is weaker than a sapling. Instead of telling us at the outset who or what the story is about, the writer starts with a participial phrase and slides in low gear to another participle. That conceals the subject and leaves us baffled.

The weakness of the first sentence in the story is compounded by the lack of a finite verb, one with a tense. The second sentence is weak because it rests on *are* and *has been,* both forms of a linking verb, *to be. Are* is in the active voice but expresses no action, so it's static.

In the second sentence of the story, *but* is incorrect. *But* implies that what is to follow changes course or is contrary to what might be expected. If police are plentiful, I wouldn't expect trouble. It might be more logical to write, "Police are out in force, *so* there has been no trouble." But I wouldn't use *so* because we can't know for sure why there has been no trouble.

The third sentence of the story refers to "victims of racial unrest." This is delusive. Unrest does not kill.

That sentence also says the victims "are *being* buried" as though it's being done now. Yet the first sentence tells us that people are *raising* fists, *singing* songs and *gathering* for the funeral. All four of those activities cannot be going on simultaneously.

*The common family name of Ng is pronounced *ing.*

Let's assume the victims were *"going* to be buried" and rewrite the opening: "A mass funeral in South Africa has drawn a vast crowd, 20-thousand blacks. As they gathered for the burial of 29 blacks, killed in riots [?], the mourners sang freedom songs and raised their fists."

Now let's look at another network weakling that's also annoying: It bounces from *ing* to *ing* like the cartoon character Gerald McBoing-Boing:

A U.S. Supreme Court *ruling* today that could affect millions of workers nationwide, a *ruling* that states may force employers to provide particular kinds of benefits in their company insurance plans, for instance, *requiring* mental health, alcohol or drug abuse services.

The subject—a ruling that could affect millions—is not followed by a verb. An incomplete sentence works once in a while, but that sentence, which is the entire item, is too long. And confusing.

When you were reading *a ruling that states,* didn't you think for an instant that *states* was a verb?

In that item, the first two *ing* words are nouns, the third is a participle. But whether an *ing* word is a participle (an adjectival form derived from a verb), a gerund (a nounlike form), or a noun, some writers often use them in threes and fours. Here's a script from the Midwest:

U.S. Agriculture Secretary Richard Lyng spent the *morning* in Buffalo County, *eating* breakfast in Gibbon and *talking* with community leaders there and *visiting* two Buffalo County farms.

Is there something in a writer's first *ing* that triggers a mechanism in his mind that sends a stream of *ings* flowing into his copy? Just asking. This script comes from elsewhere:

President Reagan and his wife, Nancy, are *continuing* their August vacation in Southern California, but correspondent _____ _____ is *saying* the president and his wife are *taking* a break from the routine of the presidential ranch near Santa Barbara.

News reflects change, so I keep saying that *continues* or *continuing* is an unsatisfactory word to use in a lead because it tells the listener that whatever has been going on is still going on.

That lead-in implies that the correspondent is going around saying something. And saying it and saying it. And in the next lead-in, the same writer keeps doing it:

> Big-city mayors from across the country are *meeting* in New York
> City *talking* about drug-*trafficking*. And correspondent _____
> _____ is *saying* a great deal of attention is *being* paid to the
> latest drug fad, the *smoking* of crack.

One possible explanation for writers' *ing*-ing is that they want to tell listeners that events are going on at this very moment, even as we're speaking, and they think *ing* imparts immediacy. An occasional *ing* may add zing, but a cluster can cloy. And can make a story soft, ungrammatical, illogical, or false.

One of the most disagreeable of all *ings* is the mistaken use of a participle as the main verb in a sentence, as in this network lead-in:

> Japan's transport minister today ordering inspections of all Boeing
> 747's now in use in the country. . . .

On the same newscast on the same day, another leaden lead-in:

> Pope John Paul *continuing* his visit to Africa with a stopover in
> Zaire.

Writers who lean on *ing* may not be ingbats, but they ought to ditch that feeble Inglish.

Word Champs

Let's mark the end of the year by awarding No-Bell Prizes. All these prize-winning scripts were broadcast by networks as news—not parody.

The first non-bellringer takes the prize for misleading lead-in:

> Japan's drive to be number one, the excellent Japanese
> education system, teenage suicides, schoolyard bullying and
> extortion at school. Some or all of these elements are in
> tonight's report from Tokyo by _____ _____.

Some or all sounds like the legalistic language of a prospectus. In fact, the correspondent said nothing about "Japan's drive to be number one." After the anchor broadcast that item, I wondered whether the writer would be emboldened to write a lead-in like this for a shootout: "Sex. Drugs. Greed. Treachery. Violence. Sudden death. Some or all those elements figure in tonight's report from. . . ."

Even if the writer had written the lead-in accurately, he'd have done it incorrectly. Starting with a list and *then* telling listeners why is like giving a recipe, then telling what it's for.

Prize for startling comeback:

> At least three people were dead tonight and three more missing
> as. . . .

Were dead—but no longer dead? Those who were killed *are* dead. The dead *were* oil workers. Even if the writer had lined up his tenses correctly, his opening was weak because he began with numbers and backed into the action.

Prize for resistible lead:

> In the 'what-else-is-new?' department, the U.S. dollar rose again
> today.

Prize for negating the positive:

> The chairman of the P-L-O, Yasir Arafat, had no kind words
> for President Reagan today.

One of Strunk and White's elementary rules of usage is: "Put statements in positive form." The lead would be far stronger this way: "The chairman of the P-L-O, Yasir Arafat, denounced President Reagan today as 'a robot and a parrot.'"

Prize for superfluous use of prepositions:

> European space scientists phoned NASA today for emergency
> help in fixing their . . . space probe that's meeting *up with*
> Halley's comet. . . .

Meet up with is substandard English.

Prize for ambiguity:

> For the first time since 1962, it appears that a woman will be
> executed next month.

Was her execution forecast in 1962?

Prize for lucidity in the heat of battle:

> The lobby of the Commodore Hotel became a battleground as
> Terry Waite held a news conference with the foreign press about
> the fate of four American hostages . . . It was a classic Beirut
> scene—Waite trying to be calm as Druse and Amal militiamen
> fought an intense street battle outside.

Was the lobby a battleground—or not?

Prize for quick-change artistry:

> What was a tragic accident on Sunday has now become a possible
> murder investigation.

This is a strange world, but how can an accident become an investigation?

Prize for absurd new word:

That's an embarrassment, a *pozzible*—a puzzle and a possible future trouble spot for. . . .

Prize for sensitive opening line:

We had hoped not to have to report it, but an Ohio doctor said today, 'There were just too many strikes against him.' He was speaking about that little boy. . . .

Prize for redundancy:

Hundreds of worried parents stood face to face with armed soldiers outside a Soweto police station.

Armed soldiers? Aren't they comrades-in-arms of *armed* gunmen? Prize for hard questions put to listeners in a lead-in:

What's cutting into the steelhead trout population in the ship canal? Some deadly disease? Or is it only Herschel and his friends?

Prize for gratuitous explanation:

Now, we didn't lead with this story because, frankly, we feel strongly about not raising any false expectations.

Whenever I hear someone say "frankly," I wonder whether he's saying that because he's usually not frank.

Prize for mangling syntax, consumer reporters' division:

Well, first I want to tell you these are not new products. These are when you borrow it from somebody else.

Prize for mangling syntax, anchors:

Foreigners found themselves jeered at, spat at and had their cars overturned.

Did the foreigners have them overturned to collect insurance? Prize for most informative first sentence:

Winter kills and snow is dangerous. Yet another reminder has happened in a small town along the coast of the Japan Sea. . . .

Reminders don't *happen.* Seacoast is land on the edge of a sea, but where is the coast of a sea? *Japan Sea?* Is that anywhere near the Sea of Japan? Prize for hype and tripe:

By the rules, what goes up must come down, but that was before the rule-breaking, record delay-breaking bloops [*sic*], foul-ups and bleepers mission of space shuttle Columbia.

By staying in space longer than planned, Columbia did not—and could not—break those rules. Besides, those are *laws* of gravity.
    Prize for iffiness:

> And if you love the ancient canal city of Venice, good news this morning.

But how's the news if we don't love cities with flooded streets?
    Prize for clear thinking:

> For many Americans, the biggest problem with having babies is not having babies.

Such a problem is inconceivable—but so are all those scripts.

Soup of the Month

If Broadcast Newswriting were a company on the Big Board, I'd be fairly bullish: Its sources are inexhaustible, its products indispensable, its consumers insatiable.

But some of the company's products are faulty, with words misused, language abused, stories confused. Most of the faults, though, are preventable or correctable. And executives say they're bearing down on the assembly lines. The company's shares may be attractive because its assets are undervalued, so the outlook could be favorable.

I was asked to evaluate the company by Joe Tiernan, editor of the *Communicator*. He asked me because I hold newswriting workshops at radio and TV stations. In my travails across the country, here's what I've found in the company's plants:

1. Most of the products are serviceable and many are commendable, but some are deplorable.
2. News directors have so many responsibilities that most N.D.s lack time to oversee their writers.
3. Some N.D.s who do have the time lack the experience in writing and teaching to train writers.
4. Quality control is inadequate. The missing link in many cases is an editor, or a good one. Unless a script is edited skillfully along the way, the assembly line is no better than a bucket brigade: the product arrives at the end of the line just as it started out.

Those minuses are offset somewhat by pluses that indicate a hunger for improvement:

1. News directors tell me how highly they rate newswriting. And how they'd like to have newswriting that's more professional.

2. Writers—including reporters, producers and anchors—also tell me how much *they* value good writing. Many acknowledge shortcomings and say they want to write better.

3. Newspeople ask me to recommend books on newswriting so they can sharpen their skills. Several textbooks carry a good chapter or section on newswriting; I recommend three whose treatment of writing is the most extensive—and effective: *Writing News for Broadcast* by Edward Bliss Jr. and John M. Patterson (published by Columbia University Press); *Broadcast News,* 2nd Ed., by Mitchell Stephens (Holt, Rinehart and Winston); *Broadcast Journalism* by Mark W. Hall (Hastings House).

If the quality of broadcast newswriting has been declining, as some people contend, it may be due partly to newcomers whose goal is to become anchors, not writers, who have only an uneasy acquaintance with English, and who are short on journalistic basics and street smarts. For example, a script that I read after it was broadcast illustrates several common problems in writing, reporting and editing:

> And, [name of co-anchor], in case you didn't know it, [name of city] Mayor _____ _____ has proclaimed January as National Soup Month. In honor of the event, the Campbell's Soup Company brought their Soupmobile here to _____ . One of the three stops they made today was here at the Salvation Army. _____ city employees as well as some of _____'s needy stood in line to warm up. The Soupmobile is making a ten-city tour of the country. It will be here for two more days before the chefs on board pack up and move on to _____ for a three-day stop.

The lead-in and voice-over are riddled with flaws from start to finish: Why should an anchor deliver the news to a co-anchor? And why pretend the co-anchor may be unaware of it? Why use the mayor's first name? And why not get the company's name right—Campbell, not Campbell's? Also, *their* should be *its*. Why does an anchor say "here" unless the Salvation Army is encamped in the studio? Who cares where the Soupmobile is going next, especially when it'll be hundreds of miles away? And who cares how many days it'll park there?

The biggest problem of all, though, is the naive approach. The event has all the earmarks of a press-agent stunt—commercialism but with no commercials. A Campbell press agent probably drafted the proclamation and arranged for the mayor to sign it. No one was hurt, I suppose, and some poor people were helped. Not to mention the press agent (and good press agents don't want to be mentioned).

The script implies that Campbell was responding to the mayor's proclamation, but any reporter who has ever covered mayors or governors knows they sign proclamations at the drop of a hint or a contribution. Why would a mayor spontaneously proclaim a National Soup Month? And how could a local official make it *national*? What a crock!

In a small town on a slow news day, it may be news when the Campbells are coming. But the news should be written with some savvy. If a writer needs seasoning, then it's up to an editor or producer or anchor or news director to set the writer straight.

No matter what size the town, every script should be read by other eyes so another company product doesn't go bad—and another writer doesn't wind up in the soup.

AS WRITERS, our goal is to do more than stay out of the soup, even alphabet soup. Our goal is to write better scripts—shorter, sharper, stronger.

Writing, though, requires far more than simply putting words on paper, as this book has reminded you: Writers must think clearly, understand language thoroughly and watch what they say, intently. You *can* improve your writing skills, but only through writing and writing and working hard at it.

And if you do all that, *you* can have the last word.

APPENDIX A

Further Reading and Reference

Writing News for Broadcast by Edward Bliss Jr. and John M. Patterson (Columbia University Press, 1978).

Broadcast News, 2d ed., by Mitchell Stephens (Holt, Rinehart and Winston, 1986).

Broadcast Journalism: An Introduction to News Writing by Mark Hall (Hastings House, 1978).*

The Word: An Associated Press Guide to Good Writing by René Cappon (The Associated Press, 1982).*

The Golden Book on Writing by David Lambuth (Viking Press, 1964).*

The Elements of Style by William Strunk Jr. and E.B. White (Macmillan, 1979).*

Writing with Style: Conversations on the Art of Writing by John R. Trimble (Prentice-Hall, 1975).*

On Writing Well by William Zinsser (Harper & Row, 1985).*

The Practical Stylist by Sheridan Baker (Harper & Row, 1985).*

The Careful Writer by Theodore M. Bernstein (Atheneum, 1965).*

Getting the Words Right: How to Revise, Edit & Rewrite by Theodore A. Rees Cheney (Writers Digest Books, 1983).

Line by Line: How to Edit Your Own Writing by Claire Kehrwald Cook (Houghton Mifflin, 1985).

Grammar for Journalists by E. L. Callihan (Chilton, 1979).*

*Available in paperback.

214

The Random House Handbook by Frederick Crews (Random House, 1984).

The Handbook of Good English by Edward D. Johnson (Facts on File, 1983).

The McGraw-Hill College Handbook by Richard Marius and Harvey S. Weiner (McGraw-Hill, 1985)

Writer's Guide and Index to English by Porter G. Perrin (Scott, Foresman, 1968).

American Usage and Style: The Consensus by Roy Copperud (Van Nostrand, 1980).

A Dictionary of Contemporary American Usage by Bergen Evans and Cornelia Evans (Random House, 1965).

Modern American Usage by Wilson Follett (Hill and Wang, 1966).*

Modern English Usage, 2d ed., by H.W. Fowler, revised and edited by Sir Ernest Gowers (Oxford University Press, 1985).*

Dictionary of Contemporary Usage by William and Mary Morris (Harper & Row, 1985).

Dictionary of American-English Usage by Margaret Nicholson (Oxford University Press, 1957).

The Writer's Hotline Handbook by Michael Montgomery and John Stratton (New American Library, 1981).*

Painless, Perfect Grammar: Tips from the Grammar Hotline by Michael Strumpf and Auriel Douglas (Monarch Press, 1985).*

The Associated Press Broadcast News Handbook, compiled and edited by James R. Hood and Brad Kalbfeld (The Associated Press, 1982).*

The Associated Press Stylebook and Libel Manual (The Associated Press, 1986).*

The U.P.I. Stylebook (United Press International, 1977).*

The Spoken Word: A BBC Guide by Robert Burchfield (Oxford University Press, 1981).*

The New York Times Manual of Style and Usage (Quadrangle, 1976).*

American Heritage Dictionary (Houghton Mifflin, 1982).*

Webster's New World Dictionary, 2d college ed. (Simon and Schuster, 1982).

Webster's New International Dictionary, 2d ed. (G. & C. Merriam, 1961).

Roget's International Thesaurus, 4th ed. (Harper & Row, 1977).

The News Business by John Chancellor and Walter Mears (Harper & Row, 1983).

Interpretative Reporting, 8th ed., by Curtis D. MacDougall (Macmillan, 1982).*

Basic News Writing, 2d ed., by Melvin Mencher (Wm. C. Brown, 1986).*

News Reporting and Writing, 4th ed., by Melvin Mencher (Wm. C. Brown, 1987).*

APPENDIX B

Grammar Hotline Directory

ALABAMA

AUBURN 36830
(205) 826-5749—Writing
Center Hotline
Monday through Thursday,
9:00 a.m. to noon and
1:00 p.m. to 4:00 p.m.; Friday,
9:00 a.m. to noon; reduced
hours during summer
Auburn University
Peter Huggins

JACKSONVILLE 36265
(205) 231-5409—Grammar
Hotline
Monday through Friday,
8:00 a.m. to 4:30 p.m.
Jacksonville State University
Carol Cauthen and Dr. Clyde
Cox

TUSCALOOSA 35487
(205) 348-5049—Grammar
Hotline
Monday through Thursday,
8:30 a.m. to 4:00 p.m.;
Tuesday and Wednesday,
6:00 p.m. to 8:00 p.m.; Friday,
9:00 a.m. to 1:00 p.m.; summer
hours, 8:30 a.m. to 1:00 p.m.
University of Alabama
Carol Howell

ARIZONA

TEMPE 85287
(602) 967-0378—Grammar
Hotline
Monday through Friday,
8:00 a.m. to 5:00 p.m.
Arizona State University
Dr. J.J. Lamberts

ARKANSAS

LITTLE ROCK 72204
(501) 569-3162—The Writer's
Hotline
Monday through Friday,
8:00 a.m. to noon
University of Arkansas at
Little Rock
Marilynn Keys

CALIFORNIA

MOORPARK 93021
(805) 529-2321—National
Grammar Hotline
Monday through Friday,
8:00 a.m. to noon, September
through June
Moorpark College
Michael Strumpf

SACRAMENTO 95823-5799
(916) 686-7444—English Helpline
Monday through Friday,
9:00 a.m. to 11:45 a.m., fall
and spring semesters; 24-hour
recorder
Cosumnes River College
Billie Miller Cooper

COLORADO

PUEBLO 81001
(303) 549-2787—USC
Grammar Hotline
Monday through Friday, 9:30
a.m. to 3:30 p.m.; reduced
hours May 15 to August 25
University of Southern
Colorado
Margaret Senatore and Ralph
Dille

DELAWARE

NEWARK 19716
(302) 451-1890—Grammar
Hotline
Monday through Thursday,
9:00 a.m. to noon, 1:00 p.m.
to 5:00 p.m. and 6:00 p.m.
to 9:00 p.m.; Friday, 9:00 a.m.
to noon and 1:00 p.m. to
5:00 p.m.
University of Delaware
Margaret P. Hassert

FLORIDA

PENSACOLA 32514
(904) 474-2129—Writing Lab
and Grammar Hotline
Monday through Thursday, 9:00
a.m. to 5:00 p.m.; occasional
evening hours; Friday and
summer hours vary
University of West Florida
Mamie Webb Hixon

GEORGIA

ATLANTA 30303
(404) 651-2906—Writing
Center
Monday through Thursday,
8:30 a.m. to 5:00 p.m.;
Friday, 8:30 a.m. to 3:00 p.m.;
evening hours vary
Georgia State University
Patricia Graves

ILLINOIS

CHARLESTON 61920
(217) 581-5929—Grammar
Hotline
Monday through Friday, 10:00
a.m. to 3:00 p.m.;
summer hours vary
Eastern Illinois University
Jeanne Simpson

DES PLAINES 60016
(312) 635-1948—The Write Line
10:00 a.m. to 2:00 p.m.,
September through May;
summer hours vary
Oakton Community College
Richard Francis Tracz

NORMAL 61761
(309) 438-2345—Grammar
Hotline
Monday through Friday, 8:00
a.m. to 4:30 p.m.
Illinois State University
Janice Neuleib and Maurice
Scharton

OGLESBY 61348
(815) 224-2720—Grammarline
Monday through Friday,
8:00 a.m. to 4:00 p.m.
Illinois Valley Community
College
Robert Howard and Robert
Mueller

RIVER GROVE 60171
(312) 456-0300, ext.
254—Grammarphone
Monday through Thursday,
8:30 a.m. to 9:00 p.m.;
Friday, 8:30 a.m. to 4:00 p.m.;
Saturday, 10:00 am. to
1:00 p.m.
Triton College
Hillard Hebda

INDIANA

INDIANAPOLIS 46202
(317) 274-3000—IUPUI
Writing Center Hotline
Monday through Thursday,
9:00 a.m. to 4:00 p.m.
Indiana University-Purdue
University at Indianapolis,
University Writing Center
Barbara Cambridge

MUNCIE 47306
(317) 285-8387—Grammar
Crisis Line
Monday through Thursday, 9:00
a.m. to 8:00 p.m.; Friday, 9:00
a.m. to 5:00 p.m., September
through May; Monday through
Friday, 11:00 a.m. to 2:00
p.m., May through August
Ball State University, The
Writing Center
Paul W. Ranieri

WEST LAFAYETTE 47907
(317) 494-3723—Grammar
Hotline
Monday through Friday, 9:30
a.m. to 4:00 p.m., when a
writing instructor is available,
during spring, summer, and
fall semesters; closed during
May and August, and mid-
December to mid-January
Purdue University
Muriel Harris

KANSAS

EMPORIA 66801
(316) 343-1200, Writer's Hotline
Monday through Thursday,
noon to 5:00 p.m.;
Wednesday night, 7:00 p.m. to
9:00 p.m.
summer hours vary
Emporia State University
Robert Goltra

*see KANSAS CITY,
MISSOURI*

LOUISIANA

LAFAYETTE 70504
(318) 231-5224—Grammar
Hotline
Monday through Thursday,
8:00 a.m. to 4:00 p.m.; Friday
8:00 a.m. to 3:00 p.m.
University of Southwestern
Louisiana
James McDonald

MARYLAND

BALTIMORE 21228
(301) 455-2585—Writer's
Hotline
Monday through Friday, 10:00
a.m. to noon, September
through May
University of Maryland
Baltimore County
Barbara Cooper, Department of
English

FROSTBURG 21532
(301) 689-4327—
Grammarphone (patented
trademark)
Monday through Friday, 10:00
a.m. to noon
Frostburg State College
Glynn Baugher, English
Department

MASSACHUSETTS

BOSTON 02115
(617) 437-2512—Grammar
Hotline
Monday through Friday, 8:30
a.m. to 4:30 p.m.
Northeastern University
Stuart Peterfreund, English
Department

LYNN 01901
(617) 593-7284—Grammar
Hotline
Monday through Friday, 8:30
a.m. to 4:00 p.m.
North Shore Community
College
Marilyn Dorfman

MICHIGAN

FLINT 48503
(313) 762-0229—Grammar
Hotline
Monday through Thursday,
8:30 a.m. to 3:30 p.m.;
Friday, 8:30 a.m. to 12:30
p.m.; Tuesday and
Wednesday evenings, 5:30
p.m. to 8:30 p.m.; summer
hours vary
C.S. Mott Community College
Leatha Terwilliger

KALAMAZOO 49008-5031
(616) 387-4442—Writer's
Hotline
Monday through Friday, 9:00
a.m. to 4:00 p.m.; summer
hours vary
Western Michigan University
Eileen B. Evans

LANSING 48901
(517) 483-1040—Writer's Hotline
Monday through Friday,
9:00 a.m. to 4:00 p.m.
Lansing Community College
Dr. George R. Bramer

MISSOURI

JOPLIN 64801
(417) 624-0171—Grammar
Hotline
Monday through Friday, 8:30
a.m. to 4:00 p.m.
Missouri Southern State
College
Dale W. Simpson

KANSAS CITY 64110-2499
(816) 276-2244—Writer's
Hotline
Monday through Friday, 9:00
a.m. to 4:00 p.m., September
through May; summer
hours vary
University of Missouri at
Kansas City
Judy McCormick, David Foster,
and Karen Doerr

NEW JERSEY

JERSEY CITY 07305
(201) 547-3337 or-3338
—Grammar Hotline
Monday through Friday,
9:00 a.m. to 4:30 p.m.;
summer, Monday through
Thursday, 8:00 a.m. to
5:00 p.m.
Jersey City State College
Harlan Hamilton

NEW YORK

JAMAICA 11451
(718) 739-7483—R-E-W-R-I-T-E
Monday through Friday, 1:00
p.m. to 4:00 p.m.
York College of the City
University of New York
Joan Baum and Alan Cooper

NORTH CAROLINA

FAYETTEVILLE 28301
(919) 488-7110—Grammar
Hotline
Monday through Friday, 8:00
a.m. to 5:00 p.m.
Methodist College
Robert Christian, Sue L.
Kimball, James X. Ward

GREENVILLE 27858
(919) 757-6728 or 757-6399—
Grammar Hotline
Monday through Thursday
8:00 a.m. to 4:00 p.m.;
Friday, 8:00 a.m. to 3:00
p.m.; Tuesday and Thursday
evenings, 6:00 p.m. to
9:00 p.m.
East Carolina University
Dr. Jo Allen

OHIO

CINCINNATI 45236
(513) 745-5731
—Dial-A-Grammar
Tapes requests—returns calls
(long-distance calls returned
collect)
Raymond Walters College
Dr. Phyllis A. Sherwood

CINCINNATI 45221
(513) 475-2493—Writer's
Remedies
Monday through Friday, 9:00
a.m. to 10:00 a.m. and 1:00
p.m. to 2:00 p.m.
University College, University of
Cincinnati
Jay A. Yarmove

CINCINNATI 45223
(513) 569-1736 or 569-1737
—Writing Center Hotline
Monday through Thursday,
8:00 a.m. to 8:00 p.m.;
Friday, 8:00 a.m. to 4:00
p.m.; Saturday, 9:00 a.m. to
1:00 p.m.
Cincinnati Technical College
John Battistone and Catherine
Rahmes

CLEVELAND 44122-6195
(216) 987-2050—Grammar
Hotline
Monday through Friday,
1:00 p.m. to 3:00 p.m.;
Sunday through Thursday,
7:00 p.m. to 10:00 p.m.;
twenty-four hour answering
machine
Cuyahoga Community College
Margaret Taylor

DAYTON 45435
(513) 873-2158—Writer's Hotline
Monday through Friday,
9:00 a.m. to 4:00 p.m.
Wright State University
Maura Taaffe

DELAWARE 43015
(614) 369-4431, ext. 301—
Writing Resource Center
Monday through Friday, 9:00
a.m. to noon and 1:00 p.m.
to 4:00 p.m., September
through May
Ohio Wesleyan University
Dr. Ulle Lewes and Mrs. Jean
Hopper

OKLAHOMA

BETHANY 73008
(405) 491-6328—Grammar
Hotline
Monday through Friday,
9:00 a.m. to 4:00 p.m.; June,
July, and August call (405)
354-1739
Southern Nazarene University
Jim Wilcox, Dept. of English

CHICKASHA 73018
(405) 224-8622
Monday through Friday, 9:00
a.m. to 5:00 p.m.; Saturday
9:00 a.m. to noon
Mrs. Underwood, retired
teacher and editor, offers this
service through her home
telephone. She is willing
to return long-distance
calls collect.
Virginia Lee Underwood

PENNSYLVANIA

ALLENTOWN 18104
(215) 437-4471—Academic
Support Center, Writing
Center Hotline
Monday through Friday, 10:00
a.m. to 3:00 p.m., September
through May
Cedar Crest College
Karen Coleman and Priscilla
Johnson

GLEN MILLS 19342
(215) 399-1130—Burger
Associates
Monday through Friday, 8:00
a.m. to 5:00 p.m.
Mr. Burger, formerly a teacher
of writing and journalism at
several colleges, offers this
service through his office,
which conducts courses in
effective writing
Robert S. Burger

LINCOLN UNIVERSITY 19352
(215) 932-8300, ext. 460—
Grammar Hotline
Monday through Friday, 9:00
a.m. to 5:00 p.m., September
through May; summer
hours vary
Lincoln University
Carolyn L. Simpson

PITTSBURGH 15104
(412) 344-9759—Grammar
Hotline
Monday through Friday,
9:00 a.m. to 5:00 p.m.,
September through mid-June;
recorder takes messages at
other times
Coalition for Adult Literacy
Dr. Mary Newton Bruder

SOUTH CAROLINA

CHARLESTON 29409
(803) 792-3194—Writer's
Hotline
Monday through Friday, 8:00
a.m. to 4:00 p.m.;
Sunday through Thursday, 6:00
p.m. to 10:00 p.m.
The Citadel Writing Center
Angela W. Williams

COLUMBIA 29208
(803) 777-7020—Writer's
Hotline
Monday through Thursday,
8:30 a.m. to 5:00 p.m.;
Friday, 8:30 a.m. to 5:00 p.m.
University of South Carolina
Laurie Demarest and Suzanne
Moore

SPARTANBURG 29301
(803) 596-9613—Grammar
Hotline
Tuesday through Thursday,
noon to 5:00 p.m.
Converse College
Dr. Karen Carmean and Eva
Pratt

TEXAS

AMARILLO 79178
(806) 374-4726—Grammarphone
Monday through Thursday,
8:00 a.m. to 9:00 p.m.;
Friday, 8:00 a.m. to 3:00
p.m.; Sunday, 2:00 p.m. to
6:00 p.m.
Amarillo College
Patricia Maddox and Carl
Fowler

HOUSTON 77002
(713) 221-8670—University of
Houston Downtown
Grammar Hotline
Monday through Thursday,
9:00 a.m. to 4:00 p.m.;
Friday, 9:00 a.m. to 1:00 p.m.;
summer hours, Monday
through Thursday, 10:30 a.m.
to 4:00 p.m.
University of Houston
Downtown
Linda Coblentz

SAN ANTONIO 78284
(512) 733-2503—Learning Line
Monday through Thursday,
8:00 a.m. to 9:00 p.m.
Friday, 8:00 a.m. to 4:00 p.m.
San Antonio College
Leon Ricketts and Irma Luna

VIRGINIA

STERLING 22170
(703) 450-2511—Writing Helpline
Monday through Thursday,
10:00 a.m. to 2:00 p.m.
Northern Virginia Community
College—London Campus
Diane M. Rhodes

VIRGINIA BEACH 23456
(804) 427-7170—Grammar
Hotline
Monday through Friday, 10:00
a.m. to noon; afternoon
hours vary; reduced hours
during summer
Tidewater Community College
Writing Center
Donna Reiss

WISCONSIN

GREEN BAY 54307-9042
(414) 498-5427—Grammar
Hotline
Monday through Thursday,
8:30 a.m. to 8:00 p.m;
Friday, 8:00 a.m. to 4:00 p.m.
Northeast Wisconsin Technical
Institute
Rose Marie Mastricola and
Joanne Rathburn

PLATTEVILLE 53818
(608) 342-1615—Grammar
Hotline
Monday through Thursday,
9:00 a.m. to 4:00 p.m.;
Friday, 9:00 a.m. to noon
University of
Wisconsin-Platteville
Nancy Daniels

CANADA

EDMONTON, ALBERTA
T5J2P2
(403) 441-4699—Grammar
Hotline
Tuesday through Friday,
12:30 p.m. to 3:30 p.m.
Grant MacEwan Community
College
Lois Drew

FREDERICTON, NEW
BRUNSWICK E3B5A3
(506) 459-3631 (residence)
—Grammar Hotline
Variable hours
University of New Brunswick
A.M. Kinloch

*Many of the services reduce hours
during the summer, and most close
during college breaks.*

Reprinted with permission from
the Writing Center/Grammar
Hotline of Tidewater Community
College, 1700 College Crescent,
Virginia Beach, VA 23456

INDEX